Building
College
Writing

◼ Acknowledgments

We would like to thank the Millikin University Writing Center staff members for their generous and perceptive assistance in field testing this book: Barbara Hope and Dorothy Romberg, who actually used the book with their students, and Linda Droll, the Center's Director. We are grateful to those instructors who were kind enough to read some or all of the manuscript: Dan McGavin, Davenport College; Tim Miank, Lansing Community College; Martha Bergeron, Vance-Granville Community College; Judy J. Hathcock, Amarillo College; Eileen B. Evans, Western Michigan University; and Martha Kearns, University of Nevada-Reno. We also thank our students from the fall of 1989 and of 1990 for their patience as we worked through several drafts. Our thanks go to Dave Wright, for his "insight"; to Homer, Clarence, and especially Ed for allowing us to use their speedy computers and laser printer; to Stuart Miller, our editor at Harcourt Brace Jovanovich; to Beverly Cory, our copyeditor; to Ruth Cottrell, who handled the production; and finally to our families—Randy (our ever-willing help in times of need), Arthur, Brittany, Stephanie, Susan, Katie, and Gavin; and Jim (your pride makes me proud), Zane, the changeling, and Dylan. *Nisi dominus frustra.*

Contents

PART 1
Grammar, Punctuation, and Usage   1

1   Subjects and Verbs   3
Verbs   3
Subjects   5
Words That Look Like Verbs   6
   Infinitives   6
   -Ing Words as Nouns   7
   Participles   8
   Past Participles   9
Seven Sentence Patterns   11
   When the Subject Follows the Verb (V+S)   11
   When Verbs Have More Than One Word (S+VVV)   12
   When Words Interrupt the Verb (S+VXV)   13
   When a Sentence Has Two Subjects (S+S+V)   14
   When a Sentence Has Two or More Verbs (S+V+V)   15
   When a Sentence Has an Understood Subject C(US)   16
   When Prepositional Phrases Separate the Subject and Verb (S+prep+V)   16
End of Chapter Exercises   18–24

2   Clauses and Phrases   25
Clauses   25
Identifying Clauses   30
   Step 1: Identify the Subject-Verb Combinations   30
   Step 2: Circle the Dependent Signals   31
   Step 3: Bracket the Dependent Clauses   31
   Sentences with Many Clauses   33
   Rules for Sentences   34
Phrases   35
End of Chapter Exercises   36–39

3   Sentence Fragments: Something Missing   41
What a Sentence Must Have   41
Fragments Without Subjects   42
Fragments Without Verbs   45

Incomplete-Thought Fragments 48
End of Chapter Exercises 51–60

4 Sentence Fragments: Something Added 61

Reviewing Verbals 61
Extra-Information Fragments 62
   Phrases with Participles 62
   Infinitive Phrases 63
   Dependent Clauses 64
   Phrases That Tell More 65
End of Chapter Exercises 66–82

5 Comma Splices and Run-On Sentences 83

Reviewing Independent Clauses 83
Joining Independent Clauses 84
   The All-Important FANBOYS 84
   Dependent Signals 86
   Semicolons 87
Avoiding Comma Splices and Run-on Sentences 87
   Using the Wrong Connection 88
   Joining Short Sentences 91
   Joining Closely Related Ideas 91
End of Chapter Exercises 92–102

6 Sentence Structure Review 103

Analyzing Sentences 103
End of Chapter Exercises 105–119

7 Commas That Separate 121

Two Independent Clauses 121
Introductory Dependent Clause 123
Other Long Introductory Elements 124
Commas for Clarity 125
Two Equal Describers 126
Commas with Quotations 127
Commas with Items in a Series 129
End of Chapter Exercises 130–142

8 Parenthetical Commas 143

When a Description Comes After the Noun 143
   Words That Describe 144
   Phrases That Describe 144
   Clauses That Provide Extra Information 145
   Clauses That Identify the Noun 146
Setting Off Other Elements 147
   Transition Words 147

        Dates with Years   *149*
        Places with State or Country Names   *150*
   End of Chapter Exercises   150–162

9   Comma Errors   163

   Too Many Commas   163
        Subject, Verb   *164*
        Verb, Object   *165*
        Dependent Clauses That End the Sentence   *165*
        Separating Only Two Items   *166*
   End of Chapter Exercises   168–181

10   Apostrophes   183

   Apostrophes to Show Possession   184
   Some Special Cases   186
   Apostrophes to Make Contractions   189
   Apostrophes to Form Plurals   189
   End of Chapter Exercises   190–200

11   Subject-Verb Agreement   201

   Subject and Verb Endings   201
   Questions Related to Sentence Structure   203
        What About Compound Subjects?   *203*
        Do Compound Subjects Ever Take a Singular Verb?   *204*
        What About or, either/or, and neither/nor?   *204*
        What About Inverted Sentences?   *205*
        What About Words That Separate the Subject and Verb?   *206*
   Pronoun Problems   210
        Indefinite Pronouns   *211*
        Indefinite Pronouns That Appear with a Modifier   *212*
        Relative Pronouns   *213*
   Other Special Cases   216
        Collective Nouns   *216*
        Quantities   *216*
        Titles   *217*
        Singular Nouns with Plural Forms   *217*
   End of Chapter Exercises   218–227

12   Pronoun Agreement   229

   Different Pronouns for Different Uses   229
        Subject Pronouns   *229*
        Object Pronouns   *230*
        Pronouns That Show Possession   *231*
        Pronouns That Refer to the Subject   *232*
   Pronoun-Reference Problems   223

Sexist Language   234
Questions Related to Sentence Structure   236
   What About a Compound Antecedent?   236
   Do Compound Antecedents Ever Take a Singular Pronoun?   236
   What About or, either/or, and neither/nor?   237
   What About a Pronoun That Comes Before the Antecedent?   239
Pronoun Problems   240
   Indefinite Pronouns   240
   Indefinite Pronouns That Appear with a Modifier   242
   Relative Pronouns   243
Other Special Cases   245
   Collective Nouns As Antecedents   245
   Quantities As Antecedents   246
   Titles As Antecedents   246
   Singular Nouns with Plural Forms   246
End of Chapter Exercises   247–259

13 Shift in Person   261

First-Person Perspective   262
Second-Person Perspective   264
Third-Person Perspective   266
End of Chapter Exercises   269–279

14 Shift in Verb Tense   281

Present Tense   281
Past Tense   283
Future Tense   285
Some Special Problems   287
   Quotations   287
   Books, Movies, and Such   287
End of Chapter Exercises   288–297

15 Punctuation   299

Semicolons   299
   To Link Two Closely Related Independent Clauses   299
   To Clarify Lists   300
Colons   301
Parentheses   303
Dashes   304
Hyphens   304
Brackets   305
End of Chapter Exercises   306–312

16 Parallel Structure 313
Deciding What to Make Parallel 314
Parallel Clauses and Phrases 316
Parallel Verb Forms 317
Parallel Nouns and Describing Words 319
End of Chapter Exercises 321–329

17 Misplaced Words, Phrases, and Clauses 331
Misplaced Words 331
Misplaced Phrases 333
  Prepositional Phrases 333
  Phrases with Participles 334
  Infinitive Phrases 334
Misplaced Clauses 335
End of Chapter Exercises 337–344

18 More on the Mechanics of Writing 345
Underlining or Italics 345
Question Marks 347
Periods 348
Quotation Marks 348
Capitalization 351
End of Chapter Exercises 353–362

PART 2
The Writing Process 363

19 Preparing to Write 365
Preliminary Choices 365
  Topic 366
  Audience 366
  Stance 367
  Purpose 368
  Form 368
Generating Ideas 371
  Expository Essay 371
  Descriptive Essay 372
  Narrative 373
  Persuasive Essay 374
  Sample: Generating Ideas 375

Deciding on Your Insight   376
   Sample: Choosing an Insight   379
End of Chapter Exercise   380

20 Deciding What to Include   381
Generating Topic Sentences   381
   Sample: Ideas for Topic Sentences   384
Choosing the Content   385
   Sample: Listing Specific Examples   387
Preparing to Write: A Summary   392
End of Chapter Exercise   392

21 Writing a Draft   393
Internal Paragraphs   393
   Unity   393
   Coherence   394
   Logical Sequence   396
   Sample: Drafting a Paragraph   396
Writing an Introduction   398
   The Funnel   398
   The Bait   400
   The Challenge   401
   Sample: Drafting an Introduction   402
Writing a Conclusion   406
   A Simple End for a Story   406
   A Review   407
   A Parting Shot   407
   The Implications   408
   Sample: Drafting a Conclusion   410

22 Revising Your Paper   411
First Reading: Organization   411
Second Reading: Audience and Stance   412
Third Reading: Strong Words and Sentences   413
   Use Concrete Nouns   413
   Use Active Verbs   413
   Eliminate "to be" Verbs   414
   Eliminate "There is" and "It is"   419
   Try to Combine Sentences   420
Every Reading: Punctuation and Grammar   421
Revising Your Paper: A Summary   422
End of Chapter Exercise   422

Appendix: Commonly Misused Words   425

   Index   431

PART 1

Grammar, Punctuation, and Usage

CHAPTER 1

Subjects and Verbs

This chapter describes the most basic parts of an English sentence, the subject and the verb, so that you will be able to recognize them in a sentence. If you are like most American students, you have probably studied this before. If so, please treat this as review.

▪ Verbs

Verbs are words that describe action (*jump, scream, cower, rescue*) or condition (*am, is, seem, become*).

Practice 1

Draw two lines under the verbs in the following sentences.

1. Bad poetry often <u>makes</u> good lyrics.
2. Grammar <u>bores</u> me silly.
3. Comedian Julie Brown <u>has</u> a fascinating on-screen wardrobe.

As well as telling what something does or is, verbs also give a sense of *when* something happens. Thus we speak of verbs being in the present tense (*laughs*), past tense (*laughed*), or future tense (*will laugh*)—as well as a host of other confusing tenses.

> **The verb is the word that tells action or condition and provides a sense of when the action or condition occurred.**

If you have trouble identifying the verb in a sentence, this sense of time in the verb can help. Once you think you know which word might be

Copyright © 1992 by Harcourt Brace Jovanovich, Inc. All rights reserved.   3

the verb, ask yourself if you can add *will* before the verb and in that way change the time when the action or condition takes place.

Present	**Future**
go	will go
is	will be
write	will write

For example, in many sentences, the word *trip* refers to an action (one that inevitably occurs when many people are watching you do it). But in the following sentence, can you add *will* before the word *trip*?

> A trip to the mall puts my bank balance in jeopardy.
>
> A *will* trip to the mall puts my bank balance in jeopardy.

No, you can't, so *trip* is not the verb. You can add *will* before *put*, however, so *put* is the verb in that sentence.

> A trip to the mall *will put* my bank balance in jeopardy.

In the next example, try adding *will* before the words *astonishment, disappearing, outside,* and *window.* Is one of these words the verb?

> To his astonishment, Isaac saw a red cape disappearing into the clouds outside the plane window.

None of the sentences you create that way makes sense. Only when you add *will* before *saw* (and change *saw* to *see*) does the sentence still make sense. Therefore, *saw* is the only verb in this sentence.

> To his astonishment, Isaac *will see* a red cape disappearing into the clouds outside the plane window.

The steps for identifying verbs, then, are as follows:

1. Look for a word that tells action or condition.
2. Check that you have the right word by adding *will* before this verb to make it tell about the future. You may have to change the verb form slightly—changing *saw* to *will see*, or *are* to *will be*.
3. If this new sentence makes sense, then you have found at least one of the verbs in the sentence (some sentences have several verbs).
4. If this new sentence doesn't make sense, try another word.

Copyright © 1992 by Harcourt Brace Jovanovich, Inc. All rights reserved.

☐ Subjects

Once you have found the verb in a sentence, you can find the subject by asking yourself, "*Who* or *what* did or was what this verb is talking about?" For example, looking at the sentence about Superman, you can ask yourself, "Who or what *saw* the disappearing cape?" The answer is Isaac, so for the verb *saw*, *Isaac* is the subject.

Looking at the sentence about the mall, you can ask yourself, "Who or what *puts* my bank balance in jeopardy?" The answer here is the trip (to the mall), so *trip* is the subject for this verb. (The answer is *not* the mall; we explain the reason for that later.)

The subject, then, is the word or group of words that tells who or what does or is something in the sentence. As it works out, the following rule is true:

> **A subject is always a noun (such as *Susan, popcorn,* or *New York*) or a pronoun (such as *I, we, he,* or *they*).**

Because verbs tell what the subject does, you can identify the subject in simple sentences with these two steps:

1. Identify the verb.
2. Identify who or what does or is what the verb is talking about.

Try this process out in the following practice exercise.

Practice 2

In these sentences, identify the subjects with a single underline and the verbs with a double underline. (Each sentence has only one subject and one verb.)

1. <u>Mr. Weasel</u> <u><u>popped</u></u> the question.
2. Frozen <u>bananas</u> <u><u>taste</u></u> even better than ice-cream bars.
3. <u>Zach</u> <u><u>spilled</u></u> enchiladas on his date's suede jumper.
4. <u>You</u> <u><u>are</u></u> a contemptible, two-timing lout!
5. Every Fourth of July, my <u>family</u> <u><u>watches</u></u> *Yankee Doodle Dandy*.
6. To my children, the <u>laundry chute</u> <u><u>is</u></u> a passage to a magical kingdom.
7. <u>Midori</u> <u><u>wore</u></u> heirloom lace at the party.

Copyright © 1992 by Harcourt Brace Jovanovich, Inc. All rights reserved.

8. One by one, the students abandoned their tests into the professor's hands.
9. The librarian often puts catchy little quotes on a stand beside the main library door.
10. These days, few people read all of Charles Dickens's books.

Words That Look Like Verbs

Unfortunately, some words in a sentence look so much like verbs, you could almost conclude that the pesky things are intentionally trying to fool you. As you look for verbs, don't be confused by these verbals, which can never be the main verb in a sentence: infinitives, *-ing* words used as nouns, and participles.

Infinitives

Infinitives look like verbs but always have the word *to* before the verb form.

    I want *to swim* in the moonlight.

No word with *to* in front of it, no matter how much it seems like a word that tells action or condition, can *ever* be the main verb in a sentence.

Practice 3

Circle the infinitives in sentences 1–3.

1. I tried to ignore that my dentist had been drinking, but when he started to drill, I felt I had to speak up.
2. Oil-free makeup works best to cover pimples.
3. Iris was never one to quibble over details.

Rewrite the sentences in exercise 4 as one sentence, using this pattern:

    Melissa jogs every morning.

    She wants to wake herself up.

    Melissa jogs every morning to wake herself up.

4. Carmela took huge doses of vitamin C.
   She wanted to guard against colds.

   _____

   _____

5. Write a sentence with an infinitive in it.

   _____

   _____

-Ing Words As Nouns

A word that ends in *-ing* can also never be the verb on its own. Sometimes these *-ing* words actually serve as nouns (a noun names a person, place, or thing), such as *skydiving* in the following sentence:

> Even the thought of *skydiving* terrifies me.

If you're confused about this, try adding *the act of* before the *-ing* word. For example:

> (The act of) Driving a stick shift makes me feel like a racecar driver.

Practice 4

In sentences 1–4, all the *-ing* words look like verbs, but they are actually nouns. Circle these *-ing* words.

1. My Aunt Margot enjoys hunting husbands on safari.
2. Teasing our assistant trainer, a favorite pastime of everyone on the basketball team, drives her crazy.
3. After sipping cherry cordial, we played mah-jongg in the parlor.
4. The space alien took off in a hurry after watching *Miami Vice*.

Combine the sentences in exercise 5 to make one sentence, using this pattern:

> John detests something.
>
> It is typing his own papers.
>
> *John detests typing his own papers.*

5. Nick enjoys many activities.
   One activity is eating salsa and chips in front of *Monday Night Football.*

   _____

   _____

6. Write a sentence with an *-ing* word as the subject.

   _____

   _____

Participles

Some *-ing* words (called *participles*) act as describing words on their own, telling about the noun. With a helping verb (*has, is, was, were,* and so forth), an *-ing* word can be part of a verb, but *only* with a helping verb. The complete verb must include both the *-ing* word and the helping verb. So the rule holds true: An *-ing* word on its own can *never* be the verb.

Practice 5 _____

In sentences 1–4, look for the *-ing* words. Some *-ing* words are used as nouns or on their own as describing words and are therefore not part of the verb. Circle these *-ing* words.

(Hoping) for a check, Tasha tore into the envelope.

Some *-ing* words are used with helping verbs and are therefore considered part of the verb. Underline the complete verbs twice (helping verb and *-ing* word):

I am going.

1. Egbert Peasewater II is kissing Gloria Wonderbilt on the fire escape.
2. The angry girl climbing the stairs stomped her feet.
3. After chasing away the dog, she disappeared into her bedroom.
4. He had been planning to visit Beirut but, thinking better of it, headed for Monte Carlo instead.

Past Participles

Confusion can also arise over a past-tense verb form—the past participle—which is sometimes used as a verb and sometimes as a describing word. When a past-tense word tells what a person, place, or thing did, then the past-tense word is a verb.

> He wrinkled his brow. She wrinkled her hair.

This past-tense word can also tag onto helping verbs to become part of the verb.

> He had had an enormous meal. He had spattered ketchup on his tie. He had dribbled mustard on his knee. He had spilled coffee on his lapel. He should have been more careful. He was going to blow this interview.

But when this same past-tense word describes an object, it is *not* serving as a verb.

> His suit was wrinkled. (*Wrinkled* describes his suit.)
>
> The wrinkled linen still looked good. (*Wrinkled* describes the linen.)
>
> Wrinkled into furrows, the man's forehead never relaxed. (*Wrinkled* describes the man's forehead.)

Practice 6

In sentences 1–6, underline the complete verbs twice. Circle the participles that serve only to describe something.

1. My daredevil sister, (perched) upon the shaky ladder, laughed scornfully at my obvious concern.
2. (Assured) of his popularity, a rock star can burp at will.
3. The hair, cut and (shaped) by the girl's little brother, looked ghastly.
4. (Hoping) to hide it, she wore a cap to dinner.
5. No one was (fooled).
6. She ended up (wearing) hair shorter than her brother's—and he had been (sporting) a military buzz.

Copyright © 1992 by Harcourt Brace Jovanovich, Inc. All rights reserved.

Combine the two sentences in exercise 7, using a participle as in this series:

> Karen went to the library.
>
> She hoped to find a quiet place to study.
>
> *Karen went to the library, hoping to find a quiet place to study.*

7. My daughter spent Saturday at the mall.
   She frittered away her entire baby-sitting hoard.

   My daughter spent Saturday at the Mall, frittering away her entire baby-sitting hoard.

8. Write a sentence with a phrase that includes a participle (either -ing or past-tense form). Put this phrase either at the beginning of the sentence or at the end.

   Hoping to reach the top, the climber never looked down.

Exercises

In the following sentences, identify the subject (underline once) and the verb (underline twice). Don't be confused by infinitives (*to* + verb), *-ing* words used as nouns, or participles without a helping verb.

1. She is dancing like a cow on ice.
2. Judging too harshly often brings judgment in return.
3. Ariel promised to study with me.
4. Disgusted by the litter on the beach, I wanted to head straight home again.
5. Jack convinced me to join him in cleaning up a small stretch of beach.
6. To our surprise, many others joined us.
7. Running a detective agency rarely satisfies Phillippa's thirst for danger.
8. David wanted to win a BMX, but not a hot pink one plastered with My Little Pony decals.

9. Looking closely, he found the hole in the balloon.
10. Finally finished with his term paper, Tim dragged himself to breakfast.
11. To jump on a bed long enough is to ruin it.
12. My fancy French sauce is curdling before my eyes.
13. Stepping boldly into my doorway, the stray dog turned challenging eyes upon me.
14. I gave him only a tiny morsel to eat.
15. I am feeding him still.
16. Hakeem dragged himself slowly toward class, worrying each step about forgetting his speech, so carefully memorized.

☐ Seven Sentence Patterns

Subject-verb is the most basic sentence pattern in English:

> Velma waits at the restaurant.
>
> Rodney snoozes.
>
> Rodney is history.

Fortunately, our language has more variety than is found in these simple statements, but with the variety comes added complexity. There are seven more complex sentence patterns that you should learn to recognize.

When the Subject Follows the Verb: V + S

In some sentences, the usual order is reversed, and you have to look *after* the verb to find the subject.

> From behind the potted palm stepped the eavesdropper.
>
> At the head of the family table sits my mother.
>
> There is a beetle in the broth.

This pattern includes questions, in which the subject almost always follows at least part of the verb.

> Am I gorgeous or what?
>
> Does your baby sleep through the night yet?
>
> Where is your oxygen mask?

Practice 7

Combine the pairs of sentences in exercises 1 and 2, putting the subject *after* the verb.

1. This sound came from somewhere within the spooky house.
   An eerie voice bellowed.

   _____

   _____

2. On the roof, something stands.
   It is an energetic rooster.
   (Can you avoid *is* in your combined sentence?)

   _____

   _____

3. Write a sentence in which the subject follows the verb.

   _____

   _____

When Verbs Have More Than One Word: S + VVV

Often, the verb in a sentence has extra words called helping verbs. The extra words that slip in before the verb include *can, would, could, should,* and *will*—words that help to change the tense of a verb, but which themselves cannot be changed. You can also add any form of the helping verbs *to be* and *to have* and make a verb with more than one word.

> I could have been a contender.
>
> By then, my father will have heard the worst.

Practice 8

Add something to sentences 1 and 2 as indicated. For example:

> Annie and Abigail tell the truth at the trial.
>
> (Add *should have* to the verb and change it as necessary.)
>
> *Annie and Abigail should have told the truth at the trial.*

1. I thought twice before volunteering to debate my logic professor.
   (Add *will* to the verb and change it as necessary.)

   _____

   _____

2. The happy snowman enjoyed the summer sunshine.
   (Add *would have*.)

   _____

   _____

3. Write a sentence in which the verb tense requires more than one word for the verb.

   _____

   _____

When Words Interrupt the Verb: S+VXV

Certain words often come between the parts of a verb: *not, ever, never, only, always, just, really, already, often.*

> When the going gets rough, you could always quit.
>
> Jamal, dear, the plumber has already fixed that toilet.
>
> The Trojans could not detect the Greeks hiding inside the giant wooden horse.

Again, this pattern includes questions, in which the subject often interrupts the verb.

> When will you be coming home?
>
> Must you stay out so late?

Practice 9

In sentences 1 and 2, insert the extra word indicated to modify the verb.

1. I will stay up to watch the late late movie tonight.
   (Insert *probably*.)

2. Perhaps the tiger will consider eating you.
   (Insert *only* in such a way that you might escape.)

3. Write a sentence in which one of these words interrupts the verb: *not, never, really, often, already, always*.

When a Sentence Has Two Subjects: S + S + V

In some sentences, two subjects are doing the same thing, so they share the same verb. We say that such sentences have a compound subject.

> Cautiously, Karen and her little sister peered into the steam room.
>
> Silver-studded leather and pink hair rarely raise eyebrows anymore.
>
> Thorny roses and blackberry brambles tangled over the gravestone.

Practice 10

Combine the pairs of sentences in exercises 1 and 2, using the pattern S + S + V. For example:

> Vampires draw blood.
>
> Lab technicians draw blood.
>
> *Vampires and lab technicians draw blood.*

Seven Sentence Patterns   15

1. In the Middle Ages, kings hunted with falcons.
   Princes hunted with falcons.
   Even common soldiers hunted with falcons.

   _____

   _____

2. Because they have no teeth, ducks grind their food rather than chew it.
   Geese grind their food rather than chew it.
   Other beaked animals grind their food rather than chew it.

   _____

   _____

3. Write a sentence in which two or more subjects do the same thing.

   _____

   _____

When a Sentence Has Two or More Verbs: S + V + V

You won't always find a different subject for every verb. In many sentences, one subject is doing two or more things.

> The black Porsche's tires squealed and spun, leaving burned rubber behind.
>
> Utterly enchanted, Horatio worked up his courage and asked for her telephone number.
>
> At the last moment, Jill unlatched her suitcase and added a can of Mace.

Practice 11

Combine the sentences in exercise 1, constructing a sentence that follows the pattern S + V + V.

1. This happens when Indians greet each other.
   They lift their hands up.
   They put the palms softly together.
   They bow their heads slightly.
   They say "Salaam," which means "Peace."

   When Indians greet each other, they lift their heads up, put their palms softly together, bow their heads slightly, and say "Salaam," which means "Peace".

Copyright © 1992 by Harcourt Brace Jovanovich, Inc. All rights reserved.

2. Write a sentence in which one subject does two things.

The boy ran then fell in the pond. (handwritten)

When a Sentence Has an Understood Subject: C(US)

A sentence with an understood subject is commonly called a command. Commands are easily recognized as "parent talk." For example:

> (You) Get back up to your room this instant!
>
> Don't come down until your bed's made!
>
> And get rid of that dirty underwear!

In such sentences, you won't find the subject for the verb because it is unstated, but understood to be "you."

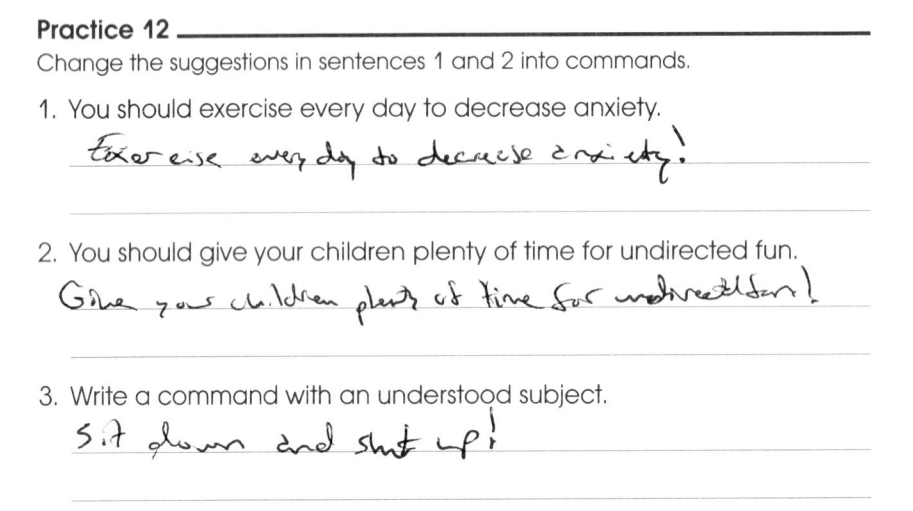

Practice 12

Change the suggestions in sentences 1 and 2 into commands.

1. You should exercise every day to decrease anxiety.

   Exercise every day to decrease anxiety! (handwritten)

2. You should give your children plenty of time for undirected fun.

   Give your children plenty of time for undirected fun! (handwritten)

3. Write a command with an understood subject.

   Sit down and shut up! (handwritten)

When Prepositional Phrases Separate the Subject and Verb: S+prep+V

Prepositions are those little words such as *in* and *by* that are used in phrases with nouns. When in doubt about whether a certain word is a preposition, think of a mountain and use the word to describe your relationship to the mountain: I am *above* the mountain; I am *around* the mountain; I am *at* the mountain; I am *from* the mountain; I am *on* the mountain; I am *under* the mountain; I am *beside/behind/in/off* . . . and so forth. As

Seven Sentence Patterns   17

always, the system has a few exceptions, such as *during, except,* and that most common preposition, *of,* but perhaps you can remember these. A prepositional phrase includes the preposition and the noun following it, as underlined in the following sentences:

> Hide yourself <u>under those branches</u>.
>
> The cat curled itself <u>around her neck</u>.
>
> The tornado hit <u>during the soccer finals</u>.

Practice 13
Complete the sentences in exercises 1–4 to answer the given questions. Use prepositional phrases.

1. Where did he hide it? Kenyon hid the much-coveted *Sports Illustrated* (where?) _under the couch_

2. Where did he jump? Spot jumped _over the gate_

3. What dessert did she eat? She ate a piece _of cheesecake_

4. Which one did he forget? He remembered all the answers _except number 10._

5. Write a sentence with a prepositional phrase, using an object other than *the mountain*.
I will get icecream, since I can't have cake.

Prepositional phrases that describe the subject usually come right after the subject of a sentence.

> The <u>legs</u> [of the chair] <u>broke</u> under their weight.
>
> The <u>rose</u> [beside the bed] <u>shed</u> its petals on her pillow.
>
> The <u>juggler</u> [outside the stadium] <u>stole</u> the crowd.

While adding valuable detail to the sentence, these prepositional phrases might sometimes confuse you when you are trying to find the true subject. When identifying the subject and verb, therefore, you need to ignore any prepositional phrase.

Copyright © 1992 by Harcourt Brace Jovanovich, Inc. All rights reserved.

Practice 14

In sentences 1–3, put brackets around the prepositional phrases that come between the subject and the verb; then underline the true subject once and the verb twice.

1. The sound [of rain on the roof] woke me from a restless sleep.
2. The sweat [of a thousand remembered nightmares] beads my brow at the thought of speaking [before a crowd].
3. Like lions waiting [in the Roman Colosseum] the fleas [in my carpet] wait for my blood.

Using prepositional phrases, combine the pairs of sentences in exercises 4 and 5; then put brackets around the prepositional phrases.

4. The pie disappeared.
   It was on the windowsill.

   The pie on the windowsill disappeared.

5. There were many boxes.
   The boxes were in the mail room.
   Only one had any mail in it.
   (Start this sentence with *Only one*.)

6. Write a sentence with a prepositional phrase separating the subject and the verb.

   The man in the window looks fake.

Exercises

For each sentence in the following three sets of exercises, first identify the subject with a single underline and the verb with a double underline. Then decide which sentence pattern it follows. Using the eight listed patterns, write the corresponding letter code in the blank before each sentence.

        S + V   Simple sentence.
        V + S   Verb comes before subject.

Copyright © 1992 by Harcourt Brace Jovanovich, Inc. All rights reserved.

Seven Sentence Patterns   19

S+VVV   Verbs have more than one word, including *will, would, could, should,* and *can,* and helping verbs with participles.
S+VXV   Extra words interrupt the verb.
S+S+V   Two or more subjects with one verb.
S+V+V   One subject with two or more verbs.
C(US)   Command with an understood subject.
S+prep+V   A prepositional phrase separates the subject and the verb.

Set 1

S+V+V 1. I covet Christie Brinkley's body but instead need Roseanne's wardrobe.
V+S   2. Too swiftly pass the days before my linguistics final.
       3. Never judge a textbook by its price.
S+V
       4. Her eyes shone more brightly than the diamonds at her throat.
S+S+V 5. The birds and bees and my girlfriend kept me from studying outdoors.
S+V   6. The cafeteria will have a separate smoking room soon.
S+p+V 7. Course material beyond my comprehension inspires me to snooze.
S+V+V 8. The eyes of many an early-morning philosophy student grow vague and blurry.
V+S   9. Remember to walk the armadillo.
S+V+V 10. Luxuries pamper the body but spoil the soul.

Set 2

S+S+V 1. Kip and Cam sneaked in after midnight.
S+V+V 2. Not having even begun, I will never, ever finish *War and Peace* by tomorrow.
S+V   3. Josefina, an unquenchable optimist, hopes to lose ten pounds by the weekend.

Copyright © 1992 by Harcourt Brace Jovanovich, Inc. All rights reserved.

Chapter 1 Subjects and Verbs

4. He won the lottery but squandered the prize.
5. Phyllida pulled on the miniskirt and wished for health-club hips.
6. Shawnella and her friends howled their approval at the Elvis impersonator.
7. The quality of mercy becomes diluted when mixed with prejudice.
8. A firefighter and a phoenix rose from the ashes.
9. Last summer, Payam and Lisa hiked in the Pariah Canyon.
10. Beneath the porch is a possum of preposterous proportions.

Set 3

1. Furtively following his wife, the health-food addict finally caught her eating animal crackers.
2. The achievement of my dreams and expectations depends entirely on the strength of my morning cup of coffee.
3. My two-year-old son, Mohammed, pushed the antique lamp over, then clapped his hands with glee.
4. Watching at home, I can guess all the answers before the contestants.
5. On the show, though, I would probably lose all capacity to think.
6. A red, red rose and a candlelight dinner appease my anger any day.
7. Just clean up the dishes afterward.
8. What animal walks on four feet in the morning, two feet at noon, and three feet in the evening?
9. This riddle of the Sphinx stumped all but Oedipus.
10. A human being crawls as a baby, walks on two feet as an adult, and uses a cane as a senior citizen.
11. Oedipus guessed the riddle but got more trouble than reward.

Copyright © 1992 by Harcourt Brace Jovanovich, Inc. All rights reserved.

Seven Sentence Patterns   21

   12. Read the full story in a book of Greek myths.

_____

Sentence Combining

Combine each group of sentences into one sentence. In your combined sentences, identify the subjects with a single underline and the verbs with a double underline.

1. Crickets rub their wings together.
   They do this to attract a mate.
   (Construct a simple sentence—S+V.)

   Crickets rub their wings together to attract a mate.

2. Social insects care for their young.
   Social insects divide the work among their group.
   Social insects have at least one queen.
   (Construct a sentence with more than one verb—S+V+V.)

   Social insects have at least one queen, they care
   for their young and divide work among their group.

3. Termites are social insects.
   Ants are social insects.
   Some bees are social insects.
   A few wasps are social insects.
   (Construct a sentence with more than one subject—S+S+V.)

   Termites, ants, bees, and wasps are
   social insects.

4. Some termites build mounds forty feet high.
   These termites are in Africa.
   (Construct a sentence with a prepositional phrase—S+prep+V.)

   Some Termites [around Africa] build mounds
   forty feet high.

5. Insects do cause problems for people.
   This does not always happen.
   (Construct a sentence with an extra word interrupting the verb—S+VXV.)

   Insects do cause problems for people, so
   this does not always happen.

Copyright © 1992 by Harcourt Brace Jovanovich, Inc. All rights reserved.

22 Chapter 1 Subjects and Verbs

6. Here is an example.
   Bees provide honey.
   Bees pollinate our plants.
   (Construct a sentence with two verbs—S+V+V.)

   Bees provide honey and pollinate our plants
   for example.

7. Insects also help us.
   They dispose of dead plants.
   They dispose of dead animals.
   They provide food for other animals.
   They loosen soil for crops.
   (Start with the first sentence, and attach the other sentences with -ing words.)

   Insects also help us by disposing of dead plants,
   disposing of dead animals, providing food for other animals,
   and loosening soil for crops.

Paragraph Editing Practice

Read through the following paragraphs. Then go back through them, marking the subjects with a single underline and the verbs with a double underline.

A. My husband's Aunt Eva lives in Monterey, California. She is now seventy-six. For ten years, she has made *jyaudz* (pronounced jowd-za) in her own factory. These little Chinese dumplings have pork, onions, ginger, scallions, and Chinese cabbage in them. Also called "potstickers," they are highly prized by the Chinese residents of Monterey and by other people in the know. The only worker, Aunt Eva painstakingly grinds the ingredients together. Then she folds about 300 per day, each one perfectly shaped. After ten years, her sign outside says: "Eva's Jyaudz Factory: Over 700,000 Made."

B. The grand opera *Carmen*, composed by Georges Bizet, was first produced in 1875. The opera tells the story of Carmen, a Spanish cigarette girl. Her fiery temper and beguiling charm fascinate the men around her. Don José, a corporal of the dragoons, falls in love with her. Forgetting his duty, he joins a band of smugglers. Having ruined Don José's career, Carmen turns her charms upon Escamillo, a popular bull-

Copyright © 1992 by Harcourt Brace Jovanovich, Inc. All rights reserved.

fighter. Spurned by this fickle creature, Don José stabs his faithless lover and then weeps over her body. Escamillo emerges from the bullfighting ring to discover his loss. This tragic story of love and betrayal has enchanted audiences for over a hundred years.

Review Exercises

1. List five prepositions. _____

2. Write sentences that include each of the following:

   a. An -ing word used as a noun _____

   b. An infinitive _____

   c. A participle _____

3. Write an example of each given sentence pattern.

   a. S+V   Simple sentence

   b. V+S   Subject following the verb

   c. S+VVV   Verbs with more than one word

   d. S+VXV   Words interrupting the verb

   e. S+S+V   Two or more subjects

Copyright © 1992 by Harcourt Brace Jovanovich, Inc. All rights reserved.

f. S+V+V   Two or more verbs

g. C(US)   Command with an understood subject

h. S+prep+V   Prepositional phrase between subject and verb

4. Underline the subject and verb in each sentence you wrote in exercise 3. Mark subjects with a single underline and verbs with a double underline.

CHAPTER 2

Clauses and Phrases

☐ Clauses

A *clause* is a group of words that has a subject and a verb. *Independent clauses* (as opposed to dependent clauses) can stand alone as a sentence; they offer a complete thought. To qualify as a sentence, a group of words must have at least one independent clause.

Practice 1

The following sentences show some of the different ways that subjects and verbs can be combined to form an independent clause. Each has a subject-verb combination. Underline subjects once and verbs twice.

1. Mrs. Rutherford refuses to sit on anything except genuine antiques.
2. She shops at only the snootiest boutiques.
3. Sarah and Shelley snuggled down under the leaves.
4. Stanley pounded on the drum.
5. Yola heard, jumped, ran, and vanished.
6. Walter spit.
7. Dance!

As you can see, independent clauses can be long or short, have one subject or two, have one verb or many more, and can even be a one-word command. The distinguishing feature of an independent clause is that it can stand alone. It does not leave you with that incomplete, so-what feeling.

An independent clause has three characteristics: a subject, a verb, *and* **a complete thought.**

Dependent clauses, though, leave you wondering. In the following group of words, identify the subject and the verb:

> After my husband gallantly carried me over the threshold.

As you see, this clause does have a subject and a verb, but even so, the thought of the sentence is obviously incomplete. We call such incomplete thoughts *sentence fragments*. "What happened next?" you wonder. Adding an independent clause will complete the sentence.

> [After my husband gallantly carried me over the threshold], he had to spend a month in traction.

Note that the added independent clause could stand alone ("He had to spend a month in traction"), but the dependent clause gives extra information that explains the independent clause. Note also that the independent clause could come before the dependent clause:

> My husband had to spend a month in traction [after he gallantly carried me over the threshold].

Mistaking a dependent clause for an independent clause can lead to sentence fragments, so learning to recognize dependent clauses can be very useful. The distinguishing feature is the dependent signal that precedes the subject of the dependent clause. *After* is the dependent signal in the sentence about the gallant husband. Other dependent signals include the following words:

after	how	until	which
although	if	what	whichever
as	in order that	whatever	while
as if	since	when	who
because	so that	whenever	whom
before	than	where	whose
even if	that	whereas	why
even though	though	wherever	
ever since	unless	whether	

These dependent signals always come *before* the subject and the verb (although in some cases, as we will explain, the dependent signal can do double duty and serve as both the subject and the dependent signal). How can you know that the word before the subject and verb is actually a dependent signal, and therefore makes the clause a sentence fragment? Try this: Move the word you suspect is a dependent signal from before the subject and verb to after the verb.

1. If you can't fit this word in after the verb—in other words, if the sentence makes sense only when the word precedes the subject and verb—you almost certainly have a dependent signal.
2. If you *can* fit this word after the verb in the sentence, and the sentence still makes sense, you almost certainly do *not* have a dependent signal.

Here's an example. Let's try moving the word from before the subject and verb (which we have marked) to after the subject and verb:

> *Because* <u>you</u> <u>asked</u> so nicely, you may type up the report on the group project.
>
> <u>You</u> <u>asked</u> *because* so nicely, you may type up the report on the group project.

The new arrangement makes no sense, so *because* is in fact a dependent signal.

In the next example, notice how you can move *perhaps* from before the subject to after the verb.

> *Perhaps* you could cut my hair after practicing on someone else.
>
> You could *perhaps* cut my hair after practicing on someone else.

Do you see that wherever you put the *perhaps*, the sentence still makes sense? Try this system with the sentences in Practice 2. Then for more practice in using dependent signals, complete Practice 3.

Practice 2

In these sentences, a word precedes each of the subject-verb combinations (which are marked with underlines). *Circle* this word if it is a dependent signal. *Leave the word unmarked* if it is not a dependent signal.

1. Then <u>he</u> <u>will not mind</u> (if) <u>I</u> <u>borrow</u> his notes.
2. <u>I</u> <u>am impressed</u> (that) <u>he</u> <u>sold</u> the plate at all; however, <u>I</u> <u>am stunned</u> that <u>he</u> <u>sold</u> it for $500.
3. (When) <u>I</u> <u>came</u> to college, <u>I</u> <u>discovered</u> (that) <u>math textbooks</u> <u>are</u> the perfect cure for insomnia.

Copyright © 1992 by Harcourt Brace Jovanovich, Inc. All rights reserved.

28 Chapter 2 Clauses and Phrases

Practice 3

After each of the listed dependent signals, add the words *I went to the store* and then follow this dependent clause with a comma. Can you sense the incomplete feeling? Next complete each sentence with an independent clause of your own. The first one has been done as an example.

1. After *I went to the store, I came home.*

2. Before _____

3. Although _____

4. Whenever _____

5. Unless _____

6. Until _____

7. If _____

8. Even if _____

9. When _____

10. Because _____

In some dependent clauses, the dependent signal acts as the subject. These double-duty words—*who, which, that,* and *whoever*—are both underlined and circled in the following sentences:

> She is a comedian [(who) appeared on *Saturday Night Live*].
>
> This is the lamp [(that) has shed light on countless students' studies].

Practice 4

Complete the following sentences, putting a verb directly after the dependent signal *who, that,* or *which*.

1. I am a student who _____

   _____

2. This is that car that _____

   _____

3. This is the misplaced letter, which _____

   _____

Occasionally these double-duty words (*who, which, that,* and *whoever*) help to form dependent clauses in the middle of a sentence, directly after a noun.

> The student [who is coming toward us] has competed in the Olympics.
>
> The home team, [which won the game], hopes to make the play-offs.

When identifying dependent clauses, then, don't be confused by these double-duty words, serving as both the dependent signal and the subject of the dependent clause.

Practice 5

Combine the following sentence pairs, using a double-duty word (*who, which, that,* or *whoever*) to start the second part of each sentence. For example:

> Paul usually rides his bike.
>
> Paul likes fresh air.
>
> (Use a *who* to add the information from the second sentence.)
>
> *Paul, who likes fresh air, usually rides his bike.*

1. Hank is more likely to go naked in a snowstorm than wear a three-piece suit.
   He shops almost exclusively at L. L. Bean.
   (Use the double-duty word *who* just after *Hank* to insert the information from the second sentence.)

   _____

   _____

Copyright © 1992 by Harcourt Brace Jovanovich, Inc. All rights reserved.

2. Scientists think that fireflies flash their lights to warn off predators. They (the fireflies) taste bad to night-feeding birds.
   (Use the double-duty word *which* to include the information from the second sentence.)

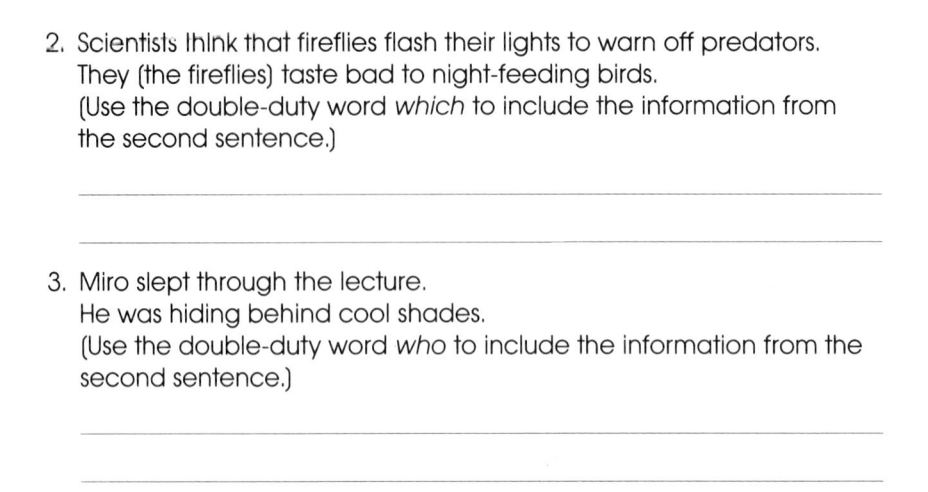

   _____

   _____

3. Miro slept through the lecture.
   He was hiding behind cool shades.
   (Use the double-duty word *who* to include the information from the second sentence.)

   _____

   _____

◻ Identifying Clauses

As we state at the beginning of this chapter, being able to identify an independent clause is the easiest way to avoid sentence fragments. This section will offer a three-step process for identifying clauses, both independent and dependent.

Step 1: Identify the Subject-Verb Combinations

A sentence can have many subjects and many verbs, but no matter how many of each the sentence has, or how they are arranged, certain subjects and verbs will belong together. Finding these combinations is the first step in identifying clauses.

Practice 6

Identify the subjects (single underline) and verbs (double underline) for the following sentences.

1. Hurry home. (Command)
2. Tawanda hurried home. (S+V)
3. Tawanda and William hurried home. (S+S+V)
4. Tawanda and William hurried home and changed their clothes.
   (S+S+V+V)
5. Tawanda hurried home, and William went with her. (S+V, and S+V)

Copyright © 1992 by Harcourt Brace Jovanovich, Inc. All rights reserved.

6. Tawanda hurried home, William went with her, and Ben stayed here.
   (S+V, S+V, and S+V)

As you try to identify clauses, begin by finding the first verb, then find the subject or subjects that go with that verb, and then look for the next verb. Sometimes this verb will belong to the same subject, and sometimes this verb will have its own subject. Keep going until you have identified all the subject-verb combinations. Watch carefully for commands, which have an understood subject, "you." Look at the subject-verb combinations that have been marked in the following sentence:

> My roommate always wears royal blue when he intends to ask a girl on a date because he thinks that the shade deepens the color of his eyes.

Step 2: Circle the Dependent Signals

For each subject-verb combination you have identified, look to see if a dependent signal precedes it. Circle these dependent signals. They will tell you which clauses are dependent clauses. Watch carefully for an understood *that*, which is often left out.

> I hoped I could go.
>
> He promised I would see Santa.

> I hoped [((that)) I could go].
>
> He promised [((that)) I would see Santa].

Circling these dependent signals will help you find the dependent clauses, as in the following sentence:

> My roommate always wears royal blue (when) he intends to ask a girl on a date (because) he thinks (that) the shade deepens the color of his eyes.

Step 3: Bracket the Dependent Clauses

Identify each dependent clause, including the dependent signal and all the other words that go with the dependent clause's subject-verb combination. The remaining clauses are independent clauses. In our sample sentence, then, the only independent clause is "my roommate always

32 Chapter 2 Clauses and Phrases

wears royal blue," a clause that could stand alone as a sentence. An independent clause has three requirements:

1. A subject.
2. A verb.
3. No dependent signal.

In the sample sentence, the dependent clauses that follow the independent clause provide extra information.

> My roommate always wears royal blue [(when) he intends to ask a girl on a date] [(because) he thinks] [(that) the shade deepens the color of his eyes].

Practice 7
Go through the three-step process for the following sentences, each of which has one dependent clause and one independent clause. The first sentence has been done as an example.

> Underline subjects once and verbs twice.
> Does a dependent signal precede any of the subject-verb combinations? Circle these dependent signals.
> Bracket dependent clauses.

1. [(After) the harvest ended], the canning began.
2. The fiesta in the mall stopped (until) the siesta ended.
3. (If) she asks me, I will agree.
4. (If) she does not ask me, I will ask her.
5. (Whenever) a New York Giants game comes on TV, there go my best intentions to study.
6. (Until) the wind blowing across the prairie stops, stay in the storm cellar.
7. (Because) Greg wanted a letter from his girlfriend and needed a check from his parents, he raced to his mailbox after his morning class.
8. Beth and Takesha missed their classes (when) they slept in.
9. Mei-Lin had never promised (that) she would work for me.
10. Joe smashed his computer screen (when) his disk crashed for the third time.

Copyright © 1992 by Harcourt Brace Jovanovich, Inc. All rights reserved.

Identifying Clauses   33

11. [(Although) I commute sixty miles round trip every day,] I have not yet had an accident.
12. [(Whatever) the salesman says,] get it in writing.
13. Go with the wrecking crew [(if) you can.]
14. The trucker stopped [(when) he saw the accident.]
15. There are only seven days [(until) spring break starts.]

Sentences with Many Clauses

Not all sentences have only one dependent clause and one independent clause. The following exercise set provides practice in analyzing more complex sentences.

Practice 8

Use the same three-step process to identify the clauses in the following sentences, which have differing numbers of clauses. The first sentence has been done as an example.

   Underline subjects once and verbs twice.
   Circle dependent signals.
   Bracket dependent clauses.

1. [(Whenever) my roommate comes in smiling], I know [(that) a romantic story is coming].
2. [(When) I am least expecting it,] from somewhere deep within me comes the insistent urge to see the ocean.
3. I feel as if I have lost my place in the family [(because) my little brother has moved into my room at home.]
4. [(Although) I think that I would be happier teaching children than selling stocks,] I am majoring in business to make my husband happy.
5. [(After) he finally managed to break in,] the burglar looked around in dismay at the remnants of packing materials scattered around the house.
6. [(Even if) designers decide that women should wear only short skirts this season,] my sister will continue to wear her full-length skirts so that she can sit on the floor of her kindergarten classroom.

Copyright © 1992 by Harcourt Brace Jovanovich, Inc. All rights reserved.

34   Chapter 2   Clauses and Phrases

7. Although better known for playing football, my hefty brother also sings a powerful bass.
8. When I drove home last Thanksgiving, there was snow on the ground.
9. The librarian refused to admit that our library did not have anything on my topic.
10. After the car slipped across the greasy patch on the highway, it rammed against the barricade and bounced across both lanes before it finally stopped on the soft, grassy field beside the road.
11. Ramón refused to go to the party because he had forgotten to make any appetizers, and even though she had remembered to make appetizers, Jill refused to go to the party because she had already eaten them.
12. Winona has a strange feeling that she had an assignment due yesterday, but she cannot be certain because she skipped class.

Rules for Sentences

Based on the sentences in Practice 8, answer these questions:

1. Can a sentence have only one dependent clause and nothing else and still be a complete sentence? _no_
2. Can a sentence have only one independent clause? _yes_
3. Can a sentence have both a dependent clause and an independent clause? _yes_
4. To be a sentence, a group of words must have at least one of what kind of clause? _Independent_
5. An independent clause has what three characteristics? (page 25) _subject + verb + complete thought_
6. Can a sentence have more than one dependent clause? _Yes_

Copyright © 1992 by Harcourt Brace Jovanovich, Inc. All rights reserved.

Phrases

A phrase, although also a group of words, conveys an idea without a subject or verb. The underlined words in the following sentences are phrases:

> The galoshes <u>on the porch</u> have holes in their soles.
>
> <u>Lifting the lid</u>, I was shocked to see a frog in the frying pan.

Phrases on their own—no matter how long they are—can never be complete sentences because they do not have the necessary requirements for a sentence: a subject, a verb, and no dependent signal.

Practice 9

Read the following groups of words and identify each with the appropriate letter code:

    IC   Independent clauses (subject, verb, and no dependent signal).
    DC   Dependent clauses (subject, verb, and a dependent signal).
    P   Phrases (groups of words without a subject or verb).

_DC_ 1. If you should ever witness a drug transaction.
_DC_ 2. When the baby swung her legs.
_IC_ 3. I loved his brains far better than his brawn.
_DC_ 4. As soon as I eat this disaster.
_P_ 5. Fishing for compliments.
_IC_ 6. My stomach cries out for Pepto-Bismol.
_DC_ 7. Inside my pretty head.
_P_ 8. But for a nasty headache.
_IC_ 9. I have only myself to blame for the crumbs.
_P_ 10. Splashing ink on her shoes.
_IC_ 11. The high chair rocked dangerously.
_DC_ 12. Since I not only made my bed but also bought it.
_P_ 13. Beyond the moon.
_IC_ 14. Never spend more than your credit-card limit.

Copyright © 1992 by Harcourt Brace Jovanovich, Inc. All rights reserved.

____ 15. Jumping as far as possible into the crystal clear waters of the lake.

Sentence Combining

Combine each group of sentences into one sentence.

1. Craig did not want to devote his entire college career to football practice.
   That is why he quit the team.
   (Use *because*.)

2. Elena read a book about Thoreau.
   She told me that Thoreau invented a process.
   The process was for making pencils.
   (Use *after*.)

Paragraph Editing Practice

Read the following paragraphs. Then go back through them, marking the subjects with a single underline, the verbs with a double underline, the dependent signals with a circle, and entire dependent clauses with brackets. Write in any understood signals, such as *that*.

A. When you go into the kitchen to make cookies, a sauce, or some other delicacy, thank Fannie Farmer for inventing the standard measuring cups and spoons that you use. Until Fannie Farmer introduced the idea of level, precise measurements, cooks in America relied on vague instructions, such as "two large spoonfuls" or "a quantity of milk." She became the Boston Cooking School's director. Then, in 1896, Fannie Merritt Farmer compiled the famous *Boston Cooking-School Cook Book*.

Copyright © 1992 by Harcourt Brace Jovanovich, Inc. All rights reserved.

Even today a version of Farmer's cookbook stands on many cooks' shelves.[1]

B. Even though most people would classify fairy tales as children's literature, Jakob and Wilhelm Grimm intended their collection for both adults and children. The Brothers Grimm, who collected original tales from storytellers, friends, neighbors, and from older collections, included some fairly violent stories, such as "Hansel and Gretel" and "Little Red Riding Hood." Although these stories shocked many critics, most people, young and old alike, loved the stories. Even today people are drawn to these tales, perhaps because, as the Grimms believed, "these primitive expressions reflect the emotions, dreams and desires of every human being."[2]

Review Exercises

There are four terms that you absolutely, no-fooling, *have to know* to understand the rest of the book. Describe how to recognize each in a sentence.

1. Subject _____

2. Verb _____

3. Independent clause _____

4. Dependent clause _____

5. List five dependent signals. _____

---

[1] Better Homes and Gardens, *Heritage Cook Book* (Des Moines, IA: Meredith Corporation, 1975), p. 312.

[2] Lily Owens, "Introduction," in *The Complete Brothers Grimm Fairy Tales* (New York: Avenel Books, 1981), n. p.

Copyright © 1992 by Harcourt Brace Jovanovich, Inc. All rights reserved.

After each of the following sentences, write the letter code for the sentence pattern it illustrates. (You may want to mark subject-verb combinations.)

S+S+V	Two or more subjects.
S+V+V	Two or more verbs.
C(US)	Command with an understood subject.
V+S	Subject follows the verb.
S+S+V+V	Two subjects, two verbs.
S+prep+V	Prepositional phrase between subject and verb.

6. Ignore my warning at your deadly peril! _____

7. Mai and Kerry rushed up the apartment stairs. _____

8. Mac read the letter, then tore it into shreds. _____

9. From across the murky river waters drifted an eerie wail. _____

10. Renoir's radiant colors and streaks of light create illusions of the sun's brilliancy and bring his subjects to life. _____

11. The crisp coolness of a perfect fall day makes my hands itch for a football to throw. _____

Misused Words: affect/effect

Almost always, *affect* is a verb and *effect* is a noun.

Affect as a verb means to influence.

> How could a diet of pizza and coke *not affect* you?

Effect as a noun means a consequence or result.

> The *effect* of too much pizza is too much middle and behind.

Very rarely, *effect* becomes a verb and means to bring about.

> We can *effect* a compromise.

Watch for these words. Because so many people misuse them, we will sometimes do so in our essay editing exercises as well, so that you can have practice correcting this error. Complete the following sentences, using the correct form of either *effect* or *affect*.

1. You should have known the _____ of ketchup on raw silk.

2. The vacuum has always had a frightening _____ on our cat.

3. Your sad story _____ me deeply, but I refuse to postpone the exam.
4. When will the mental _____ of an earthquake wear off?
5. Because I have asthma, smoke _____ me badly.

CHAPTER 3

Sentence Fragments: Something Missing

▢ What a Sentence Must Have

When editing your work, one of the first things to watch out for is sentence fragments. You know what a sentence must have:

A sentence must have at least one independent clause.

You also know what an independent clause requires:

To be an independent clause, a group of words must meet three requirements: It must have a subject, it must have a verb, and it cannot have a dependent signal.

Practice 1

The following groups of words may be missing subjects or verbs. Whenever possible, do the following:

   Mark the subject-verb combinations.
   Circle the dependent signals.
   Bracket the dependent clauses.

Then, put a check mark by the entries that have at least one independent clause. The first one has been done as an example.

✔ 1. I lost my marbles, or did you find them in the cuckoo's nest?

_____ 2. My mom, my most faithful and devoted Little League fan.

_____ 3. Although I rented an ugly apartment, I was able to transform it with paint, plants, and prints.

_____ 4. Am happier counting calories than counting inches and pounds.

_____ 5. Singles on *Love Connection*, often humiliated by their dates and yet continuing to risk rejection.

Copyright © 1992 by Harcourt Brace Jovanovich, Inc. All rights reserved. **41**

6. Early morning walks with my husband, which saved my marriage.

7. After the pilot sang on the plane, he landed in Spain where it seldom rains.

8. While visiting every zoo from here in Brownsville, Texas, to Manhattan, bought enough stuffed animals to create our own zoo.

9. He allowed himself to fall for his young philosophy professor, a charming but married woman.

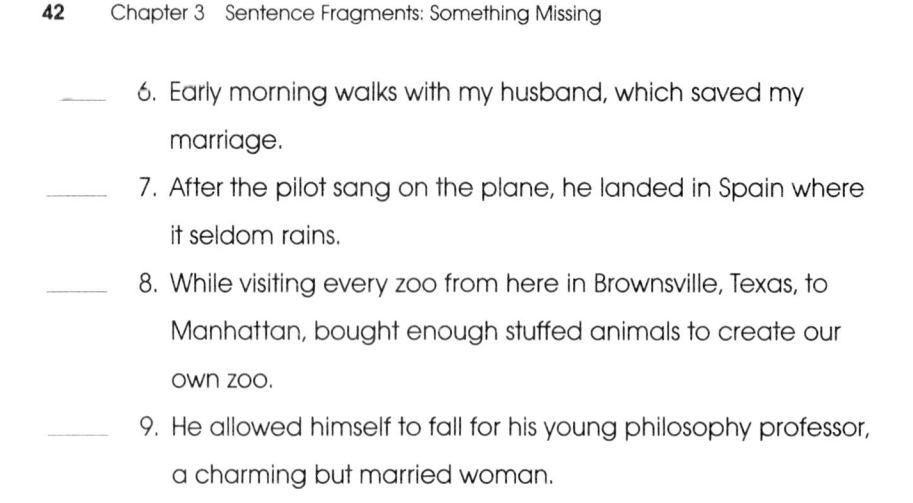

The entries that do not have at least one independent clause are called *sentence fragments*, which are rarely acceptable in the formal writing that is expected in college. This chapter explains how to avoid certain sentence fragments.

☐ Fragments Without Subjects

If you try to mark the subject-verb combinations in the following paragraph, you will find that none of these "sentences" has a subject.

> After falling into the icy blue water. Kicked off her heavy hiking boots, slipped off her sweater, and grabbed the nearby, floating oar. Then climbed onto the overturned boat. And started paddling for shore.

Why might you create these sentence fragments? Sometimes, after writing a good sentence, you might decide to tell something else the subject did. Instead of adding this information to the original sentence, you might create a second, flawed sentence that has no subject. Subject-verb combinations must live together in the same sentence—no divorce allowed! Each of the examples on the left should be one sentence, not two. To help you sort out the problems, the subjects have been underlined once, the verbs twice, and the dependent clauses have been bracketed. Compare each example with the corrected version on the right.

Copyright © 1992 by Harcourt Brace Jovanovich, Inc. All rights reserved.

Incorrect	Correct
Charles made a map of his hometown. But forgot to give it to his fiancée and her parents.	Charles made a map of his hometown but forgot to give it to his fiancée and her parents.
She knew [(that) she needed to lose a few pounds] so she skipped the raw vegetable. And ate only one helping of double-fudge cheesecake.	She knew [(that)she needed to lose a few pounds] so she skipped the raw vegetable and ate only one helping of double-fudge cheesecake.

In all these examples, the sentence fragment begins with one of the seven coordinating conjunctions. These conjunctions join two parts of a sentence:

for, and, nor, but, or, yet, so

The first letters of these seven words form the acronym *FANBOYS*. It's an easy way to remember these seven conjunctions.

Practice 2

For practice in writing complete sentences with coordinating conjunctions, combine the following pairs of sentences. Use only one subject (S + V + V) as in this sentence:

Rashid threw on a bathrobe and scrambled down the fire escape.

How do you punctuate these sentences? When a sentence has only one subject but two verbs, you don't need a comma before the FANBOYS.

1. Vera went to the horror movie.
   She lost her voice screaming.

   _____

   _____

2. Sophie threw up a desperate shot.
   She missed the basket.

   _____

   _____

Copyright © 1992 by Harcourt Brace Jovanovich, Inc. All rights reserved.

Students often make the same sentence fragment error with transition words, such as *then*.

Incorrect	**Correct**
He threw down the computer disk. Then stomped on it with his foot.	He threw down the computer disk, then stomped on it with his foot.
Sherrie put the pizza into the oven. Then forgot to turn it on.	Sherrie put the pizza into the oven, then forgot to turn it on.

To edit this error, change the period to a comma and add the sentence fragment to the complete sentence.

Practice 3

To review, mark the subject-verb combinations in the following sentences (single underline for subjects and double underline for verbs). Put a box around the FANBOYS (*for, and, nor, but, or, yet, so*).

1. At birth, baby pandas weigh only four ounces but can grow to weigh over 200 pounds as adults.

2. Alberto has not had a date in six months and is thinking about taking out an ad in the Personals.

3. In the morning, give me coffee, hot and black, and then leave me alone.

4. The prince, after defeating the dragon, tried to untie the fair damsel but almost fainted from her bad breath instead.

Combine the sentence pairs in exercises 5 and 6, using only one subject with two verbs (S + V + V).

5. Berti stayed up all night typing her paper into the computer. Then she forgot how to work the printer.

_____

_____

6. We will go to a movie tonight.
We will eat a late supper.

_____

_____

Edit the following paragraph, eliminating sentence fragments. If you have trouble with any of these, first underline the subject-verb combinations, and then make certain each verb has a subject to go with it.

7. Once and only once, I looked down. And found money. I am not talking about spare change or even a shiny silver dollar. There on the sidewalk, a hundred-dollar bill, green, newly minted, crisp as a garden-fresh salad, was smiling up at me. A sweet gift had fallen from heaven. And landed at my feet. Unfortunately, I had seen the bill slip from a woman's purse only moments before. Then fall to the sidewalk. Still in sight, she was halfway up the block. Sighing, I shouted. And hurried after her.

☐ Fragments Without Verbs

In this paragraph, none of the apparent sentences has a verb:

> Movies [that come out right at the beginning of a long, hot summer]. Scary thrillers, suspenseful adventures, gory horror stories, [which appeal to adolescents]. These kids, [who are looking for a way to escape the afternoon heat]. Dark, cool theaters, an overflowing box of popcorn, their friends around them, and a monster of the midway on the loose.

As happens in the paragraph above, sometimes the information with the subject of a sentence becomes so long and so detailed that you lose track of your original subject, which still doesn't have a verb to go with it. Look at this "sentence" (actually a sentence fragment):

> The groupie in purple spandex tights, a lime-green tunic, black leather vest, and mustard-colored scarf.

As long as this sentence fragment is, it lacks a verb. What, you might ask, did this brightly dressed groupie *do*? Burp? Kiss Michael Jackson? Sit on a dozen eggs? With this sentence fragment, you can't know.

In some instances you might create long descriptions by adding clauses or descriptive phrases after the subject. Look at the following sentence

Copyright © 1992 by Harcourt Brace Jovanovich, Inc. All rights reserved.

46 Chapter 3 Sentence Fragments: Something Missing

fragments. In the first example, *who* is a dependent signal that serves as the subject of the dependent clause.

Sentence Fragment	Complete
Professors [who lecture on one thing and test on something completely different].	Professors [who lecture on one thing and test on something completely different] drive me crazy.
My teeth, [the only natural set that I will ever have].	My teeth, [the only natural set that I will ever have], are disintegrating rapidly.

These sentence fragments begin with long, descriptive subjects. Perhaps because these subjects are so long, you might sometimes feel you have to stop the sentence, creating a sentence fragment. When this happens, you will usually follow a missing-verb sentence fragment with another sentence that completes the thought. Using our groupie sentence, notice that when it is written correctly, all the information fits into a single sentence.

Incorrect	Correct
The groupie in purple spandex tights, a lime-green tunic, black leather vest, and mustard-colored scarf. She crowded ahead of me in the ticket line.	The groupie in purple spandex tights, a lime-green tunic, black leather vest, and mustard-colored scarf crowded ahead of me in the ticket line.

Practice 4

Sentences 1–6 have long, descriptive subjects. Underline the subjects once and the verbs twice, and then bracket the dependent clauses. Notice how widely separated the subjects and verbs are.

1. The shimmering, blue waters and the shining, sandy beach [of the lake] [behind my parent's cabin] look good enough to be [on a travel brochure].

2. Our last car [which lasted through three children and a St. Bernard] became a fiery sacrifice [at the nearby firefighters' training school].

3. His only brother, [who worked in Alaska for many years, but who now has moved to Mexico for some warmth,] refuses to visit [in the winter].

Copyright © 1992 by Harcourt Brace Jovanovich, Inc. All rights reserved.

Fragments Without Verbs   47

4. The large, heavy textbook that you dropped on my sore toe has accidentally been kicked into the mud.
5. The jackrabbit, determined yet hopelessly outclassed, beat the coyote with wit rather than muscle power.
6. Stamps that have printing flaws, such as superimposed images or misspelled words, are worth thousands of dollars to collectors.

For practice in correctly writing sentences with long, descriptive subjects, combine the sentence pairs in exercises 7 and 8. Even though the subject begins to seem long, continue the sentence until you have at least one independent clause.

7. There was an enormous, multicolored mural with boldly painted figures.
   It covered one wall of the college gymnasium.

   There was an enormous, multicolored mural with boldly painted figures covering one wall of the college gymnasium.

8. There was a small, pig-tailed child with tears running down her face, whimpering softly for her mother to come home.

For exercises 9–11, insert the information from the second sentence into the first sentence to combine them.

9. The pajamas had figures of Cupid on them.
   I wore the pajamas last night.

   The pajamas, I wore last night, had figures of Cupid on them.

10. Amy will be arriving at our house any moment.
    Amy is my children's favorite baby-sitter.

    Amy, my children's favorite baby-sitter, will be arriving at our house any moment.

11. Katie must have an asbestos tongue.
    She loves to eat the hottest possible Indian curries.

    Katie loves to eat the hottest possible Indian curries, she must have an asbestos tongue.

Copyright © 1992 by Harcourt Brace Jovanovich, Inc. All rights reserved.

Practice 5

Edit the following paragraph, eliminating sentence fragments.

The ruggedly handsome biker[in black leather.]He spied a woman leaning back against his shiny new Harley-Davidson. Apparently she was taking a break without regard to his property. She had her nerve! The biker, who had every intention of jerking her to her feet. He saw her peaceful, pretty face and instantly forgave her. Besides, she was wearing a Harley T-shirt.

☐ Incomplete-Thought Fragments

The following paragraph seems strange because all the "sentences" are actually dependent clauses.

> [When she found the knife in the butler's closet]. [Although Agatha thought] [that she had finally solved the maddening murder]. Unfortunately, [because the knife was embedded in the butler himself]. [If he didn't do it].

Why do people use dependent signals, the way this writer did repeatedly? You know that an independent clause has a subject and a verb. If you want to show a relationship between two independent clauses, you can add a dependent signal to one of these clauses. The dependent signal shows the relationship. For example, here are two independent clauses:

> She found the knife in the butler's chest. She opened the door.

As written, you cannot know how these independent clauses relate to each other. If you add a dependent signal either to the first or to the second independent clause, a relationship becomes clear:

> She found the knife in the butler's chest [when she opened the door].
>
> [When she found the knife in the butler's chest], she opened the door.

Copyright © 1992 by Harcourt Brace Jovanovich, Inc. All rights reserved.

You could also have used the following dependent signals: *before, because, after,* or *while*. Try inserting them into the sentence, before either the first or the second independent clause, to see how the relationship between the independent clauses changes.

As soon as you add a dependent signal, of course, the clause ceases to be independent and becomes dependent, and *a dependent clause cannot stand alone as a complete sentence.* When you fail to attach a dependent clause to an independent clause, you create a sentence fragment.

Being able to recognize a dependent signal makes your job much easier, and yet, unlike the FANBOYS, dependent signals do not easily form an acronym—a memorable word made up of their beginning letters. We discussed earlier how to identify dependent signals (try moving them, and if you can't, you probably do have a dependent signal); however, the only truly reliable way to identify dependent clauses is to develop a sense for the incomplete feeling that these clauses give you.

When analyzing sentences, first remember to watch out for dependent clauses in which you choose to leave out the *that*. Second, remember that four dependent signals—*who, which, that,* and *whoever*—can serve double duty as the subject and the dependent signal. Watch for these words.

Practice 6

In the following sentences, put a single line under the subjects, a double line under the verbs, and a circle around the dependent signals. Put a check mark beside the sentences in which a dependent signal serves as the subject of its clause (these have the double-duty dependent signals *who, which, that,* or *whoever*).

1. Because three hours later his friend was sober, Alonzo dug the car keys out of the flower pot, owning up to his theft.
2. ✓ Jared, who refused to take typing in high school, has spent a fortune on typing services.
3. After he saw the bullet hole in the office door, my brother decided to look for work elsewhere.
4. ✓ Mendelssohn's oratorio *Elijah*, which tells the Biblical story, contains one of the most beautiful musical exhortations to trust God, "O Rest in the Lord."

Copyright © 1992 by Harcourt Brace Jovanovich, Inc. All rights reserved.

50   Chapter 3   Sentence Fragments: Something Missing

5. Even though the bomb exploded right next to my new pickup, not an inch of its glossy red surface was marred.

6. Pippi's favorite professors (meaning whoever require the least work) usually offer classes at the wrong time for her to take.

7. I missed the last bus that would have taken me to work on time.

8. Isaac Asimov has written well over 200 books, which surely must be some kind of record.

Practice 7

Combine the following sentence pairs, using a dependent signal to create a dependent clause. The first few signals are given as clues. How should you punctuate these sentences? If the dependent clause goes before the independent clause, you need a comma following it:

When my uncle laughs, his eyebrows jump.

If the dependent clause follows the independent clause, you do *not* need a comma:

My uncle's stomach jiggles when he laughs.

1. First, she promised to share her inheritance with him. Then he proposed marriage. (*after*)

2. Perhaps Dexter was carrying the treasure map somewhere on his body. If not, we were going to have a long search. (*unless*)

3. I had to climb up the trellis outside my window most Friday nights. Then my father let me stay out past midnight. (*until*)

Copyright © 1992 by Harcourt Brace Jovanovich, Inc. All rights reserved.

Incomplete-Thought Fragments   51

4. In Jefferson Airplane's song "White Rabbit," the Dormouse says, "Feed your head."; but
In the book, Lewis Carroll's Dormouse says no such thing.

_____

_____

5. Although I would happily kiss some of the beasts around me,
I had a hope they would turn into royalty.

_____

_____

6. I don't care for rock music. Although
I rarely recognize the groups my friends rave about.

_____

_____

Exercises

Set 1

The correctly written sentences in Set 1 show one of the following three patterns. Refer to this list as you identify each sentence with the appropriate letter: A, B, or C. The first one has been done as an example.

- A — *S + V + V*: A sentence with one subject and two verbs, this pattern occasionally causes unintentional missing-subject fragments.
- B — *Long descriptive subjects*: This sentence pattern occasionally causes missing-verb fragments.
- C — *Sentences with dependent clauses*: This sentence pattern occasionally causes incomplete-thought fragments.

__B__ 1. Later, the settling dust and the gaping, jagged-edged windows wouldn't let me forget the terrifying force of the tornado.

__A C__ 2. Whether I stay or go, the sun will rise, and you will live.

__C__ 3. As the much-anticipated concert date approaches, more and more students scurry to buy Grateful Dead tickets.

__C__ 4. After my boyfriend found out I wasn't really a blond, he dumped me for a redhead (and they say *women* can't make up their minds!).

Copyright © 1992 by Harcourt Brace Jovanovich, Inc. All rights reserved.

52 Chapter 3 Sentence Fragments: Something Missing

_B_   5. Arthur, the eldest of five siblings and the only boy in the bunch, has decided to give his parents one more chance to produce the longed-for brother.

~~A~~ B   6. A temple of doom, a lost ark, some spicy intrigue, and an incredibly handsome man turned out to be a money-making combination.

_A_   7. I intend to make more money than my parents and live on less than I make.

_B_   8. The cheerleader having trouble catching her breath between gulps of Gatorade looks exhausted.

_C_   9. Ukiyo clawed his way up the embankment to the side of the road, then tried vainly to flag down help for his bleeding sister.

_B_   10. Eventually, when all my seven siblings have left home and graduated from college, my mother and father will take a long-anticipated cruise around the world.

_C_   11. Ivan thought through the story of Midas, then reconsidered choosing a major solely for financial reasons.

_A_   12. The doll moved its plastic lips and said, "Buy me!"

Set 2

Correct the following sentence fragments.

1. I choked down the sushi, but gagged on the sake.
2. In my dream, I felt the rope slip from my grasp, and screamed so loudly that I woke myself up.
3. Abstract art, which only to the uninformed appears to be sloppy splotches of spilled paint, is worth a fortune.
4. My son didn't realize that he had picked up my political science paper, and put down the pages for our puppy.
5. If babies are too young to flirt, why does my little girl look up at me through the fluttering lashes of a southern belle?

Copyright © 1992 by Harcourt Brace Jovanovich, Inc. All rights reserved.

Incomplete-Thought Fragments 53

6. The chocolate chip cookies, still warm from the oven, the chips moist and oozy, the flavor bursting with each bite are *the 2 sellers*.
7. My mother's original song, which helped me remember the presidents' names, *was a big hit*.
8. I'll sing it to you, if you'll give me your green jelly beans.
9. Cafeteria food, that much insulted continual banquet of undercooked french fries, overcooked vegetables, unflavored meat patties, and oversalted soup, *is very nasty*.
10. When he winked and smiled, the flirtatious man unknowingly revealed a slipping set of false teeth.

Set 3

Correct the following sentence fragments.

1. I chauffeur my daughter to early-morning band practice, then my son to his school next, and only rarely have time to deliver myself on time to my classes.
2. My parents, who live in the same house with me, but not in the same world, *are very old fashioned*.
3. The dancer who wiggled so well to the beat of Club MTV, *got a spot in a video*.
4. The Doberman pinscher looked at me with eyes bold and frank and dangerous, then dared me to come one step closer.
5. If you are ever alone in a strange city, head for a library and you will surely find old friends.
6. May you be blessed with the gifts of Blarney Castle's Cormac McCarthy, who went out unarmed to face his foes, and talked them into leaving him in peace.
7. The alert grandmother jumped up, charged across the room, and grabbed the baby before he could crawl too close to the fire.
8. The rugged brick walls of my dormitory and the green lawn around them, *is unsanitary*.

Copyright © 1992 by Harcourt Brace Jovanovich, Inc. All rights reserved.

54 Chapter 3 Sentence Fragments: Something Missing

9. The second game of the season, when the school mascot got out of her double-gauge steel cage,
10. The sports magazine that lures subscribers not with game plays but with hot swimsuits and hotter models.

Paragraph Editing Practice

Read the following paragraphs. Then go back through them, editing any sentence fragments that you find.

A. She dreamed of lace and satin and love everlasting. But found out the hard way that Weston was looking for a meal ticket. She couldn't compete with a doctor or lawyer for a man with a heart of fool's gold.

B. Winter days filled with wildly driven snow, a chill draft that sweeps in each time the door opens, and a twinge in the shoulders that no sweater can take away. These days demand a blazing fire in the hearth and a steaming mug of cocoa in hand. One year, on the first really snowy day, my crazy father, whose ideas of fun admittedly seem strange to civilized folk. He had a sudden longing for ice cream. He built up the fire, gathered the family in front of it. Then dashed off to the nearby Dairy Queen for Blizzards. It was so much fun that now my family always welcomes winter with this tradition.

C. When the king joked that the princess would marry the first clod at the royal ball to trod on her silken slippers. She called his bluff and wore steel-toed boots. The princess made it through the evening a free woman. No man was foolish enough to dance with her.

D. Quinn heard a shot outside in the dark. He quickly put out the lantern and grabbed for his .44. Then headed for the cabin door, loading three more bullets into the cylinder as he went. He slowly slid the door open a crack and peered out. With no moon, the night was too dark to

Incomplete-Thought Fragments 55

see anything. Suddenly, the door swung wide and knocked Quinn off his feet and the gun out of his hands. A shadowy outline filled the doorway, the outline of—a woman?

"Quinn Rarebit," the figure yelled, "get yourself up off that-there floor. You're goin' to get hitched."

He knew now that it was Annie McOakley, his fiancée of five years. She stood determinedly over him.

"Aw, Annie, you know I love you. But you just can't get a man with a gun."

"Maybe not, handsome," she replied, thrusting the barrel of his own gun into his face, "but I can get *you* with a gun. And this-here preacher man, too."

Quinn, who know when he was licked, got himself up off the floor.

Essay Editing Practice

Read straight through the following essay, reading for meaning and content first. Then go back through the essay, editing any sentence fragments that you find.

How I Spend My Summer Vacations

My father keeps telling my sister and me to get a summer job. Working at a taco stand, bagging groceries, pumping gas, or typing in a secretarial pool. These would satisfy him. But really, how can anyone **profane** the long, lazy freedom of summer by signing away whole shifts of time? All summer, a friend of ours who worked at a door factory. She took half-finished door frames from one assembly line. And flung them onto another so that the frames could slide under a paint sprayer. She ended the summer richer in purse, stronger in body, and absolutely **impoverished** in spirit. College offered her a break from the summer. My sister and I, far wiser, have always found ways to have both the money and the fun.

Copyright © 1992 by Harcourt Brace Jovanovich, Inc. All rights reserved.

One summer we started a housekeeping service. Employers who pay the same wage no matter how hard the employee works, they miss an obvious incentive to finish the job quickly. Instead of agreeing to work for an hourly wage, we figured out how many hours the job would normally take, calculated the pay at $5 an hour, then offered our services for that flat rate. A job that would take a normal yawner and dawdler four hours, for example, we would agree to do for $20. After we whipped through the job in forty-five minutes, we would have the rest of the time to play. Unlike my friend, we went back to college richer in purse, tanner in body, and quite self-satisfied in spirit.

The next summer we opened a lawn-care business. This time, when we went out to line up contracts, we took our father's push mower, and calculated the cost according to how long it took us with this dinosaur. Then we showed up the rest of the summer with my uncle's riding lawn-mower and zipped through the job, earning fat fees in record time.

This next summer we will rent food service apparatus and take my mother's barbecued ribs on the road. Her sauce tastes spicy-sweet, with just the right touch of tang and flash of flavor to make everyone dream about the next bite, even before they have swallowed. We will go to county fairs, city celebrations, craft sales, outdoor festivals, and any other gathering that will rent us a concession. As good as those ribs are, they'll do more than make us rich. After this summer, we will be famous!

Our father, who is a college professor and therefore addicted to hard work for little money, he says we take after our uncle, who made his first million before he was twenty-five. We hope so.

Writing Practice

Choose a topic below and write two to three paragraphs on that topic. If you need help writing a paragraph, please refer to Chapter 21, which describes how to develop a paragraph. First concentrate on getting down what you

Copyright © 1992 by Harcourt Brace Jovanovich, Inc. All rights reserved.

want to say. Then, after writing a first draft, reread your paper to check for sentence fragments and other errors in grammar and punctuation.

A. What summer jobs are available to young people in your town? List five or six jobs and choose three to write about. Before writing your paragraphs, make notes to describe the activity and explain why you would or would not choose this job. Then write the paragraphs.

B. What are the advantages or disadvantages of working for yourself? Make a list of four or five advantages and disadvantages, then take notes for two paragraphs. In the first paragraph, describe three advantages. In the second, describe three disadvantages. Close with a short third paragraph, stating your conclusion on whether you would want to work for yourself.

C. Like many young people, the person speaking in this essay dreams about making a lot of money for only a little work. Her father, however, has chosen to pass up a big salary to work as a professor—a job requiring long hours (even in the summer for most professors) and yet paying little. Many other people also pass up high-paying jobs to do something they love, something creative, or something to help people. Make two lists comparing the advantages and disadvantages of a high-paying job that you might dislike versus a low-paying job that you would enjoy. Pick out three disadvantages of both and write a paragraph; pick three advantages of both and write another paragraph; then decide which type of job you would choose and write a final paragraph.

Misused Words: it's/its

It's is a short form of "it is." Use this contraction only when you can insert *it is* in its place.

>*It's* a gray day when the home team loses.

>How could you forget that *it's* our one-month anniversary?

Its signifies possession. As a possessive pronoun, *its* serves the same function in a sentence as *his* does.

>The family piano lost *its* rhythm when my brother left home.

>My roommate hopes to pass *his* test.

>My pet dog hopes to find *its* bone.

Copyright © 1992 by Harcourt Brace Jovanovich, Inc. All rights reserved.

Complete the following sentences, using either *its* or *it's*.

1. The mail had __its__ regular share of bills today.
2. Coffee loses __its__ sass without caffeine.
3. __It's__ going to be one of those why-am-I-in-college weekends.
4. The test is missing __its__ fourth page. Can I just skip it?
5. She has been remembering that __it's__ not just the brilliant who pass. __It's__ also the diligent.

Review Exercises

Set 1

For each of the following, write P for phrase, DC for dependent clause, or IC for independent clause.

__IC__ 1. Stop writing in that library book!
__DC__ 2. Whenever she glances across the cafeteria.
__IC__ 3. A pigeon sat on the statue's nose.
__P__ 4. Wishing for summertime.
__P__ 5. Before I knew what "exam" meant.

Set 2

Underline the words in the following list that could serve as the only verb in a sentence.

have	to dash	sensing	promise
am drawing	come	dances	am wishing
swam	bothering	to match	will learn

(underlined: have, sensing, promise, am drawing, come, dances, am wishing, swam, to match, will learn)

Set 3

In the following sentences, underline subjects once and verbs twice, put a circle around the dependent signals, and then bracket the dependent clauses.

1. At the age of thirty-five, Paul Gauguin gave up a promising business career to become a painter, achieving fame for his South Seas paintings.

Copyright © 1992 by Harcourt Brace Jovanovich, Inc. All rights reserved.

Incomplete-Thought Fragments 59

2. Unlike most Impressionist artists, Edgar Degas painted mostly indoor scenes.
3. Most people do not know that Vincent van Gogh became a lay preacher in his twenties and worked as a missionary in a mining section of Belgium.
4. When Pablo Picasso went to Paris in 1900, he began painting first in blue tones, which became his "blue period," and then in rose.
5. Rembrandt's masterful use of dark backgrounds and piercing shafts of light in portraits allowed him to reveal both the features and character of a subject.
6. Any parent would appreciate Mary Cassatt's warm and loving portraits of children with their mothers.
7. My daughter, who just came in from seeing her first opera, *Hänsel and Gretel*, said that she loved it, but I don't think she is ready to see *The Ring of the Nibelungen*.
8. The computer that an accountant uses will not necessarily meet the needs of a poet.
9. The sudden storm of summer, noisy as a spoiled child in a tantrum, spends its temper quickly, and the peaceful sun returns.
10. Becky, who spent four years studying Spanish in high school, began to think in Spanish after only one month in Spain.
11. Novelists whose plots depended on the Berlin Wall must be wondering what to write about next.
12. Our dorm resident, who seems to be friendly, can turn mean and nasty if she ever finds a student playing her *Honeymooners* videos without permission.
13. A medieval castle, the setting for grand romances and sweeping legends, actually felt cold and damp and not in the least cozy.

Copyright © 1992 by Harcourt Brace Jovanovich, Inc. All rights reserved.

Set 4

Write a complete sentence using each of the following dependent signals. Be sure to include at least one independent clause in each sentence.

1. Whenever I go to the mall, I just have to buy something before I leave.
2. Because of the terrorist attacks we will be going to war soon.
3. Until summertime comes back I will always have a coat around.
4. Although they are tired, they still went out last night.
5. Even if she begged & pleaded, I still wouldn't take her back.
6. The pen, which bust in my book bag was worth fifty dollars.
7. The game that was cancelled over the weekend, will get played on Thursday.
8. The customer who lost they wallets will be here in a couple of minutes.

Dictionary Practice

Look up the words printed in bold type and provide a brief definition for each word as it appears in the sentence.

1. But really, how can anyone **profane** the long, lazy freedom of summer by signing away whole shifts of time?
   profane: _____

2. She ended the summer richer in purse, stronger in body, and absolutely **impoverished** in spirit.
   impoverished: _____

CHAPTER 4

Sentence Fragments: Something Added

▪ Reviewing Verbals

For a complete sentence, you need a subject and a verb without a dependent signal. There are certain words called verbals, including infinitives, -ing words, and past participles. Because these verbals look so much like verbs, you might be tempted to use them as your verb in a sentence. You can recognize *infinitives*, such as *to go, to see*, or *to cry*, because they always have the word *to* before the verb form.

>He is going to play Grendel in a musical version of *Beowulf*.

-Ing words can never be the sentence verb on their own. If there is a helping verb (*has, is, was, were*, and so forth), then *-ing* words act as part of a complete verb, as in the following sentence:

>She was carrying the wedding cake when she fell.

Past participles used with a helping verb also become part of the complete verb:

>He had given his roommate a promise.

This chapter will describe how verbals might cause you to create sentence fragments. The following practice reviews infinitives, *-ing* words, and past participles.

Practice 1

In the following paragraphs, underline the subjects once and the verbs twice, circle the dependent signals, and bracket the dependent clauses. Then put a box around the verbals, including the infinitives and the *-ing* words or past participles without helping verbs.

A. Relying on a career in professional sports would be a mistake for most college athletes, especially in football. Most experts agree that only 50 percent of college football players have gone on to play in the NFL. Furthermore, among those playing in the NFL, all will become at least partially disabled because of leg and back injuries.[1]

B. Long ago, Europeans made up stories about the dangers that were faced by spice hunters. Arriving on the scene, hunters supposedly found poisonous snakes guarding the trees. To reach the pepper, spice hunters had to burn down the trees, in that way killing the snakes. Because of the burning, the pepper was always black. Far from requiring such desperate measures, peppercorns actually grow on vines as berries, and they become black and wrinkled from the sun drying them out.

☐ Extra-Information Fragments

Sometimes you might want to add extra information to an otherwise complete sentence, but believing that your sentence is getting too long, you separate the extra information and create a sentence fragment. When you add this information as phrases or dependent clauses, you need to do so *within* the sentence.

Phrases with Participles

You might add information in a phrase that includes a participle, but no helping verb.

> Roland slammed his books down on the library table, *waking* up the girl at the next table.

> Fidelia got up before dawn every day last semester, this *being* the only time she could fit exercise into her busy schedule.

> The book of "Knock, Knock" jokes arrived yesterday, the one *sent* by my brother for my birthday.

---

[1] Rick Telander, *The Hundred Yard Lie: The Corruption of College Football and What We Can Do to Stop It* (New York: Simon & Schuster, 1989).

Practice 2

Combine the sentences in exercises 1–3, using an -ing phrase for each. Remember that you can put the phrase either before or after the main clause.

1. Leroy walked through the library.
   As he did this, he looked for his roommate.
   His roommate was the person who had taken his final paper by mistake.

   _____

   _____

2. The guest speaker repeatedly popped vitamin C tablets into his mouth.
   He was trying to ignore his worsening cold.

   _____

   _____

3. The clown shuffled down the main hall of the Academic Building.
   The clown handed out flowers to everyone.

   _____

   _____

4. Write a sentence of your own with an -ing phrase before or after the main clause.

   _____

   _____

Infinitive Phrases

Sometimes you might add information with a phrase that begins with an infinitive.

> I returned to the cosmetic counter *to show* the clerk what her lipstick had done and to get my money back.

> Jilly and Jerry went down to the bank *to take* out their last bit of money.

Practice 3

Combine the sentences in exercises 1 and 2, using a phrase with *to* + verb (an infinitive) somewhere in each sentence.

1. Most parents prefer this.
   They have their babies in a hospital.

2. Some parents, however, would rather stay home.
   They do this to experience the joy of birth among loved ones.

3. Write your own sentence with a *to* + verb (infinitive) phrase either before or after the independent clause.

Dependent Clauses

Sometimes you might add information that begins with a double-duty dependent signal (*who*, *which*, *that*, or *whoever*).

> The psychologist kept insisting that Napoleon was dead, *which* made me very angry.

> I have decided to keep my brother, *who* surprised me with a birthday cake.

Practice 4

Combine the following pairs of sentences by attaching the information from the second sentence with a double-duty dependent signal.

1. Romy says that she doesn't even own a dress.
   This doesn't surprise me.

2. T.J. has been searching for Douglas.
   Douglas forgot to return T.J.'s car keys.

3. Check out the new dance.
   It comes right before mine in the variety show.

   _____

   _____

Phrases That Tell More

You might add information in phrases that tell more about certain aspects of the sentence.

> Sloan broke up with his girlfriend just before finals, *the best time possible for his grades.* (The phrase tells more about the time, "just before finals.")
>
> I manage each year to pay the car insurance on my Mercedes, *in spite of my perpetual poverty.* (The phrase tells more about how the writer pays.)
>
> The girl down the hall lost my favorite wool skirt, *handmade by my mother.* (The phrase tells more about the skirt.)

Practice 5

Combine the sentences in exercises 1–3, using a phrase to add extra information in each sentence.

1. My father calls every Saturday at 6 A.M.
   This is the only time during the weekend that he can catch me.

   _____

   _____

2. This happens after most of my big exams.
   I go out on the track and jog three miles.
   This is a good way to work off my anxieties.

   _____

   _____

3. Nothing can beat movies for relaxation.
   Movies can distract a student from studying.
   Studying is a necessary discipline at college.
   (Use *although* as a dependent signal to begin this sentence.)

   _____

   _____

Copyright © 1992 by Harcourt Brace Jovanovich, Inc. All rights reserved.

Exercises

The sentences in these two exercise sets show one of the following four patterns. Refer to this list as you identify each entry with the appropriate letter: A, B, C, or D. Then edit the sentences, correcting any fragments that you find. Be aware that all of these patterns might cause you to create unintentional extra-information sentence fragments.

- A An added phrase that includes a participle: He ran, *hoping* to escape.
- B An added phrase that begins with an infinitive: *To pass*, you should study.
- C An added clause that includes a double-duty dependent signal (who, which, that, whoever): My roommate, *who studies endlessly*, misses all the fun.
- D An added phrase that further describes some aspect of the sentence: I did the problems, *one by one*.

Set 1

C   1. November days often dawn gray and dreary. The perfect days for staying in bed.

B   2. Yoshiro refused absolutely to give me another week to consider his proposal.

A   3. My roommate borrowed my new silk dress and washed it in the dormitory laundry machines, ruining it.

D   4. I caught a fish one day and—what a surprise—it came out of the water, all slimy and gooey from industrial waste.

A   5. To work is to play, sweltering in the ninety-degree day.

A   6. It is such a strange plight. To work in the twenty-degree night.

C   7. Benjy never goes Dutch on our dates. Which usually consist of peanut butter sandwiches in front of his VCR.

A   8. In the spring, tulips and daffodils and a flourish of other flowers bring new life to my garden, rivaling even Christmas in excitement.

Extra-Information Fragments   67

Set 2

_B_ 1. To trounce every other contender in the field. I have to leave my gentle nature in the locker room.

_C_ 2. My wife recently passed the real estate licensing exam. Which she claimed was harder than any other test she had ever taken.

_C_ 3. I advised her to save her astonishment for the broker's exam. Which must make linear algebra look easy.

_A_ 4. My wise and thrifty father ignored the woman's sales pitch for buying a stair-climbing machine. Pointing to his readily available and completely free staircase.

_B_ 5. Please help me finish all my brussels sprouts. Just this once.

_A_ 6. Think how hard it must be to stay happy and British. Smiling with a stiff upper lip.

_B_ 7. I do solemnly promise to eat every last ounce of Heavenly Hash before you return.

Sentence Combining

Combine the sentence pairs in these exercises.

1. Garry Trudeau took twenty months off from his successful comic strip, "Doonesbury."
He did this to care for his newborn twins.

_____

_____

2. I sat hopefully through the competition until the fifth pianist played the Khachaturian concerto.
This ended my dream of winning.
(Use *which*.)

_____

_____

Copyright © 1992 by Harcourt Brace Jovanovich, Inc. All rights reserved.

68   Chapter 4   Sentence Fragments: Something Added

3. How foolish it all seems.
   It is the crunch of football helmets, the grunts of escaping tension, the brief, mad folly of healthy humanity heaped upon itself.
   (Add the second sentence as extra information after the first sentence.)

   _____

   _____

4. He slipped stealthily into the second-story window long after his curfew.
   My teenage son came face to face with a burglar.
   (Start the sentence with *Slipping*.)

   _____

   _____

5. As early as age fourteen, my sister began saving money.
   She did this to buy a deluxe ticket on the Orient Express.

   _____

   _____

6. To many people, physics is a mystery.
   It is baffling, befuddling, and belittling.
   (Add these three descriptive words at the end of the sentence.)

   _____

   _____

7. To me, physics is a key to the universe.
   It unlocks its mysteries.
   (Use an *-ing* participle.)

   _____

   _____

8. The first clue that I had company was the periscope.
   It appeared above the tub rim halfway through my makeup routine.
   (Use *which*.)

   _____

   _____

Paragraph Editing Practice

Read straight through each of the following paragraphs for content and meaning. Then go back through each one, editing any sentence fragment errors that

Copyright © 1992 by Harcourt Brace Jovanovich, Inc. All rights reserved.

you find. If these paragraphs seem difficult to understand, don't be surprised—that difficulty shows exactly why professors dislike sentence fragments so much. Like you, they have difficulty reading and understanding the intent of a piece of writing when students leave sentence fragments in their papers.

A. Horror movies aren't scary anymore. They are just gory instead. Old-time movies frightened rather than disgusted their audiences. The old Frankenstein flicks, for example, were almost pleasantly chilling. They kept viewers in suspense. Without making them sick. Furthermore, while the movie monsters of yore occasionally butchered, they did so only in black and white. Which makes the blood seem so much less deadly. Living color, on the other hand, shocks so much more because the blood flows bright red. Gushing, spurting, and dripping nicely for the nauseating pleasure of horror fans. Perhaps without color, ordinary monsters would never have turned into bloody mass murderers.

B. It must have been chance. That at the dance the breakers blew the lights. Hilda Brown began to frown. There'd be no dance that night. Young Hilda Brown threw down her crown. Stamping with dismay. She was to be the queen, you see. At her school soiree. Her arms went out. She flailed about. Screaming at her date, "I'll never be 'Her Majesty.' I'm utterly irate!"

C. Last fall, my daughter Alexis tried to hide a truancy by forging a new date on an old written excuse. Carefully fished from the kitchen trash. The next evening, she sought to atone for her sins by doing her homework in double time. She was serene until 8:00 P.M. when her teacher called to confirm her absence from school on Monday. After a brief conversation with Alexis's teacher, I learned that my apparently healthy daughter had been sick the day before. With the same "serious" illness she had just gotten over. I was furious, and Alexis was undone. To this day she skips school only on weekends and holidays.

Copyright © 1992 by Harcourt Brace Jovanovich, Inc. All rights reserved.

D. The Olympics are getting too commercial even for me. An advertising executive. The networks now offering competition breaks between the commercials. Instead of retired athletes pitching beer, I want to see current athletes, caught up in the most intense moments of their lives. The networks, which pay more and more for the rights to televise the Olympics, will see more and more viewers turn away, if they don't show more competition.

Essay Editing Practice 1

Read straight through the following essay, reading the first time for content. Then go back through and edit any sentence fragments that you find. Watch for incorrect use of *affect* or *effect* (*affect* is usually a verb, *effect* is usually a noun).

My Home, the Space Colony

Before entering my parent's farmhouse, I stopped and looked around me. In one direction stretched the rising slope of the space colony's circular outer edge. With a small city nestled among the trees across a gently winding river. Then the slope gradually disappeared behind the solar panels of the ceiling. In the other direction flourished fertile rice fields. One of the colony's main food sources. This slope rose to where an **azure**-blue lake glistened in the sunlight, and then it, too, disappeared behind the solar panels.

I knew that if I walked in either direction, I would always have the sensation of being at the base of this artificial valley, for the colony was constructed in a giant wheel. The colony's ground, its land, water, trees, and so forth, filled the outer edge of the wheel. Solar panels formed the inner edge. Giving us a blue sky. Once each week, my father and I hiked entirely around the four-mile colony. Both for exercise and for the pleasure of reacquainting ourselves with each **vista** of our world.

My parents, who brought me to the space colony when I was six, thought at first that the colony would seem claustrophobic to us. The walls closing in on us, and the continuously curving shape of the land making us dizzy. Now, at eighteen, after twelve years on Alpha Terrace (Alterra, for short), I actually found comfort in the cradle-like terrain.

I went upstairs and slipped the diskette for my history text into my Microslate so that I could read my notes from the morning's history lecture. The class had been a total waste. Earth-side history professors who beamed lectures to space colony universities should choose their lecture topics more carefully. Even before Schnizzle Whiskers began speaking, I knew more than he did about how space colonies had effected human civilization.

First, no one—not even Schnizzle Whiskers—could count the enormous technological benefits that the colonies had given humanity. In particular, the whole area of recycling took off with the colonies. Everyone on Earth and in the colonies used recyclable packaging. Eliminating the need to dispose of plastic, cardboard, and other wrapping materials. People also carried portable computerized libraries like my Microslate, which conserved on paper and the wood pulp and energy that paper required. They had also learned to purify their air and water more completely and quickly. All these technological advances, so necessary to Earth's environment, had occurred because space colonies required a more efficient management of resources than Earth did—or rather, than Earth realized it did.

Space colonies also offered living space. After all, Mother Earth had run out of room. Japan had built whole cities underground. China had begun to allow only one out of three families to have a child. Even the United States had finally figured out a system. Whereby only homes with no more than two children could receive television signals. Men and women, fearful of losing weekend sports and daytime soaps, went in droves to family planning centers. Each country, in turn, had dealt with the problem as it could, but no one had ever solved it. Even colonies provided only a partial solution.

Far more necessary and beneficial than living space, however, was the new frontier that space colonies offered. Before space colonies became common, Earth-siders had felt imprisoned. Without any opportunities for the pioneers among them to spread out and seek new horizons. Space colonies had given these pioneers a new world to conquer. Sparking their hope and ambition. The world had also needed the hazards that the new world of space colonies inevitably held. At times this danger seemed too extreme. An entire colony had perished a few years earlier when its energy panel malfunctioned. On another colony, explosions sent the station veering out of its orbit toward certain destruction. When the air purification system faltered on our own Alterra, we also had a few tense hours. Yet I believed that colonists came partly *because* of the danger. Without danger could there be challenge? And without challenge could there be conquest? That pioneering spirit, that common danger, and that ultimate conquest of an alien environment had rejuvenated humanity. Giving it a unified, adventurous, and invigorating spirit once again. For this, humanity owed the most to the colonies.

I glanced down at my Microslate and grinned. At least I wouldn't have to study for my exam. I already knew more about colonies than old Schnizzle Whiskers. I picked up the phone to call A'lesha. Maybe she could meet me at the swimming hole.

Writing Practice 1

Choose a topic below and write two to three paragraphs on that topic. (See Chapter 21 for instructions on writing a paragraph.) First concentrate on your message—what you want to say. Then read back over your writing to check for the sentence fragments explained in this chapter, as well as errors in spelling, grammar, and punctuation.

Copyright © 1992 by Harcourt Brace Jovanovich, Inc. All rights reserved.

sometimes uncontrollably. Without the possibility of either fighting or fleeing, we freeze, unable to deal with our problems at all.

If you suffer from test anxiety, you can try the following techniques to control your anxiety. Some people can reduce their anxiety by talking themselves out of it. Reminding themselves again and again how long they have studied, how well prepared they are, how familiar they have become with their notes. Don't be surprised if this positive self-talk has little effect on your fears, however. After years of fearing tests. Your response to them has probably ceased to be a rational response. Perhaps at first you really hadn't studied well enough, and your fear made sense. As time passed, the response of fear came even when you had studied well. By now, your anxiety may have lapsed into an emotional response without any rational basis.

Deep-breathing techniques reduce tension more successfully. Initially, we respond to danger by taking a short, sharp breath. With a real enemy, this shallow breath prepares us to fight or flee. With a test as an enemy, we can't respond physically, so this shallow breathing merely builds tension. Our bodies need a steady supply of oxygen, so it is no wonder that shallow breathing makes us extremely tense. Take a few shallow breaths. The tension begins in your lungs. Spreading to your shoulders, your arms, your neck, and finally invading your entire body. You can consciously reduce this tension by taking in long, slow breaths. First, forcefully expel the old air from your lungs, and then slowly fill your lungs with new, fresh air. Repeat this process two or three times whenever you begin to feel breathless.

With this slow breathing, you can practice relaxation. Imagine that you are sitting at the desk in class, reaching for the test, writing your name, reading the first question. Can you feel the tension building? If you feel it in your shoulders and neck, roll your shoulders once or twice. And then imagine all the tension sliding down your arms and out through your hands. To relax your face, fake a yawn, stretching your cheek and

Copyright © 1992 by Harcourt Brace Jovanovich, Inc. All rights reserved.

jaw muscles, and then expel a long breath, letting the tension in your face recede with it. Finally, tense each leg in turn and then stretch it out. Again imagining the tension leaving the leg.

As you sit at your desk, the dreaded test before you, flexing your muscles and breathing deeply in and out. Close your eyes for just a moment, clear your thoughts, and picture waves on a beach rolling gently in, flowing gently out, over and over again. Picture yourself in this scene. The sun against your face, the breeze in your hair, the birds overhead. Breathe in as the waves come in, and breathe out as they recede. Now, bring yourself calmly and slowly back to the classroom, and begin the test.

You have had years, unfortunately, to develop your fight-or-flight response to taking a test. Mastering these techniques won't necessarily take years in return, but for these techniques to do you any good, you will have to practice them diligently before you get to the test. Going through each step as described. With mastery of these techniques comes the reward of a test well taken.

Writing Practice 2

Choose one of the following topics to write about. As you write, concentrate first on what you want to say. Then go back over your writing, looking for errors in grammar and punctuation.

A. List three or four of the most relaxing scenes you can imagine, including the scene mentioned in this essay if you would like, or using a panoramic picture from a magazine like *Arizona Highways*. Then divide this picture into three sections—top, middle, and bottom; left, middle, and right; near, farther, and farthest. Jot down a few descriptions for each section, and then use your notes to describe this scene in three paragraphs.

B. Describe a frightening experience you have had. Begin by taking

Copyright © 1992 by Harcourt Brace Jovanovich, Inc. All rights reserved.

CHAPTER 5

Comma Splices and Run-On Sentences

▣ Reviewing Independent Clauses

In this chapter, we look at two common types of sentence errors. In order to avoid them, you have to be able to recognize independent clauses. The following review will tell you if you can do that.

Practice 1

For the following entries, underline subjects once and verbs twice, circle dependent signals, and bracket dependent clauses. Then, in the space before each entry, write how many independent clauses each entry has. (Any clause without a dependent signal is an independent clause.)

_____ 1. Clarissa refused to miss an episode of *Designing Women* as a result she never went out on Monday nights.

_____ 2. Tests terrify me, they make my skin crawl.

_____ 3. Ellan worked full-time as a homemaker, genuinely fulfilled by a life of service to her family.

_____ 4. Lavar saw the dog coming, however he never suspected that the dog would bite him.

_____ 5. Bruce hates to houseclean he ignores the mess in his apartment.

_____ 6. Guess what I finally passed a philosophy test.

The sentences in this exercise that have two independent clauses have been written incorrectly. What punctuation is used between the independent clauses in these incorrect entries?

7. _____

8. _____

Joining Independent Clauses

When trying to link two independent clauses, you may be tempted to use one of two incorrect methods. First, you could incorrectly put a comma where a period belongs. If you do this, you create a *comma splice*. Second, you could put nothing—no punctuation at all—where a period or semicolon belongs. If you do this, you create a *run-on* sentence (also called a *fused* sentence).

This does not mean that a sentence can't have two or more independent clauses. It can, but you must write it correctly.

The All-Important FANBOYS

> To link two independent clauses, the only word that you can use between the clauses is a coordinating conjunction (a FANBOYS—*for, and, nor, but, or, yet, so*).

Practice 2

Mark the subjects (single underline) and verbs (double underline) in the following sentences. Then put a box around the conjunctions.

1. I shall be smiling extra sweetly at Donna this week, for she has tickets to NCAA tournament games.
2. Enormous rain slickers defend against the torrents, and they also ward off appreciative second glances.
3. I have never seen one of the *Friday the 13th* movies, nor do I intend to.
4. The time is right, but my bed beckons me back to sleep.
5. Please lend me the use of your brain for the next two hours, or I will surely fail my organic chemistry final.
6. I have always dreamed of spending a week at the renowned Peninsula Hotel in Hong Kong, yet dreams have little value on the current exchange.
7. Alli's husband never had the nerve to tell her that he was cheating, so where did he get the nerve to break her heart?

Copyright © 1992 by Harcourt Brace Jovanovich, Inc. All rights reserved.

Joining Independent Clauses   85

All the sentences in Practice 2 have only two independent clauses, but occasionally you might want to construct a sentence with more than two independent clauses.

In a string of three or more independent clauses that are so closely related that they belong in one sentence, you need to put a FANBOYS only before the last one.

Cameron crept furtively up the dorm steps, she fended off the ravenous wolves in the hallway, and she finally sat down in her dorm room to enjoy her pizza.

Don't put a comma before the FANBOYS unless what comes after the FANBOYS can stand alone as a separate sentence. In other words, put commas before a FANBOYS that links two independent clauses (S + V, FANBOYS S + V).

Practice 3
Combine the sentences in exercises 1–7, using a FANBOYS for each sentence. You will need to remove unnecessary words.

1. This happened at the Churchmouse Antique Store.
   Alice pounced on what she hoped were silver candlesticks.
   They were only tin.

   _____

   _____

2. In my heart, I know that Elvis Presley is dead.
   That same heart skips a beat when a tabloid claims he is still alive.

   _____

   _____

3. My cat is terrified of the bulldog next door.
   Because of this, she stays inside.
   She gazes out the front picture window.
   (Begin this sentence with *Because*.)

   _____

   _____

Copyright © 1992 by Harcourt Brace Jovanovich, Inc. All rights reserved.

4. This is according to a literary tale.
   Lord Byron's college didn't allow dogs.
   Because of this, he brought a bear instead.

   _____

   _____

5. The professor, who wanted the students to study hard, threatened failing grades.
   None of them cared.
   (Use a FANBOYS before adding the second sentence.)

   _____

   _____

6. Fast cars enthrall me.
   I would gladly spend my first fifty thousand on one.
   (Use a FANBOYS.)

   _____

   _____

7. I need some laughs.
   Let's play Pictionary.
   (Use a FANBOYS.)

   _____

   _____

Practice 4

1. Write a sentence of your own that has two independent clauses combined with a FANBOYS.

   _____

   _____

2. Write a sentence that has three short independent clauses, combined with one FANBOYS before the last clause.

   _____

   _____

Dependent Signals

> You can link two independent clauses by changing one into a dependent clause.

Inserting a dependent signal before one of the clauses helps show the relationship between the clauses.

Separate independent clauses	**Linked with dependent signal**
Manuel keeps a picture of his grandmother propped up on his desk. She was the first to believe that he would go to college.	Manuel keeps a picture of his grandmother propped up on his desk *because* she was the first to believe that he would go to college.
We threw an enormous party. We went home to wait anxiously for our grades.	*After* we threw an enormous party, we went home to wait anxiously for our grades.

Semicolons

You can join two independent clauses, as long as they are closely related ideas, by using a semicolon (rather than a period) at the end of the first independent clause.

Some people bite their fingernails because they are nervous; I bite mine to make my mother nervous.

Warm-blooded people like to bake brown in the sun and dive into cool waves; cold-blooded people prefer to dive into a snowbank and then bake cozy-warm in front of a blazing fire.

Be warned, however. You may feel tempted to use semicolons too frequently. In actual practice, most writers use semicolons sparingly. In your own writing, try to rely more heavily on the first two methods described: Use a FANBOYS (also called coordinating conjunction), or make one of the clauses dependent.

☐ Avoiding Comma Splices and Run-On Sentences

Perhaps if you can understand why you might combine independent clauses incorrectly, you can avoid this in your own writing. This section tells you about three situations in which you are apt to create comma splices and run-on sentences.

88 Chapter 5 Comma Splices and Run-On Sentences

Using the Wrong Connection

One common error arises when you try to use something other than a FANBOYS between the two independent clauses. As you know, only the seven coordinating conjunctions (*for, and, nor, but, or, yet, so*—or FANBOYS) can join independent clauses. Using any other word will create either a comma splice or a run-on. To help you see how easy it is to make this mistake, complete the following practice exercise.

Practice 5

Each of the following entries has two independent clauses. For each entry, first mark the subject-verb combinations and bracket the dependent clauses. (Remember, if you think perhaps you have a dependent signal before the subject and verb, try moving this word somewhere else in the sentence. If you can move it and the sentence still makes sense, you *do not* have a dependent signal.)

Next mark each entry with one of the following letter codes, and correct the ones that have errors.

> OK   *Correct:* If the entry has a FANBOYS between the two independent clauses, the sentence has been written correctly.
>
> RO   *Run-on:* If the entries have no punctuation between the independent clauses, the entry is a run-on. (It doesn't matter if there are commas elsewhere in the sentence; it only matters that there is no punctuation at the end of the first independent clause.)
>
> CS   *Comma splice:* If the entries have only a comma between the two independent clauses (no FANBOYS), the entry is a comma splice.

1. Porter came grudgingly to the Greek play then he left halfway through.

2. He thought the flimsy costumes were great however, he couldn't stand the chorus's moans.

3. Wendy loves hamburgers, and her father loves fixing them.

4. Oscar's father played for the San Diego Chargers, therefore Oscar was allowed to sit with the team at any home game.

5. Anne meant to convince her professor to give an extra day instead, her professor assigned extra homework.

6. Tito played soccer in high school overseas, thus he easily made the first-string team.

Copyright © 1992 by Harcourt Brace Jovanovich, Inc. All rights reserved.

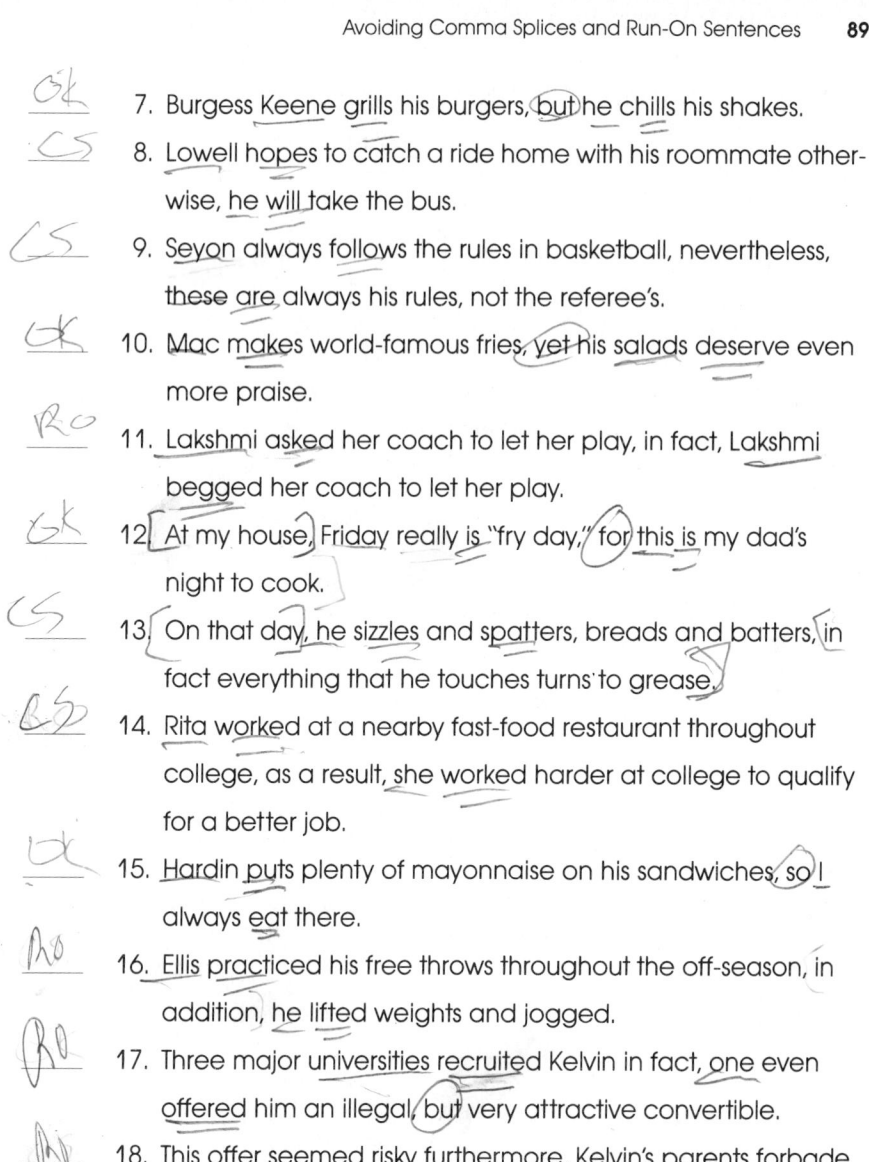

Avoiding Comma Splices and Run-On Sentences   89

7. Burgess Keene grills his burgers, but he chills his shakes.
8. Lowell hopes to catch a ride home with his roommate otherwise, he will take the bus.
9. Seyon always follows the rules in basketball, nevertheless, these are always his rules, not the referee's.
10. Mac makes world-famous fries, yet his salads deserve even more praise.
11. Lakshmi asked her coach to let her play, in fact, Lakshmi begged her coach to let her play.
12. At my house, Friday really is "fry day," for this is my dad's night to cook.
13. On that day, he sizzles and spatters, breads and batters, in fact everything that he touches turns to grease.
14. Rita worked at a nearby fast-food restaurant throughout college, as a result, she worked harder at college to qualify for a better job.
15. Hardin puts plenty of mayonnaise on his sandwiches, so I always eat there.
16. Ellis practiced his free throws throughout the off-season, in addition, he lifted weights and jogged.
17. Three major universities recruited Kelvin in fact, one even offered him an illegal, but very attractive convertible.
18. This offer seemed risky furthermore, Kelvin's parents forbade acceptance.
19. I love eating at Daisy Quid's house, for she excels at dreaming up ice-cream delights.
20. Richie, who sat out his first football season, gained a lot of practice, also, he went into the pros a year older and stronger.

Copyright © 1992 by Harcourt Brace Jovanovich, Inc. All rights reserved.

Now go back to the twenty sentences in Practice 5 and circle the words that are used incorrectly as coordinating conjunctions. These are *transition words*. They show the following relationships between ideas:

>Contrast: *however, on the other hand, nevertheless, instead*
>Sequence: *first, second, then, also, after this, later, finally*
>Example: *for example, for instance*
>Reinforcement: *actually, in fact, indeed, of course*
>Cause/effect: *therefore, for this reason, consequently*
>Summary: *in conclusion, therefore*

The transition words in Practice 5 show a relationship between independent clauses, but unlike the FANBOYS, they must not be used to combine sentences into one sentence. You can make your own list of the words that most frequently cause run-on sentence errors by writing the words you circled in the Practice 5 sentences.

_____

_____

In college papers, these transition words are the villains that cause most run-ons and comma splices. Look them over again. Remember: You cannot use these words to combine independent clauses. Use *only* the FANBOYS—seven words, easily remembered, an exclusive list—*only* the FANBOYS to combine independent clauses.

Practice 6

Combine the following sentences as indicated for practice in the distinction between FANBOYS and transition words.

1. People in China favor pork.
   They keep a household pig, fed on food scraps and waste.
   (Use a FANBOYS.)

   _____

   _____

2. Again combine the two sentences in exercise 1, this time using one of the transition words you listed from Practice 5.

   _____

   _____

3. Most Chinese families eat the pig.
   Some families must sell the pig at market.
   (Use a FANBOYS.)

   _____

   _____

4. Again combine the two sentences in exercise 3, this time using one of your listed transition words.

   _____

   _____

Joining Short Sentences

Another type of run-on sentence happens when you believe that a short exclamatory sentence, or any short sentence, doesn't deserve its own punctuation. Look at the following pairs of sentences, and notice how tempting it might be to attach the short sentences to their longer companion thoughts. The subjects and verbs have been underlined for you.

Incorrect	Correct
I am thirsty could I have a drink?	I am thirsty. Could I have a drink?
He made the championship baseball team and the Dean's List now that is impressive!	He made the championship baseball team and the Dean's List. Now that is impressive!

Because they are brief, these short exclamations or questions appeal to readers. Attaching them to another sentence defeats that benefit.

Joining Closely Related Ideas

Here's another common source of run-on errors: You might believe two or more sentences are so closely related that they belong in the same sentence, so you put them all together. These can be fixed in several ways.

Incorrect	Correct
For an easy main dish, heat some bottled cheese sauce, then pour it over some corn chips.	For an easy main dish, heat some bottled cheese sauce. Then pour it over some corn chips.

Copyright © 1992 by Harcourt Brace Jovanovich, Inc. All rights reserved.

| I came, I played, I triumphed. | I came, I played, and I triumphed. |
| I realize [that money can't buy happiness] I will settle for everything else [it can buy]. | I realize [that money can't buy happiness]; I will settle for everything else [it can buy]. |

In the list of correct sentences, notice how the errors have been fixed. The first is made into two separate sentences, the second has a FANBOYS, and the third has a semicolon. These are the three ways that you can correct a run-on or a comma splice, but be cautious about using semicolons.

Exercises

In the following four exercise sets, identify each entry with one of these letter codes:

> OK *Correct:* Independent clauses have been combined with FANBOYS.
> RO *Run-on:* Independent clauses have been combined without any punctuation.
> CS *Comma splice:* Independent clauses have been combined with only a comma (and *no* FANBOYS).

If you have trouble with any of these sentences, underline the subjects once and the verbs twice, bracket the dependent clauses, and then check for FANBOYS.

Set 1

_RO_ 1. Anna Maria's veal piccata surpasses that of the finest Italian restaurant wouldn't you agree?

_CS_ 2. Old pirate movies with swashbuckling heroes, silk-clad, feisty heroines, and villains with hearts black as muck glue me to the tube, I could watch them all night.

_CS_ 3. I get my perm at the mall tomorrow, I hope none of the other guys on the wrestling team sees me with those little pink rollers in my hair.

Avoiding Comma Splices and Run-On Sentences   93

_RO_ 4. Gosh, I'm spacey I managed to miss the Georgia O'Keeffe exhibit in New York.

_OK_ 5. I had better get a date book, or I will forget the Andy Warhol Retrospective, too.

_RO_ 6. I never watch TV shows however when a natural disaster comes on the news, I stay glued to Cable News Network.

_CS_ 7. I grew up listening to Cat Stevens, as a result, I left for college singing, "Oooh, baby, baby, it's a wild world."

Set 2

_____ 1. My pompous brother drinks only *café au lait*, so I insist on having my coffee black.

_____ 2. Shy people do have ambitions, however, those ambitions carry them only as far as their inhibitions allow.

_____ 3. My lips beg to be smeared with the shiny grease of salty, buttery popcorn, but my thighs plead to squeeze into my new jeans, one size too small.

_____ 4. I can't believe you waited until my birthday to get in touch with me besides I would have preferred a postcard to a collect call.

_____ 5. Kate is a joker and so is her son as a result they always have fun.

_____ 6. Before each work week, I always had to iron piles of oxford shirts, but now that I am back in school, I revel in glorious wrinkles.

_____ 7. Last night I caught myself wishing that life had given me more, then I wiped away the last traces of my milk chocolate ice cream with extra fudge sauce and was humbled.

Set 3

_CS_ 1. My parents swing to country music, my older brother lives for southern gospel, little Sheena is a punk rocker, and I go mad for rap, is it any wonder we fight over the car stereo?

Copyright © 1992 by Harcourt Brace Jovanovich, Inc. All rights reserved.

94 Chapter 5 Comma Splices and Run-On Sentences

CS   2. Most of the women interviewed remembered all the details of their first kiss, however, all of the men claimed to have forgotten everything.

CO   3. For example, Susannah recalled that her first kiss was on Friday, April 9, 1977, when she was seventeen years old, in contrast, Luis did not remember *his* first kiss at all, though he was certain the girl did.

CS   4. First, Rowan stocked up on tofu, dried mushrooms, dried lily buds, and bamboo shoots, then she whipped up a huge pot of her spicy hot-and-sour soup.

CS   5. Jethro finds it almost impossible to turn off the television, for the shows entertain, enlighten, and encourage him, however, this week he has finals to study for, so he has unplugged his set and will leave it turned off.

RO   6. Turn the burner off the experiment is boiling over.

OK   7. I am desperate, so could you type my paper for me?

Set 4

_____ 1. What is the matter with Madeline, she is clutching her middle.

_____ 2. Guess what, Julio does not know it, but he just received a Fulbright scholarship to study dramatic arts in Japan.

_____ 3. Is there something funny about the way I am dressed everyone is staring at me.

_____ 4. Blackbeard was the fiercest pirate ever to terrorize the Carolina coast, yet he began his life with the unassuming name of Edward Drummond.

_____ 5. What a blunder he made, Ralph admired Miranda's bright blue eyes and then asked for the name of her optometrist.

_____ 6. For Claire it was a perfect summer. The knees ripped out of her jeans, her hair bleached butter-white, and her freckles had a population explosion.

Copyright © 1992 by Harcourt Brace Jovanovich, Inc. All rights reserved.

Avoiding Comma Splices and Run-On Sentences   95

_____ 7. I always wait up for David Letterman, what a wacky guy he is!

_____ 8. I worked at a greasy spoon in Hollywood for a year, hoping to see even one celebrity, then I finally faced the fact that they never eat cheap food.

Paragraph Editing Practice

Read straight through each of the following paragraphs. Then go back and edit each, watching especially for comma splices or run-on sentences. If you have trouble, underline subjects once and verbs twice, and bracket the dependent clauses. In this way you can isolate the independent clauses and check to see if they have been combined correctly.

A.   My husband recently developed a new rose, however, he named it "Mustard Yellow." The color glows with a distinctive depth, and its scent is so richly romantic that it could put divorce lawyers out of business. Even so, no one wanted the rose until he changed the name therefore, I believe that a rose by any other name is *not* as sweet.

B.   Quite early one morning, I arose to surprise my parents with breakfast in bed, to my amazement I spied them out in the garden, laughing, holding hands, and watching the sun come up. Somewhat guiltily, I slipped back into bed. Could it really be old Mom and Pop out there? No, it definitely wasn't. Those two giggling maniacs couldn't be my parents they only appeared to be. I considered calling the cops to report the trespassers, then I decided that I had better not. After all, I was trespassing, too.

C.   I can't decide what to do. I could rewrite my rough draft of the Psych take-home final I could French braid my hair. Maybe I should ransack my closet for tonight's killer outfit. (And believe me, with my wardrobe I really will have to ransack.) Better yet, I ought to work out at the Fitness Center and indulge in a nice long whirlpool bath, then afterwards I can justify a triple-thick milkshake. Oh, I forgot, Jenni is coming

Copyright © 1992 by Harcourt Brace Jovanovich, Inc. All rights reserved.

over to borrow my Bon Jovi and Mozart tapes. She can always be coaxed into coming to the gym with me. But what will I do for the next twenty minutes?

D. Billy Jeff dropped his arm from the back of Peggy's chair onto her stiff, skinny shoulders, hoping that she would think him suave instead of scared silly. Thankfully, she didn't notice, she just stared at the movie screen. He tried to copy her intense concentration so that afterward he could impress her with his insights into the movie, all he could think about was how thin she was. Clearly, she had not gained her freshman five, or maybe she had, and it was lost in all that skin and bone. Maybe she was sick. Or maybe she had used up her food account. After the film he should ply her with steak and lobster and force-feed her a hot fudge sundae with extra whipped cream. Concern became realization, and he relaxed he must really like Peggy to worry about her so much. He hoped that this would be the first of many dates with her.

Essay Editing Practice 1

Read the following essay straight through. Then read through it again, correcting the comma splices and run-on sentence errors as you find them. Watch for misused words.

My Life as a Forty-Year-Old Student

It happened again today. My history professor announced an unexpected quiz for the next class period. The other, much younger students around me raised a chorus of complaints, which ranged from a sorority meeting to play practice to a rugby match, I only wish I had such light responsibilities. As an older, nontraditional student, I am always reminded during this **litany** of eighteen-year-old laments of just how difficult the task is that I have given myself.

Its true that sororities and play practice can be draining. Do these younger students realize, though, that I never begin my homework until after 9 o'clock? First, as a single father of three, I must get dinner on the table, even with my children's help, that takes time. After dinner, I round up whoever is supposed to clean the kitchen, then I help my children finish their homework. Finally, just as I am about to start, I have to make sure my teenager has the right jeans for the next day. All this easily takes up the early evening hours. Daytime is hardly better, of course, even though my three children are in school. Besides a part-time job and my own college work, I have many family responsibilities. Sarah might need a daisy costume for her ballet class, Jeff has soccer practice three afternoons a week, Carrie sometimes has trouble with her allergies. While my young classmates have to choose between studying in their dorm rooms or at the library, I have to choose between studying in the car outside Sarah's piano lesson or not studying at all.

Actually, I am convinced that the magic years between eighteen and twenty-two are the only sane years in which to attend college. Younger students' money problems, for example, look so appealing to me. They take baby-sitting jobs to earn money for clothes or for a midnight pizza. When finances run low, they wonder whether Mom or Dad will send an extra hundred dollars next week none has had to overrun a bank balance to buy antibiotics for a seven-year-old daughter. None has had to absorb the shock of the yearly house insurance payment or the teenage shame generated by wearing discount-brand tennis shoes. My classmates probably think that as an adult, my income is enormous, enough surely to afford a Lamborghini or at least a Mazda RX7, our thirteen-year-old Chevy Malibu knows otherwise. At any rate, as long as I am in college, if my classmates earn $10 baby-sitting, they have $10 more disposable income than my family has.

Then there are the more subtle traumas that a forty-year-old faces upon returning to college. My children's attitudes best illustrate how abrupt my transition has been. They have previously had clean laundry every Sunday morning, a hot meal every night, a handy chauffeur for their outings, and an entertaining hour together in front of the television, now they have had to adjust to underwear left damp in the washer, frozen pizza, and remembering to bring home the lemonade pitcher from their soccer games. As for the hour of television, well, I moved the computer into the family room. As I type this essay for comp class, they at least have my company if not my undivided attention.

Calm down, reader. If you are one of the eighteen-year-old students I am writing about, please know that I do understand that you also face problems. I haven't completely forgotten my own younger years. Can you believe now, however, that when I show up for class with my assignments finished and my papers neatly typed, I have had to pay as **exacting** a price as you must pay for your own completed work?

Writing Practice 1

Write three paragraphs or a complete essay on one of the following topics. As you write, first concentrate on what you want to say. Then go back and edit for errors in grammar and punctuation.

A. What are the problems of a college student just out of high school? Why do these problems occur, under what circumstances, and why aren't they a problem for older students? Choose three specific problems and write a paragraph on each.

B. What advice would a student over twenty-five give to other students over twenty-five? List a variety of suggestions, and group them into three categories—for example, study skills, time management, and coping with professors who are not used to nontraditional students. Write a paragraph for each of your categories.

C. How does a person benefit from attending college—other than financially? List advantages to attending college other than a better job, and then group these advantages into three categories (such as social, personal maturity, discipline, intellect, and so forth). Write notes on each category, describing the advantages, how these advantages may result, and why they are important. Then write a paragraph on each.

Copyright © 1992 by Harcourt Brace Jovanovich, Inc. All rights reserved.

A. Jot down some notes on different kinds of dates and how a person might dress differently for each. Choose three kinds and write three paragraphs that could serve as the body of an essay (you do not need to write the introduction and conclusion that would complete these essays).

B. List some ways that fashions have changed since you were thirteen years old, including some actual examples of different styles. Write three paragraphs about the phases of your personal fashion history, paragraphs that could serve as the body of an essay.

C. List the kinds of clothes you need right now in your life, and group these clothes into three categories. Make notes on each category, describing the clothes and why you need them—when you wear them, for what impression, and so forth. Then write three paragraphs that could serve as the body of an essay.

Review Exercises

1. Write three combinations of sentences (correctly) that someone might be tempted to write as comma splices or run-on sentences.

   a. _____

   b. _____

   c. _____

2. Using the following terms, write a rule for avoiding comma splices: *independent clauses, coordinating conjunction, comma.*

3. Using the same three terms (*independent clauses, coordinating conjunction, comma*), write a rule for avoiding run-on sentences.

Misused Words: fewer/less

Use *fewer* to describe items—things you can count one by one, such as seashells, serpents, surprises, and salamanders.

> Otis has *fewer* trophies on his shelf, but he has more prestigious ones.

Use *less* to describe amounts—things that come in a lump or all together, like pie filling, fear, fan support, or laughter.

> Otis may have fewer trophies, but he doesn't have any *less* pride.

Insert either *fewer* or *less* in the following sentences.

1. The team needed _____ turnovers to win the game.
2. If only the other team had _____ luck.
3. Shanda would end up with more cookies if she ate _____ dough.
4. Susie would prefer to eat _____ lentil casserole and _____ broccoli dishes.
5. Mr. Kyaing, the librarian, has asked for _____ noise, please.
6. You'll make _____ mistakes if you write the formula out first.

Dictionary Practice

Match each of the following words with its brief definition, using a dictionary if necessary. (Page numbers tell you where the word appears in the text.)

_____ 1. exacting (p. 98)   a. tending to change often

_____ 2. facets (p. 100)   b. the many sides of a single object

_____ 3. litany (p. 96)   c. long, repetitious chant

_____ 4. mutable (p. 100)   d. making severe demands

_____ 5. persona (p. 99)   e. image a person presents to the public

CHAPTER 6

Sentence Structure Review

■ Analyzing Sentences

In this chapter, you will practice recognizing correctly written sentences. Sometimes you will immediately recognize a given example as a sentence fragment, a comma splice, or a run-on. As the exercises become more complicated, however, you may want to follow this sequence of steps to analyze the entries.

Step 1: Underline subjects once and double underline the verbs that go with these subjects. Work all the way through the entry.

Step 2: Circle the dependent signals so that you can know whether any of the subject-verb combinations belong to dependent clauses. In marking dependent signals, remember three things.

Be careful to watch for understood dependent signals, such as *that*, which may not be written out in the sentence but still create a dependent clause.

Remember that some words serve as both the subject of the dependent clause and the dependent signal. These words include *which, who, that,* and *whoever*.

Remember that sometimes one dependent signal can serve for several subject-verb combinations:

Charis fondly remembers back to high school [(when) she finished her homework between classes, her friends rarely had to study, and her mother typed all her papers].

Copyright © 1992 by Harcourt Brace Jovanovich, Inc. All rights reserved.

Step 3: Once you have identified the subjects, verbs, and dependent signals, ask yourself this series of questions. Fill in the blanks with either *complete sentence, sentence fragment, comma splice,* or *run-on*.

1. Do you have at least one independent clause (a subject and its verb without a dependent signal before it)?
   Without at least one independent clause, you have a

   _____.

2. No matter how many dependent clauses you have, do you have at least one independent clause?
   With only one independent clause, you have a

   _____.

   If you have two or more independent clauses, then you have to ask yourself some additional questions.

3. Is there a coordinating conjunction before the last independent clause? (Whether a sentence has two or more independent clauses, a FANBOYS must precede the last one for the sentence to be written correctly.)
   If there *is* a FANBOYS before the last independent clause, then you have a _____.

   If there is *not* a FANBOYS, are there semicolons separating the independent clauses? If so, then you have a

   _____.

   If there is neither a FANBOYS before the last independent clause nor a semicolon separating independent clauses, you must ask two more questions.

4. Are these incorrectly written independent clauses separated with only a comma?
   If so, you have a _____.

5. Are the incorrectly written independent clauses run together without any punctuation?
   If so, you have a _____.

Again, in many instances you will readily recognize whether the given sentence is written correctly. If you have trouble with any of the exercises, however, use the foregoing series of questions.

Copyright © 1992 by Harcourt Brace Jovanovich, Inc. All rights reserved.

Analyzing Sentences   **105**

Exercises

In the following three exercise sets, identify each of the entries as one of these four possibilities:

> F   *Sentence fragment:* Lacking one independent clause.
> OK   *Correct:* One or more independent clauses, correctly punctuated.
> CS   *Comma splice:* Two or more independent clauses, incorrectly combined with only commas.
> RO   *Run-on:* Two or more independent clauses, incorrectly combined without any punctuation.

Set 1

__F__   1. When my mother, who is now in her sixties, was little.

__OK__   2. She lived on the wide-open prairies of Nebraska on her family's farm.

__CS__   3. Each winter morning, after putting a dress on over her long underwear, my mother would climb into thick work overalls, then top it all off with a coat, scarf, hat, and mittens, only then would she set off for her small country school about six miles from home.

__OK__   4. She took the overalls off when she got to school.

__F__   5. Because little girls in those days always wore a dress.

__F__   6. She looking so crumpled after that!

__F__   7. Because she rode a little farm pony to school each day and a bareback ride across the prairie does little to improve a dress already scrunched up under overalls.

__CS__   8. Actually, out in that prairie land, few children lived close to school, most rode ponies to get there.

__CS__   9. In the cold winter months, the prairie winds would whip snowy storms down from the frigid northern reaches of Canada, the warm ponies helped to keep the children warm.

__CS__   10. Parents put up makeshift stalls in the back of the school to give the ponies some shelter still, the ponies must have been terribly cold.

Copyright © 1992 by Harcourt Brace Jovanovich, Inc. All rights reserved.

11. So cold, in fact, that one afternoon my mother's pony ran away with her.
12. As soon as it felt my mother's leg go over its bare back, before my mother had a chance to settle in.
13. The pony took off in the direction of home he was so anxious to get to his nice warm barn.
14. She laughs now as she tells the story, but she had to hang on for dear life.
15. Especially when she got to the end of the school road and had to make a sharp left turn.
16. She was so certain she would fall off she hung on somehow.
17. That poor little pony!
18. After that her family always said that Nebraska winters caused the waters to freeze and the ponies to run.

Set 2

1. If students want to use their time to their greatest advantage and fit the most into each day, time management being especially important at college.
2. They should first make a list of everything they have to do.
3. Certainly a sensible way to begin, but not the most important step in time management.
4. With this list, students should then set priorities this means deciding what they must finish and what can wait for another day if necessary.
5. Doing the activities in this order, however, even if this list does show what is most important, ignores an undeniable human trait.
6. Each person performs his or her tasks to a certain rhythm, one person working best in the morning, another in the afternoon.

Analyzing Sentences   **107**

___RO___ 7. This rhythm flows between strength and weakness, concentration and inattention, carefulness and carelessness throughout the day, the wise student pays attention to this rhythm.

___F___ 8. Because this rhythm will help reveal when students should do certain tasks.

___CB RO___ 9. Looking at their list of important, must-do activities, students should ask themselves which will require the most concentration they should do these activities when they are most alert.

___F OK___ 10. Then they should ask which they would be most likely to shirk and avoid and do these when their motivation runs high.

___FRAG F___ 11. Those activities which they have no choice about doing, such as sitting in class or fulfilling work-study hours in the library, or those activities during which the student would never fall asleep, such as working on the school paper or doing a lab with a partner.

___OK___ 12. These activities should be scheduled for down times when students' motivation runs low, eyes droop, and feet drag.

___CS___ 13. Some activities do tend to lull a student to sleep, studying at the library, reading a literary novel, or reviewing sociology notes should be scheduled for students' most alert times.

___OK___ 14. Everybody has periods of strength and periods of weakness effective time management recognizes these times and schedules accordingly.

Set 3

___OK___ 1. When it comes to fashion, our bodies just haven't gotten the message that thin is better.

___F___ 2. Through most of humanity's history, during times of famine, drought, war, and sickness.

Copyright © 1992 by Harcourt Brace Jovanovich, Inc. All rights reserved.

3. Our ancestors struggled to get enough to eat, indeed, even now, many people on earth continue this struggle.
4. Small wonder, then, that our bodies were made to adjust rapidly to any sudden weight loss, taking drastic measures to halt the decline.
5. Operating in the dark recesses of our bodies, physical and chemical mechanisms that control how we use the food we eat (called metabolic processes).
6. The mechanisms can't distinguish between a New Year's resolution to lose twenty pounds and a life-threatening shortage of food consequently, automatic danger signals go up whenever a person starts losing weight too rapidly.
7. In order to protect itself, the body begins using food more carefully.
8. The more rapidly we diet, the more our bodies hold on to whatever we feed them to state it more grimly, the less we eat, the less we can eat to maintain a low weight.
9. The simple fact is that dieting makes it harder and harder to lose weight, the body thinks it is dying.
10. To succeed at losing weight, then, we must do it so slowly that we trick our bodies into not noticing.
11. No diets, no pills, no calorie counting, just a slight adjustment in eating habits, such as eliminating any food after 8 P.M. and refusing seconds at meals.
12. In particular, cutting back on fat seems to help long-term loss.
13. Which means eating toast, potatoes, and pasta without butter, frying in a no-stick pan, and limiting fatty meats.
14. Also, through consistent aerobic exercise, we can coax our bodies into using food more quickly.
15. A change in lifestyle would help here for example people

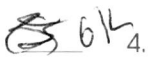

Analyzing Sentences   109

who change from a desk job to an outdoor job often achieve the most successful, long-term weight loss.

___F___ 16. Even if they weren't planning to.

___RO___ 17. So, for those of us who keep diet books on the best-sellers list, the good news is that quick-loss diets waste our time and determination the bad news is that long-term, steady exercise and consistent dietary changes offer our best hope.

___F___ 18. A solution that will cause little rejoicing among those of us who avoid mirrors.

___OK___ 19. How do the people who give us this news think we got all this weight in the first place?

Paragraph Editing Practice

Read the following paragraphs, and then go back through them editing any sentence errors that you find.

A.   Zane can be a pain. Sometimes I wonder if I spawned a monster sixteen months ago. Zane doesn't look like a tiny green creature with jagged horns, claws, and a long, spiked tail. To the naked human eye, he appears to be a pink and white, grinning, babbling, bouncing little boy, however, Mom knows better. Picture this, with superhuman strength and willpower, Zane races through the living room on toddling legs, leaps onto the coffee table, and grabs a handful of cassette tapes. Left within his reach by accident. Then, in the time it takes me to dash in from the kitchen on my all-too-human mommy legs. The irresistible tape ribbons have already been stretched, twisted, and crumpled into a sticky ball. Can it be, is this the handiwork of a human child? In my heart I know Zane is no monster, alien, or changeling left by fairies in exchange for my true offspring he is merely an energetic, curious, perfectly normal toddler. Even so, when I am cleaning behind his shell-pink ears, I cannot resist checking for signs of those jagged horns.

Copyright © 1992 by Harcourt Brace Jovanovich, Inc. All rights reserved.

B. People invent wonders for many reasons, need and greed and speed among them, however, one invention at least rose out of a young suitor's gallantry. Some time ago, Charles Menches took a friend to the St. Louis World's Fair. Flush with money and perhaps something else, he bought her both a bouquet of roses and an ice-cream sandwich. Though the roses looked beautiful against her cheeks (also flushed with something else, perhaps), they were making a mess. Spreading water all over her clean, white gloves and dripping down into her cuffs. Gallant as he was, Charles immediately saw a solution, he took the top wafer off the ice-cream sandwich, soft now from the melting ice cream, and rolled it into a cone. A perfect vase for her roses. He then rolled a second cone from the second wafer, and thus, as one story goes, was the ice-cream cone invented.

Essay Editing Practice 1

Read straight through the following essay for content. Then go back through it, editing any errors you find, including sentence fragments, comma splices, and run-on sentences.

Odysseus and the Cyclops

Long ago, fresh from his victories in the Trojan War, Odysseus decided on his way home to take a detour through adventure. With his ship and his boatload of men, he wandered the Aegean Sea looking for trouble, and when, after a great storm, he finally reached an island and managed to lead his weary crew onto shore, he found it. Wanting rest and food, he and his men entered into an inviting cave, discovering only at twilight that the cave belonged to an enormous Cyclops, an ugly giant with only one eye. The Cyclops drove his sheep into the cave, spotted the men, picked up an enormous stone. And to Odysseus and his men's great dismay closed the mouth of the cave. The men were trapped with a hungry monster who liked to eat sheep but who

Copyright © 1992 by Harcourt Brace Jovanovich, Inc. All rights reserved.

liked to eat men even better. The Cyclops quickly disposed of two of Odysseus' men.

Odysseus was stumped, he could kill the giant, but then how would they move the stone, much too large for even twenty men to budge? The next day, after the Cyclops drove his sheep out and blocked the entrance with the stone again, Odysseus came up with a plan. He first sharpened the branch of an olive tree, then when the Cyclops came back, Odysseus offered him some wine, getting him drunk. Before the Cyclops dozed off, he offered Odysseus a gift if Odysseus would tell him his name.

"My name is Nobody," Odysseus said.

"Your gift is that I will eat you last," the giant graciously responded and fell asleep, drunk.

Odysseus had been waiting for this, he and his men promptly blinded the Cyclops with the olive branch. When the Cyclops cried out in pain and anger, his giant friends came running and asked who was bothering him.

"Nobody," the Cyclops screamed, so of course his friends left him alone. An angry giant being dangerous for even other giants to deal with.

Even blind, though, the Cyclops refused to let the men escape. He sat at the entrance, feeling each sheep as it passed through to make certain that none of his delicacies was riding to freedom. What could Odysseus and his men do? There seemed no possibility of escape. Eventually the Cyclops would find them all and eat them.

Wily as ever, Odysseus saw a way out. He strapped three sheep together then he tied one of his men on underneath. The Cyclops, who carefully felt the sheep's backs, missed all the men clinging to the sheep's bellies.

Out of the Cyclops' cave with plenty of sheep to feed them on their voyage, Odysseus and his men escaped, sailing on to new adventures.

Copyright © 1992 by Harcourt Brace Jovanovich, Inc. All rights reserved.

Writing Practice 1

Write an essay on one of the following topics. Remember, as you write, concentrate on your message first. Then as you go back over your writing, concentrate on your grammar and punctuation.

A. Choose any fable, fairy tale, myth, or legend that you know (including a story of a modern-day hero such as Indiana Jones or Batman), and retell the story. First, jot down notes on what happens in the story. Then use these notes to write the story. Finally go back over it and check for any sentence errors.

B. Compare the relative strengths of Batman and Superman. Make lists of information related to their physical, emotional, and character strengths. Then write a paragraph on each kind of strength, comparing the two heroes.

C. What traits do heroes (male or female) have in common? Consider Indiana Jones, Princess Leia, and Wonder Woman (or other heroes), and list their common traits. Then group these traits into three categories. Write three paragraphs, using actual characters to illustrate your categories.

Essay Editing Practice 2

This essay has sentence fragments and incorrectly combined sentences. Read through it and then edit it to correct the problems.

The Hardest Lesson

College naturally offers students much to learn. They must find out what major is most likely to lead to a $100,000-a-year job, which chemistry professor is easiest, and whether they should study their lecture notes for the history test. Of all the lessons offered students, however, the most difficult to learn is how to wake up for a first-period class.

Some people, of course, have no problem getting up. They are easy enough to spot. The day *before* the term paper's due, they sit smugly in class. And tap the final draft piled neatly on their desk. They excuse themselves from lunch, telling everyone at the table that they have to return some library books. Before the books become overdue. They unpack their suitcases the minute they come back from break. Remarkably, they never run out of clean underwear. For these students, a simple alarm clock **suffices** to get them up.

For most students, however, an alarm clock merely becomes a prop in their dreams. Like Freddie ringing twice in a nightmare on Elm Street or a police siren intruding at the worst moment. When students hear the alarm, they rouse themselves only long enough to slap the sound off and then drift lazily back to sleep again.

Putting another alarm clock across the room requires students to get out of bed and walk across the room. Would seem to bring the sleepyheads at least to the upright position. But how the bed calls them back, sweetly, invitingly, like Jason's **sirens** driving away all memory of obligation. No path is ever so rocky and **laden** with obstacles as the one from the bed to the alarm, or so smooth and easy as the one back to the bed.

Plainly, the alarm across the room solves only half the problem. Until someone invents a device to keep students out of bed, alarm clocks will remain a minor nuisance to those who have trouble waking up. Microchips now tell toast when to pop up, the iron when to turn off, and the dryer when to stop spinning. Perhaps one day, on signal, microchips will tell blankets when to go from soft to scratchy, from warm to chilly, from comfy to stiff. And in that way repel anyone from returning to bed. What a step this will be for humanity! The person who invents these blankets can take his or her place alongside those heroes of **ingenuity**. The inventors of the wheel, the printing press, and the lollipop.

Even then, however, students who really hate to get up in the morning will probably still forget to set the alarm in the first place.

Writing Practice 2

Choose a topic below and write two to three paragraphs on it. Remember to concentrate on your message first, and then read back over your writing to check for errors.

A. Make a list of your responsibilities related to college. Group these into three or four categories, and make notes on why each category is important. Using examples to clarify each, write three paragraphs on these categories, writing the paragraphs in order of importance (most important first, least important last).

B. This author seems to think getting up is one of the hardest lessons to learn in college. List five or six other problems a college student confronts. Group these into three categories, and jot down what the problems have in common. Then write three paragraphs explaining each category of problem and using examples to clarify the category.

C. What was a problem that you or a friend had adjusting to college? Take a few notes on the problem, the way you or your friend attempted to solve the problem, and what finally happened. Then write the experience as a story.

Essay Editing Practice 3

Read through this essay, and then edit it. The problems include both sentence fragments and incorrectly combined sentences.

Tomato Trees and a Cure for AIDS

In 1989, the Exxon oil freighter *Valdez* ran aground in Alaska. Dumping over ten million gallons of crude oil into the **pristine** waters of Prince William Sound. Some scientists immediately considered a bioengineered solution. A tiny organism developed in the laboratory could actually eat the long carbon chains that made up the crude oil. And during digestion turn these chains into environmentally safe by-products, such as alcohol. No one accepted the scientists' proposal, for even though tipsy otters would have been better than dead ones, bioengineering still seems to pose too many hazards for widespread use.

The name itself seems the stuff of Frankenstein. *Bio* means life and *engineering* conveys the notion of design or manipulation therefore *bioengineering* seems to mean "the manipulation of life." In theory, the abuses seem enormous: Bioengineering could lead to more effective and therefore even more horrific chemical warfare or to an updated version of *Brave New World* in which parents design the child they want. Even unintentional results seem scary, faulty bacteria could devour the country's entire corn crop or start an epidemic.

The basketball player sitting beside you in class, though, may be glad that scientists have developed bioengineering techniques. Without bioengineering, he may have stood 3'6" high. Years ago, scientists realized that a certain hormone would stimulate human growth in children destined for shortness. Back then, they extracted the hormones from cadavers, an extremely expensive process that kept the supply limited. When bioengineering techniques improved. Scientists were able to isolate and study cells' genetic material, which tells a cell how to behave. Including how to reproduce itself and what kind of chemicals it should make. A single unit of this genetic material, like a single car in a train, is called a *gene*. Eventually, scientists were able to isolate the gene that told certain cells in the human body to produce human growth hormone. They took that gene, inserted it into the genetic material of a bacteria, and turned that bacteria into a micro-factory producing human growth hormone. With this method, much more efficient and slightly less expensive, scientists now provide growth hormone to almost anyone who really needs it.

So although the hazards seem tremendous. The benefits also cause many a heart to race. Someday bioengineering might provide a cure for sickle-cell anemia, cancer, muscular dystrophy, and even AIDS. As for food production, imagine tomato trees which, like apple trees, produce bushels of fruit every year with a minimum of labor. Less dramatic but probably more advantageous would be strains of corn, beans, wheat,

Copyright © 1992 by Harcourt Brace Jovanovich, Inc. All rights reserved.

and rice that are resistant to pests and disease or have a higher protein or vitamin content. Producing plants that can grow in desert conditions or extreme cold. This would be trickier because for these advances scientists would have to combine characteristics. Still, the Sahara in bloom is worth dreaming about.

True, we take a risk with bioengineering. However, we risk food poisoning when we eat in a restaurant, we risk terrorists when we fly across the Mediterranean. For these hazards, we set up health standards and security measures, and then we live with the risks. We can do the same with bioengineering. If we have developed the technology to transport millions of gallons of crude oil across our precious oceans. Then we had better develop the technology to clean up our inevitable messes.

Writing Practice 3

Write an essay on one of the following topics. Remember to concentrate on your message first, and then read back through for errors in punctuation and grammar.

A. Take a stand for or against bioengineering, listing reasons for your stand. Choose three of these reasons and jot down what you might include in a paragraph about each. Then write the three paragraphs.

B. Suggest three rules our society should institute to limit bioengineering. Jot down ideas on why each rule would be important, and then write a paragraph explaining each rule and the reason you believe the rule is necessary.

C. What inventions or discoveries in the past hundred years do you think have changed your life the most? Choose three, and for each one describe in a paragraph how that invention or discovery has changed your life.

Copyright © 1992 by Harcourt Brace Jovanovich, Inc. All rights reserved.

Misused Words: use/used

In the expression "I *used to* do something," meaning a habit or practice that you have had in the past, be careful to use the past participle *used*. After hearing so many people slur *used to* together, you might forget to add the *d*. Write either *use* or *used to* in the following sentences.

1. Jo and Steve ___used to___ live in Indonesia.
2. Vic and Carol ___used to___ own a fluorescent purple car.
3. Marty and Yoram ___use___ their extra money for world travel.
4. Renaldo and Bunny ___used to___ live in a townhouse.
5. Thalita and Ken ___use___ a station wagon to transport their family.
6. Steve and Isabel ___used to___ take photographs but now take only videos.
7. Randall and Rose ___used to___ want only four children.

Review Exercises

Set 1

In the following examples of comma splices and run-on sentences, circle the transition word that has been used incorrectly to separate independent clauses, and list those words on the lines following the sentences.

1. A man named Siwash George found gold first in Canada, along the Klondike River, after this, thousands of prospectors came in search of gold.
2. During this gold rush, prices skyrocketed for example, one man with a cow sold each cup of milk for $5.
3. One new arrival sold a current newspaper he had brought with him for $160, however, the man who bought it made an even bigger sale.
4. He charged a dollar from anyone who wanted to hear the paper read aloud in this way, the man cleared over a thousand dollars.

5. Some made a fortune, therefore, either through gold or other means then they went home.
6. Many others came also expecting quick riches and a quick return however, they fell in love with the land and stayed long after the gold had gone, settling the vast land called Alaska.

Transition words: _____

Now go back and correct the sentences in Set 1.

Set 2

In the following sentences, underline the subjects once and the verbs twice, circle the dependent signals, and bracket the dependent clauses. Remember that some dependent signals, called relative pronouns, can serve both as the dependent signal and as the subject of the dependent clause. Make a list of these dependent signals on the line following sentence 4 (these words will be both underlined and circled).

1. The Mayans, who inhabited Yucatan, the eastern portion of Mexico, over a thousand years ago, built towering temples.
2. Nearly half of the three million people of Uruguay live in Montevideo, which is the capital city.
3. The huge stone sculptures that sit looking across the waters surrounding Easter Island in the South Pacific weigh over fifty tons and yet were moved with only ropes and ramps.
4. These people, whoever moved the sculptures, had no metal, no wheels, and no machines.

   Double-duty dependent signals: _____
5. List eight other dependent signals. _____

Dictionary Practice

Match the following words with their definitions.

____ 1. ingenuity (p. 113)   a. bearing a load

____ 2. laden (p. 113)   b. crafty

____ 3. pristine (p. 114)   c. to be enough

____ 4. siren (p. 113)   d. clever inventiveness

____ 5. suffice (p 113)   e. unspoiled; innocent

____ 6. wily (p. 111)   f. a female mythological character who lured sailors to their destruction; temptress

CHAPTER 7

Commas That Separate

Whereas Chapter 5 explains how you might sometimes use commas *incorrectly* to separate parts of a sentence, this chapter tells you how to use commas *correctly* to separate sentence parts. Notice how the commas have been used in the following sentences:

> After getting ready for a hot date, Ivy picked up the phone to see if she could find someone to go out with.
>
> She called Vergil, Steven, and Will.
>
> Not wanting to waste the night on a video, she finally dragged out her stodgy roommates with the offer of free fajitas.

Each of these sentences requires commas to separate elements within the sentences. To explain when you need these commas, we will be using certain terms that were introduced in earlier chapters. Do the following to see if you understand these four terms.

1. Write a sentence with a *dependent clause*. _____

2. List five *dependent signals*. _____

3. Define *independent clause*. _____

4. List all the *coordinating conjunctions*. _____

◼ Two Independent Clauses

When you correctly join two independent clauses with a coordinating conjunction (FANBOYS), you need a comma before the conjunction.

The following sentences have two independent clauses, separated by a FANBOYS:

> Sami sat stiffly on the sofa, so she could impress her Great-aunt Bess.

> Jeffrey sat at the old woman's feet instead, and he was the one [who inherited her money].

These sentences require commas because they meet the following requirements:

1. Each has two independent clauses (two subject-verb combinations that have no dependent signals).
2. Each has a FANBOYS.
3. Whatever comes after the FANBOYS can stand alone as a sentence.

Practice 1

Combine the sentences in exercises 1 and 2, using a FANBOYS to separate the two independent clauses.

1. Mohan attended many recitals at the music school.
   He avoided voice recitals.

   _____

   _____

2. Then he began dating a soprano.
   He grew to enjoy classical songs.

   _____

   _____

3. Write an original sentence that has two independent clauses joined by a FANBOYS.

   _____

   _____

Please remember this rule, however:

> **If you have one subject and two verbs, you *do not* need a comma.**

> Karen walked briskly to the end of the diving board and walked just as briskly back again.

The <u>waves</u> <u>crashed</u> against the seashore and <u>frightened</u> my little boy away.

Recombine the following two sentences, this time using only one subject and two verbs.

4. Then he began dating a soprano.
   He grew to enjoy classical songs.

_____

_____

☐ Introductory Dependent Clause

When you begin a sentence with a dependent clause, use a comma to separate that introductory thought from the main part of the sentence.

These sentences have introductory dependent clauses:

[(Before) my <u>son</u> <u>had</u> his birthday party], our <u>house</u> <u>was strewn</u> with nervous tremors of raw excitement.

[(After) the <u>party</u> <u>was</u> over], our <u>house</u> <u>was strewn</u> instead with trash, enough to fill two twenty-gallon bags.

To recognize when you need this comma, look for a dependent clause at the beginning of the sentence.

Practice 2
Combine the sentences in exercises 1 and 2, using a dependent clause to begin the sentence.

1. Pedro took chemistry.
   Before he did this, he had never realized what a poor sense of smell he had.

_____

_____

2. He tried to identify a substance from its smell.
   When he did this, he found it impossible.

_____

_____

Please remember this rule:

> **If the dependent clause *follows* the independent clause, you do not need a comma.**

In the following sentences, the independent clause comes first:

> The judge refused to give Lewis any leeway [(after) she found out] [that he had been drinking].
>
> Escher's paintings make me dizzy [(when) I look at them too long].

3. Write a sentence with a dependent clause preceding the independent clause.

    _____

    _____

4. Now rewrite your sentence with the dependent clause *following* the independent clause.

    _____

    _____

☐ Other Long Introductory Elements

> **Like dependent clauses, any long introductory phrase should be set off from the main sentence with a comma.**

The following sentences have long introductory phrases:

> On Saturday morning at least, I ignore the demands of college.
>
> After spreading a bagel with cream cheese, I head into the den to watch *Muppet Babies*.

Please note the emphasis on *long*. Unless your reader must pause for clarity, please don't insert commas after just one or two words at the beginning of your sentences. With optional commas like these, the rule is this: Avoid commas unless you really need them. All the following sentences have introductory elements, but because these elements are so short, none absolutely requires a comma.

Copyright © 1992 by Harcourt Brace Jovanovich, Inc. All rights reserved.

On Friday I intend to celebrate with an elegant candlelight dinner.

Then I will see two movies [(that) I have had my eye on all semester].

After that I shall dance the entire night away.

Practice 3

Combine the pairs of sentences in exercises 1–3.

1. She was following after everyone else.
   Earline noticed the lost child.

   _____

   _____

2. Duncan will do this next.
   He will try out for the golf team.

   _____

   _____

3. This happens whenever Xavier gets into a plane.
   His stomach feels as if it will explode.

   _____

   _____

4. Write a sentence with a long introductory element (*not* a dependent clause, this time).

   _____

   _____

◼ Commas for Clarity

Of course, whatever other rule about commas you follow, always try to avoid misunderstandings, some of which can be quite embarrassing.

You can always use commas to eliminate confusion.

Notice how useful commas are in the following sentences.

Without commas

After driving my wife likes to take a long walk.

With commas

After driving, my wife likes to take a long walk.

Copyright © 1992 by Harcourt Brace Jovanovich, Inc. All rights reserved.

Before eating the raccoon washes its hands.

Before eating, the raccoon washes its hands.

By six seven stooges volunteered.

By six, seven stooges volunteered.

☐ Two Equal Describers

When you use two equal words to describe a noun (person, place, or thing), you need to separate these words with a comma.

The following sentences have equal describers:

I like a wild, wacky hairstyle, the kind that makes my father gasp and my boyfriend grin.

The dark, dreary night descended over the backyard, sending shivers up the young campers' spines.

How can you know whether the words are *equal?* Try this two-step test.

1. Reverse the order of the two words: a wacky, wild hairstyle.
2. Insert *and* between the words: a wacky and wild hairstyle.

If the sentence still makes sense, the words are equal and you need the comma.

Notice that the following examples have *unequal* describers; therefore, no comma is required between them:

Just the thought of *spicy Chinese* food causes my mouth to water.

Who would ever paint her bedroom such a *sickly green* color?

Practice 4

Try the two-step test on the describers in sentences 1–6, inserting commas where needed.

1. The four tired marchers collapsed on the couch, their pickets still clasped in their hands.

2. After climbing the rickety old ladder, the cat lost its courage to come down.

3. My precious perfect husband does the laundry every week.

4. Have you ever seen such disgustingly bratty children?

5. Sometimes lovely green ivy hides poison in its veins.

6. The bull's eyes gleamed at the sight of the bright red bicycle.

Combine the sentences in exercises 7 and 8, putting the descriptive words *before* the noun that they describe.

7. My roommate is messy.
   She is also disorganized.
   She manages to get all her assignments in on time.

   _____

   _____

8. The lost city is Machu Picchu in Peru.
   The lost city is mysterious.
   The lost city was discovered in 1911.

   _____

   _____

9. Write a sentence with two equal describers.

   _____

   _____

10. How would you recognize that you need a comma in the sentence you just wrote?

    _____

    _____

▪ Commas with Quotations

Use commas to separate most quotations from their "tags," words such as *he said* or *she remarked*.

These sentences include quotations:

> James said, "I shall drive nothing but a Mercedes."

> "Then you will have to find a remarkably rich wife," his mother replied.

Copyright © 1992 by Harcourt Brace Jovanovich, Inc. All rights reserved.

This rule always holds true when the tag comes at the beginning of the sentence, but it doesn't apply to questions or exclamations when the tag comes at the end. Notice that in the following sentences, if the order of the tag and quotation changes, the punctuation changes as well.

Tag first	**Tag second**
One day my father asked, "If you're so smart, why can't you keep track of your other earring?"	"If you're so smart, why can't you keep track of your other earring?" my father asked one day.
The fireman shouted, "Jump now!"	"Jump now!" the fireman shouted.

Please note this as well:

Commas and periods always go *within* the quotation marks, no matter how short the quoted material is.
Question marks go within the quotation marks only when the entire question has been quoted.

Practice 5

Combine the sentences in exercises 1 and 2.

1. In Texas, this happens when customers leave a store.
   Most shopkeepers say something.
   "Y'all come back now!"

2. "Can I set my alarm for 12 midnight?"
   My son asks this each Christmas Eve.

3. Write a sentence in which someone says something as a direct quotation.

■ Commas with Items in a Series

When you have three or more items in a series, use commas to separate these items. The following sentences use commas to separate items in a series:

> On a diet, I glide through the morning, trudge through the afternoon, and collapse in the evening.
>
> Cheesecake, brownie batter, and barbecued potato chips are my stumbling blocks.
>
> In the end, though, as long as I'm perceptive, passionate, and provocative, who should care about a few extra pounds?

Please note that items in a series can be words, phrases, or even clauses. If you put two or more independent clauses together, remember that they must be closely related and must have a FANBOYS before the last clause. Notice the FANBOYS in the following sentence, which has been correctly punctuated:

> We know everything as teenagers, we begin to have doubts about [what we know in our twenties and thirties], and we find out from our own teenagers [that we know nothing in our forties].

Practice 6

Combine the sentences in exercises 1 and 2.

1. Most people don't realize something.
   The Chinese invented the compass.
   They invented paper.
   They invented printing.

   _____

   _____

2. This happens in Africa.
   Chad was named for Lake Chad.
   Nigeria was named for the Niger River.
   Namibia was named for the Namib Desert.

   _____

Copyright © 1992 by Harcourt Brace Jovanovich, Inc. All rights reserved.

Chapter 7 Commas That Separate

3. Write a sentence that includes a series of three or more items.

Exercises

Why do the following sentences require commas? Write the rule after each sentence.

1. However she does it, my little sister always gets her way.

2. "It's really an easy test," said the deluded professor.

3. Big Bird, Tweety Bird, and Larry Bird are my favorite feathered friends.

4. Whatever else you do, do the dishes.

5. Jasper's vivid yellow, black-spotted overcoat makes him look like a bee.

6. Lupe says that she likes football, but she skips the games to study.

7. Having just purchased his first car, Gavin can't help showing it off.

Copyright © 1992 by Harcourt Brace Jovanovich, Inc. All rights reserved.

Sentence Practice

Each sentence in these exercises shows one of the following five patterns. Refer to this list as you identify each sentence with the appropriate letter: A, B, C, D, or E. Then correct the punctuation in the sentences.

- A *Two independent clauses (S + V comma FANBOYS S + V):* These must be properly separated with a FANBOYS. Insert a comma before the FANBOYS.
- B *Long introductory element, including dependent clauses* (Intro comma IC): Insert a comma after the long introductory element.
- C *Equal describers:* If you can switch the order of the two describers and insert *and*, then put a comma between the two words.
- D *Quotations:* Separate the tag (such as *he said*) from the quotation, except for questions and exclamations with the tag at the end.
- E *Series:* Use commas to separate three or more items in a series.

_____ 1. When Gracie was only five she thought that white eggs came from hens and that brown eggs came from roosters.

_____ 2. Now that she is six she thinks all eggs are brown until the farmer scrubs the dirt off.

_____ 3. Arthur single-handedly devoured two buckets of crispy chicken and a piece of cherry pie at the church potluck and then he launched an attack on his neighbors' barbecue.

_____ 4. Leon spotted the earnest energetic girl on the volleyball team and decided to ask her out.

_____ 5. What could be better than singing and dancing jumping and leaping rocking and rolling to rockabilly tunes?

_____ 6. Musuko said "What's the matter?"

_____ 7. "My computer has a virus" his roommate answered.

_____ 8. Imagine! Sometime before Emily Brontë was thirty years old she wrote *Wuthering Heights*.

_____ 9. She must have somehow acquired a tortured anguished soul to write a novel so filled with humanity's darkest pride and passion.

_____ 10. The coffin containing the remains of last year's Halloween decorations is safely entombed within a long low room behind the basement staircase.

_____ 11. When her boss complained about the smell Sally produced a can of air freshener and sprayed the offending Limburger cheese.

_____ 12. Asked about his plans the precocious eight-year-old gave his response with a wink and a smile.

_____ 13. "We have lift-off" the volleyball announcer said.

_____ 14. After switching from whole milk to skim milk for my health I find whole milk tastes like whipping cream.

Sentence Combining

Combine the sentences in each exercise to make one sentence.

1. Many people would be surprised to hear it.
   This happened for eleven years.
   Karl Marx, author of *Das Kapital*, contributed editorials to New York's *Daily Tribune*.
   (Use either a FANBOYS or a dependent signal.)

   _____

   _____

2. Maybe you cannot judge a book by its cover.
   You can most certainly judge a book by its title.

   _____

   _____

3. My future spouse must be kind.
   My future spouse must be witty.
   My future spouse must be in love with me.

   _____

   _____

4. I ate the roast beef happily.
   The roast beef was tough.
   The roast beef was dry.
   My proud son had cooked it.
   (Use *tough* and *dry* as descriptive words before *roast beef*.)

   _____

   _____

5. "Get your shopping bags off the hood of my car."
   A taxi driver shouted this statement.
   The taxi driver was angry.

   _____

   _____

6. "Then get your tire off my scarf."
   The woman snapped this statement back.
   She was equally angry.

   _____

   _____

7. "See you below in one piece or a thousand!"
   The parachutist said this statement.
   He said this as he leaped from the plane.
   (Combine these sentences twice, once with the tag first and once with the tag at the end.)

   _____

   _____

   _____

   _____

Paragraph Editing Practice

Read through the following paragraphs. Then edit them, looking especially for comma errors.

A.   When my grandmother was young she hated to cook. In those days, however, the woman of the house was expected to find the time to put three square, tasty meals on the table every single day. If that sounds simple, remember that she had no microwave no hot dogs no frozen dinners and no Bisquick, for heaven's sake. Also, please consider that each meal took up to an hour to prepare so she sometimes spent up to three hours a day in the kitchen which did not include doing the dishes.

    Not surprisingly on some days Granny had better things to do with her time. She would get so busy quilting or tatting or whatever women in her day did for fun that she would forget all about cooking supper. Even so, Granny had things figured. A few minutes before Grandpa Dan was due in from the fields she would throw some onions on the grill. My how the rich brown smell of those onions would fill the air. Grandpa would come in and start salivating. "Supper's almost ready" Granny would call. "Why don't you set the table for me?" In the time it took Grandpa to put the plates and glasses out Granny would have whipped together some grilled steak and home-canned green beans to eat with those onions. My Granny June was not just quick. She was also clever.

B.   Nine times in the past week I stubbed my toe on a crack in the sidewalk. Not only that yesterday I bit my tongue four times, once when I was drinking lemonade. I was never accident-prone until I met Donna Mayberry. Blond green-eyed completely irresistible Donna sits next to me in biology class and she has altered the course of my life. As a "real cool dude" I never used to stutter and turn three shades of red when I talked to a female. My hands never felt like boxing gloves and my glasses never fogged up. For goodness sakes my fly used to stay zipped. Now as soon as Donna turns to me and says "Hi" I become a nerd. I can think of only two causes for this strange **metamorphosis** from graceful king moth to clumsy caterpillar. Either I am crazy or I am crazy in love. It must be love because a stubbed toe never felt so good.

Essay Practice 1

Read straight through the following essay. Then go back through it, inserting commas to separate parts of sentences (as studied in this chapter).

The Real Miracle

Americans love television. They eat their Crunch-Munchies in front of the morning news programs pretend to dust during the soaps and let Johnny make them drowsy enough for sleep. But whatever Americans watch, as long as they are tuned to the networks, they see a lot of commercials. These thirty-second slices become the basis for people's individual dreams and desires even though the life that the commercials present is so often unattainable. The way television commercials portray family life is especially unrealistic.

On television commercials children always cooperate. Car commercials, for example, regularly show three smiling creatures happily climbing into the back seat of cars but these creatures only masquerade as children. For one thing real children never get ready on time. They begin looking for their shoes when Mom grabs her car keys. Only after an exhaustive ten-minute search do they find the shoes, one wedged behind the cereal boxes in the kitchen cabinet and the other under the pile of towels molding in the bathroom. Then, when real children do come to the car, they arrive with their shirts on backward their hair clinging weakly to yesterday's rubber band plum jam on their chins and the wrong homework. And here is the clincher. Real children never willingly give up the window seat. Every child knows that whoever ends up in the middle is obligated to complain until the car reaches its destination. Clearly, under their disguises the creatures masquerading as children in the commercials must actually be robots. If car companies could sell them with the cars gross profits would increase a thousandfold.

Also unrealistic is the way television families talk to each other. Almost every commercial selling feminine hygiene products, for example, shows daughters asking their mothers for advice. Where but on television could these miraculous encounters exist? In real life girls ask friends know-it-all sisters their boyfriends or even the man in the moon but they never ask their mothers. Similarly, on television commercials families sit around the kitchen table and talk about the new brand of macaroni and cheese Mom bought about new boyfriends or about Dad and son playing ball together. In real life, families cannot afford to talk at meals. They might miss Willard congratulating another centurion or Vanna prancing across the stage.

Most painful of all to watch television families always seem to get along. Dad brings home a computer and the family gathers around and watches Mom work on family accounts. In real life Mom first comments that the family cannot afford this luxury. She then mutters a complaint about this being one more ploy to get her to do the family accounts. In real life children crowd around trying to punch keys and they yell "It's my turn," and "When do I get to do it?" and "Why didn't you buy any computer games, Dad?" On television when older daughters come home to visit Mom they settle down for a mellow companionable cup of Irish Mocha Mint. In real life, daughters eventually end up complaining. Their mothers never praised their successes enough never encouraged their efforts enough never were around enough when they needed them and most of all never understood them.

Ultimately commercials about families can become disheartening disillusioning and just plain painful. Who knows how many products have been purchased in hopes of achieving the fantasy family and how many tempers have been lost because real life will never measure up to the commercials? This is especially ironic because real life far exceeds fantasy. Families don't need the false perfection portrayed on commercials. In spite of all the frustrations complaints distractions and defeats American family life endures and even prevails. It is a miracle that exceeds three children crowded into the back seat without arguing.

Copyright © 1992 by Harcourt Brace Jovanovich, Inc. All rights reserved.

Writing Practice 1

Choose one of the following topics to write about. (See Chapters 19–22 for information on writing an essay.) Concentrate on your message first, and then read back through to check for errors in punctuation and grammar.

A. Think of reasons why people who live in the same house might not communicate well. Choose three reasons, and jot down one or two examples to illustrate each, using examples from your own life, the news media, books, or popular media. Write a short essay using this information.

B. Why do people need families? Choose three reasons and write a paragraph about each, describing ways that your family or the families of friends have met these needs. List reasons and choose three to focus on. For these, jot down why each need exists and ways that families meet this need. Then write a short essay using this information.

C. What are the three most important rules for family members to follow? Choose three rules and list examples, descriptions, and reasons why you have chosen each. Then write a short essay using this information.

Essay Editing Practice 2

Read through the following essay, and then edit it. Watch for and correct all kinds of errors.

Steel-Toed Boots and a Seat at the Game

All the marches in Washington, the banners demanding equality, and the speeches **denouncing** sexism have had some big results for women. While they have yet to achieve certain jobs (professional football player and president of the country making an odd **juxtaposition**), women now seem to have more choices in life than men do. In fact, although my wife disagrees, I believe women have taken some of what men once held distinct and have **relinquished** little in return.

Take clothes, for example, with the possible exception of a man's athletic supporter, women wear everything that a man does. Including his boxer shorts. Women don tuxedos steel-toed boots three-piece suits and hard hats, in addition to their **plethora** of feminine apparel. Not only can women wear more different items, but the items they wear can

Copyright © 1992 by Harcourt Brace Jovanovich, Inc. All rights reserved.

be more varied. A woman's collar offers almost infinite variety in hue, plunge, and flounce. A man's collar instead offers the singular variety of a button on the flap. The same **variance** holds true for sleeves, shirt fronts, underwear, and belts. Most enviable of all, women can choose clothes that hide their flaws. My wife regularly wears oversized shirts to camouflage her hip depository. With what can I hide my stomach stash?

More than just clothes, however, women have more freedom in how they spend their day. Even if staying home were an option for a man (and who could face his bowling buddies if he did?) think how poorly he would fit in. Women, who have **wrested** from men membership in the New York Stock Exchange, have **tenaciously** reserved from men membership in the Wednesday afternoon bridge club. Women drop their children at "Mother's Day Out." And indulge in coffee **klatches**, learn petit-point needlepoint and plot neighborhood garage sales. Men have no place among these **hallowed** endeavors. Indeed, lowly man has more hope of infiltrating the Mafia than slipping unnoticed into a coupon swap.

And speaking of petit-point consider the hobbies men must now share. While women hold almost exclusive right to all forms of needle-point and craft work, men have **relinquished** sole ownership of their most cherished leisure pursuit. Sitting anything but demurely among the spectators at any major sports event, even boxing, the gentle women of this land let their guard drop. Excognito, they yell and scream with abandon, more rotor in their rooting than the men around them, my wife included. At our house, when the Oklahoma-Texas game comes on, my wife races our fourteen-year-old son for the best spot on the couch. On Thanksgiving, because my wife refuses to miss the Turkey Day games, we declare the kitchen closed and order pizza. She behaves worse during the NCAA tournament. Everything from the laundry to our love life **languishes** as the final games approach. So even in their hobbies women have more options.

Copyright © 1992 by Harcourt Brace Jovanovich, Inc. All rights reserved.

After so many centuries of limited choices, of corsets and high heels, of bound dreams and **fettered** intellects, women's multiplicity of choices probably comes fairly and behind time. Even so, will they eventually share their gains? I grant them their dresses freely, of course, and have no desire to take up their barbaric habit of leg-shaving, but what about a Wednesday afternoon poker game? Now *that* I could handle.

Writing Practice 2

Write on one of the following topics. (See Chapters 19–22 for information on writing an essay.) Concentrate on your message first, and then your punctuation and grammar.

A. In what ways have women made gains in the last twenty or thirty years? Choose three ways and list possible examples that would demonstrate these gains. Then write a short essay.

B. In what ways do women still need to make gains? Choose three, listing examples of discrimination or prejudices that would support your claim. Then write a short essay.

C. The writer of this essay says women have relinquished little in return to men. Do you believe this? Think of three ways that men have gained as a result of the women's movement, giving examples from popular media, books, or your own life if possible to demonstrate your claims. Then write a short essay, using your notes.

Misused Words: to/too/two

To comes from the word *toward*. If you can substitute *toward*, you need the word *to*. You also use *to* with infinitives and with certain common phrases, such as *in addition to*.

He carried the suitcases *to* the car.

Copyright © 1992 by Harcourt Brace Jovanovich, Inc. All rights reserved.

Two has an extra *o*, so use it when you are discussing something extra, such as *too much energy* or *too little luck*.

The trunks were *too* heavy for him.

Two rarely causes problems; use it for the number.

Write *to* or *too* in the following sentences.
1. Come with me, please, _____ the masquerade.
2. That would cost _____ much money.
3. But I would be _____ disappointed if we didn't go.
4. Do you really have enough money _____ pay for your ticket?
5. You have _____ little faith in me.
6. No, I am _____ familiar with your habits. You intend for me _____ buy your ticket, don't you?

Review Exercises

Insert commas as needed in sentences 1–6.
1. Driving down the wrong way at the grocery store parking lot my wife ran into another car.
2. She remained poised during the police report and then did her shopping as if nothing had happened.
3. She drove our dented maroon car home came inside without unloading the groceries went straight to the shower and cried in private.
4. Everyone was glad that no one was hurt but if that was true why did she cry?
5. Much later she was able to smile and joke about it.
6. She said "After all that I didn't even have the grocery coupons I needed."

7. Write five places you need to use commas to separate parts of a sentence.

   a. _____
   b. _____
   c. _____
   d. _____
   e. _____

For exercises 8–15, identify each entry as one of the following:

OK	*Correct.*
F	*Sentence fragment:* Lacking an independent clause.
RO	*Run-on:* Two independent clauses joined without any punctuation.
CS	*Comma splice:* Two independent clauses joined with a comma only.

_____ 8. In the days of the great Egyptian kingdoms, the pharaohs were buried with furniture, food, jewelry, and other treasures.

_____ 9. As well as anything they might need to make their afterlife comfortable.

_____ 10. The Vikings also took their treasured possessions with them, these included weapons, tools, chests of robes and furs, favorite horses and hunting dogs, and sometimes even a slave or two.

OK 11. Always thinking ahead, the Egyptians and Vikings arranged for transportation in their different heavens.

F 12. The Egyptians taking a boat-shaped bier with them into their burial vaults, in honor of their sun god Ra and the vessel he rode across the sky each day.

OK 13. Rich Viking warriors were buried with their warships, which they would use in Valhalla.

F 14. Where Odin, the chief of the Viking gods, presided, along with Thor and Freya and a host of other great Norse heroes.

142   Chapter 7   Commas That Separate

C.S 15. The Egyptians and the Vikings shared many similarities in their burial customs, most noteworthy they convinced themselves that at least some among them would defy death and take their greatest treasures with them.

Dictionary Practice

Look up the words in bold print and provide a brief definition for each word as it appears in the sentence.

1. I can think of only two causes for this strange **metamorphosis** from graceful king moth to clumsy caterpillar.

    metamorphosis: _____

2. Women don tuxedos, steel-toed boots, three-piece suits, and hard hats, in addition to their **plethora** of feminine apparel.

    plethora: _____

Match the following words with their brief definitions.

_____ 3. denounce (p. 137)   a. to pine or suffer neglect

_____ 4. fetter (p. 139)   b. variation

_____ 5. hallowed (p. 138)   c. to place two or more things side by side

_____ 6. juxtapose (p. 137)   d. to criticize or accuse, especially publicly

_____ 7. klatch (p. 138)   e. sacred

_____ 8. languish (p. 138)   f. an informal gathering

_____ 9. relinquish (pp. 137, 138)   g. to restrain

_____ 10. tenacious (p. 138)   h. to gain forcibly

_____ 11. variance (p. 138)   i. to give over, especially with regret

_____ 12. wrest (p. 138)   j. persistent in clinging to something

Copyright © 1992 by Harcourt Brace Jovanovich, Inc. All rights reserved.

CHAPTER 8

Parenthetical Commas

Can you see a common purpose for the commas in this paragraph?

> Lacey, my foolhardy sister, knows no caution. If you knew what she dared, dear friend, you would never date her. A girl like Lacey, plucky and persuasive, can be unhealthy for a guy. Her last boyfriend, who seemed like an impulsive enough fellow himself, gave up on her after she shaved her head for a Halloween party.

All the commas in the paragraph above are *parenthetical commas,* so called because the commas set off information that isn't absolutely necessary to the sentences. Look again at each sentence. Couldn't the writer use parentheses instead of commas? The parentheses would make too strong a break, though, so commas were used instead, as weaker, less intrusive parentheses.

Because these commas act like weak parentheses, their distinguishing feature is that they never dance alone. Using one alone should appear as strange to you as using one parenthesis would. The only time these commas dance alone is when the parenthetical information comes at the beginning or end of the sentence (because, of course, you would never start or end the sentence with a comma). This chapter describes where you might use parenthetical commas.

■ When a Description Comes After the Noun

A description that follows a noun can take one of four forms: words that describe, a phrase that describes, a clause that adds extra information, or a clause that identifies the noun. Some but not all of these forms will need parenthetical commas.

Copyright © 1992 by Harcourt Brace Jovanovich, Inc. All rights reserved.

Words That Describe

If describing words follow the noun, use commas to set them off.

My kitten, <u>frisky and sharp-clawed</u>, costs me more in pantyhose than in cat food.

Because the underlined words describe the noun that precedes them, they must be set off on both sides with commas. If these same words come *before* the noun they describe, no commas are necessary.

My <u>frisky and sharp-clawed</u> kitten costs me more in pantyhose than in cat food.

Practice 1

Combine the sentences in exercise 1 into one sentence, putting the word or words that describe after the noun.

1. The storm clouds hovered.
   They were dark and gloomy.
   They stayed on the horizon.
   They were there throughout the picnic.

   _____

   _____

2. Write a sentence in which two words that describe the noun come *after* the noun.

   _____

   _____

Phrases That Describe

When phrases that follow a noun provide extra, unnecessary information, these phrases should be set off with commas.

The key word here is *unnecessary*—unnecessary to the meaning of the main independent clause. The extra words may be interesting, enlightening, or informative, and therefore may actually improve the sentence. Nevertheless, the main independent clause would be clear without these words.

Copyright © 1992 by Harcourt Brace Jovanovich, Inc. All rights reserved.

T.S. Eliot, *not the easiest poet to read*, gave us the whimsical, entertaining characters of the theatrical production *Cats*, an extremely popular musical.

The Dallas Cowboys, *my favorite football team*, has not seemed the same without Tom Landry on the sidelines.

Practice 2

Combine the sentences in exercise 1, adding the extra information after the noun.

1. There was a patch of ice.
   It was hidden under a thin blanket of snow.
   It caused Luis to fall.
   He was my uncle.

   _____

   _____

2. Write a sentence in which you add extra information after the noun.

   _____

   _____

Clauses That Provide Extra Information

> **When an entire clause follows the noun, if you can cross out this clause and *still know the identity of the noun*, then this clause should be set off with commas.**

If, on the other hand, you must have these words to restrict the identity of the noun, then you should not put commas around the clause.

In the following sentences, the subjects are clearly identified. The writer could be talking about only one person or holiday. Consequently, the information after the subject has been put between commas.

James, [(who) has delusions of grandeur], pays his suite-mate to bring him coffee on a silver tray each morning.

The Christmas holidays, [(which) begin early with advertising and linger long with payments], fortunately come only once a year.

Practice 3

Combine the sentences in exercise 1 as instructed.

1. Professor Harrison's make-up test was worse than the original.
   I took it last night.
   (Use *which* to attach the second sentence.)

   _____

   _____

2. Write a sentence in which a clause that does not restrict the noun follows the noun.

   _____

   _____

Clauses That Identify the Noun

Sometimes you can't cross out the entire clause following a noun because it provides necessary details.

> **When readers need the information to identify the subject—to know whom or what you are referring to—then the information in a clause following the noun should *not* be set off with commas.**

In the following examples, because you need the information to identify the subject, the clauses that follow these subjects have not been set off with commas.

> The rake [(that) I bought yesterday] has already fallen apart.

That is, of the many rakes that the writer of this sentence may own, it is the one bought yesterday that fell apart.

> The sportscaster [(who) did the commentary on last night's game] didn't know when to stop.

That is, of the many sportscasters now working in the media, it was the sportscaster for last night's game that this writer is criticizing.

Practice 4

Combine the sentences in exercise 1 using a clause that identifies the noun.

1. The house sold for over a million dollars.
   It was the house my sister-in-law designed.

   _____

   _____

2. Write a sentence in which a clause that identifies the noun (and therefore does not need commas) follows the noun.

   _____

   _____

Combine the sentences in exercises 3 and 4, using a phrase or clause after the subject.

3. Camels are ideally suited to life in dry climates.
   They can last six months without drinking in the cooler winter months.
   (Use *which*.)

   _____

   _____

4. A certain camel can do something.
   This camel has gone without water for a long period of time.
   This camel can drink up to thirty-five gallons of water in less than six minutes.

   _____

   _____

■ Setting Off Other Elements

In addition to setting off unnecessary descriptive material that follows a noun, commas are sometimes used to set off transition words from the rest of the sentence. Commas are also commonly used in certain forms of dates and geographical references.

Transition Words

> When transition words cause a definite break in the flow of the sentence, these transition words should be set off with

> **commas; if the transition words fit smoothly into the sentence, you should leave commas out.**

As discussed in Chapter 5, transitions show the reader how one topic or subject relates to another. Among the most common transitions are the following:

> Contrast: *however, on the other hand, nevertheless, instead*
> Sequence: *first, second, then, also, after this, later, finally*
> Example: *for example, for instance*
> Reinforcement: *actually, in fact, indeed, of course, certainly*
> Cause/effect: *therefore, for this reason, consequently*
> Summary: *in conclusion, therefore*

You can place these words anywhere in the sentence—at the beginning, in the middle, or at the end. You choose the location depending on what you want to emphasize or how you want the sentence to sound.

Commas around transition words are optional. How do you know if you need them? Usually transition words that need commas require readers to pause. In the sentence you are reading right now, for example, the transition words clearly interrupt the flow of the sentence. When this happens, the words should be set off on both sides with commas (unless, of course, the transition words occur at the beginning or end of the sentence, in which case you would need only one comma).

> Mariko already has a date for Friday and, besides, wouldn't like a movie with that much violence.
>
> Sally, on the other hand, owns all the Rambo movies on video and so would probably love to go with you.

Sometimes, however, commas intrude on readers, making them pause where they don't need to. If you feel the commas are intrusive, leave them out, as in the following sentences:

> *Perhaps* I should admit some of my antisocial eating habits before you move in.
>
> I'm often in a rush and *consequently* drink straight out of the milk carton.
>
> I *also* dip straight into the peanut butter jar, devouring whole spoonfuls.

I have been known to slice into a roommate's icing and *then* artfully rearrange the top to hide my indiscretion.

But *certainly* I promise not to do any of this to your food.

Practice 5

Rewrite sentences 1–3 twice each, inserting the transitions in parentheses. First put them at the beginning of the sentences; the second time, put them somewhere within the sentences.

1. Antique furniture can gleam with an inner beauty. (certainly)

2. My old furniture comes from the local secondhand store. (however)

3. The only time it shines is when an exposed nail catches the light. (unfortunately)

4. Write a sentence with a transition that requires commas.

5. Now write a sentence with a transition that does not require commas.

Dates with Years

When a sentence includes a complete date (month, date, year), the year should be set off with commas.

The date August 6, 1945, marks the birth of nuclear fear.

On December 17, 1903, the Wright Brothers shed our ties to earth and headed us toward the stars.

Treat the year as extra information and put a comma both *before* and *after*.

Places with State or Country Names

As with complete dates, complete locations require commas before and after the state or country name.

Thousands of cows wander the streets of Calcutta, India, looking for food.

Tiny Snook, Texas, annually produces statewide basketball championships.

Again, always remember to insert the second comma *after* the state or country; parenthetical commas never dance alone.

Practice 6

Write a sentence that tells when and where someone was born, such as:

I was born on February 2, 1955, in Basim, India.

Exercises

Set 1

Sentences 1–8 demonstrate the correct use of parenthetical commas. Identify each sentence with A, B, C, or D to show which comma rule applies.

- A   When a description comes after the noun.
- B   With transitions.
- C   Dates with years.
- D   Places identified with state or country names.

_____ 1. She did very well on the test, which hardly surprises me.

_____ 2. The Edgar Allan Poe House in Philadelphia, Pennsylvania, is where the poet wrote "The Raven."

_____ 3. Poe lived in this house, however, for only three years.

Copyright © 1992 by Harcourt Brace Jovanovich, Inc. All rights reserved.

Setting Off Other Elements   151

_____ 4. On December 29, 1890, U.S. troops massacred over 400 Sioux at Wounded Knee.

_____ 5. Be sure to visit the Buffalo Bill Museum in Denver, Colorado.

_____ 6. Felicia cooks a mean steak, grilled to perfection and oozing with flavor.

_____ 7. I actually enjoy my sixty-mile commute, the calmest time in my schedule.

_____ 8. On November 4, 1981, Henry Cisneros became the first Mexican-American mayor of San Antonio.

Set 2

Edit the following sentences, inserting commas where needed. Some may already be correct.

1. The United States Army first used an armored tank during World War I when on September 12 1918 troops manned a French Renault tank in the Battle of St. Mihiel.
2. My husband who has grand dreams speaks unceasingly of trekking the supposedly breathtaking wilderness of Patagonia a South American region in southern Chile and Argentina.
3. To get my permission to go however he must promise not to do any mountaineering.
4. He has never scaled the Andes one of the most challenging ranges in the world so I would be sick with worry until he was safely home.
5. I refuse to ice-skate with poor Aggie who never would take lessons because she clings like a drowning rat to the rink's outside rail.
6. I also avoid skating with my friend Sasha an accomplished show-off who preens through the center of the rink for all to admire.
7. When Martin Luther King Jr. was assassinated on April 4 1968 he was in Memphis Tennessee protesting on behalf of striking sanitation workers.

Copyright © 1992 by Harcourt Brace Jovanovich, Inc. All rights reserved.

8. On the day Harmonia the daughter of Mars and Venus was married to King Cadmus she received a necklace fatal to all who possessed it.
9. Poor Harmonia also received a robe covered with crimes which later made all of her children wicked.
10. Finally as if they had not already suffered enough Harmonia and Cadmus were turned into serpents. And you think you have problems?

Sentence Combining

Combine the sentences in each exercise into one, using as few words as possible.

1. There is a *matamata* turtle.
   It lives in South America.
   It sucks fish into its mouth like a vacuum cleaner.
   (Use *which*.)

2. The common snapping turtle is an aggressive hunter.
   It has powerful jaws.
   The turtle clamps onto prey.
   This prey includes large fish and even ducks.
   The turtle will not let go.
   (Start this sentence with a *When* dependent clause.)

3. This happens when the alligator snapping turtle gets hungry.
   The alligator snapping turtle is the common snapping turtle's cousin.
   This cousin is lazy.
   It opens its mouth.
   It wiggles its bright red tongue.

Setting Off Other Elements 153

4. Fish see the bright red tongue.
   The fish are swimming by.
   They mistake it for a worm.
   They think the worm is juicy and tempting.
   They swim right into the turtle's gaping jaws.

5. The hawksbill turtle has shells.
   People use their shells for combs and jewelry.
   The shells are tough and durable.

6. Sea turtles swallow a lot of sea water.
   Sea water is salty.
   Sometimes sea turtles swallow too much sea water.
   They must rid their bodies of this salt.
   They do so by shedding big tears.
   The tears are also salty.
   (Start this sentence with a *When* dependent clause.)

7. Sea turtles lay their eggs under the sand.
   They return to the same beaches each year.
   They usually lay their eggs at night.
   (Use *which*.)

8. Turtles lived with the dinosaurs.
   Turtles have changed little since those days.
   (Use *which*.)

Copyright © 1992 by Harcourt Brace Jovanovich, Inc. All rights reserved.

9. Sea turtles vary from freshwater turtles.
   Sea turtles cannot withdraw into their shells.
   They regain a little protection.
   Their skin is tough.
   Their skin is scaly.
   (Use *but* in this sentence.)

   _____

   _____

Paragraph Editing Practice

First, read straight through the following paragraphs. Then reread them, inserting commas where they belong. Watch for and correct any misused words.

A. Contrary to popular campus myth, the amount students worry before a big exam has nothing whatever to do with the grades that the students receive. Nicomi a first-year student and therefore new to the game studied little before her first Intro to Religion exam. She breezed through the test, calm confident and relaxed, naturally expecting to do well since she had always paid attention in Sunday School. She failed. Long before her next Intro to Religion exam, she began worrying about another failure. In the mornings heaping a large helping of anxiety onto her cafeteria tray she digested Krishna with her cornflakes and Buddha with her buttered toast. After lunch exhausted from her late night studying she would fall asleep over her books. In her dreams C.S. Lewis and Bertrand Russell those two great **antagonists** would engage in heated debates over whether Nicomi would or should pass her test. They could never agree. Dinner led to more studying, which led to restless fretful sleep. Nicomi in short worried day and night, so much in fact that when the next exam came much to soon she flunked again. Having worried way too little and then way too much, Nicomi finally learned that like Goldilocks with her porridge a little worrying is just right.

B. Because she had just read *Romeo and Juliet*, **winsome** Samantha convinced George kindly and wildly romantic to elope that very afternoon telling him she was **destitute** and of age. George regretted his hasty marriage of course when he discovered too late that Samantha was only fourteen. Samantha's parents enraged and vengeful accused George of criminal cradle-robbing and had him arrested. George who had long dreamed of marital bliss spent his wedding night in the county jail. Samantha **notorious** for her imaginative mischief was sent to boarding school in Switzerland. She lasted a month before being expelled.

Essay Editing Practice 1

Read straight through the following essay. Then reread it, inserting parenthetical commas where needed.

Summer Jobs

"What are you doing this summer?"

One by one the four college friends sharing their last meal before the summer described their summer jobs, one in a fast-food restaurant, one in a family business, and one at a nearby amusement park.

"What about you?" All eyes turned toward the fourth friend at the table.

"Don't you remember? I'm going out to Redmond Washington. I've got an internship with Microsoft."

The expression that came into the other friends' eyes mingled jealousy, admiration, and curiosity. Why hadn't they bright as they were, thought of an internship?

An internship usually set up through the career development center at colleges or universities offers more than just a nice salary. First as its most practical benefit a job with a respected company like Apple,

Amana, or Procter and Gamble along with a good recommendation looks good on a resume. At a time when entry-level positions with the better companies are becoming more and more competitive, this jewel can catch a recruiter's eye and help a student to make the first cut. Why do recruiters value this experience so much? The answer lies in the other benefits that students gain from internships.

These positions allow students to do some hands-on exploring into the kind of job they want. During an internship, a student may find that she detests having to promote products and therefore could never be a salesperson. Another student may discover that his muscles cramp up when he sits in front of the computer all day. For some students then the hands-on experience of an internship helps to determine their major. Even if students have already chosen their major however many choices about their eventual job await them. Where will they work, under what size of a company, in what department, and doing what kind of work? An internship gives students an opportunity to try out one specific professional job and with that experience have a standard to build their ambitions upon.

Perhaps most enlightening however, internships allow students to see the life of a professional. The negative side of this means seeing people work long hours, rushing to meet a deadline, answering to supervisors and team leaders, and having someone regularly expect results. The positive side means discovering the joys of a team effort, gaining the honest respect and esteem of colleagues, and enjoying the coffee breaks, department parties, comfortable furniture, and company perks that are all part of holding a professional position. All these benefits so gratifying and appealing can help students remember why they are in college and can encourage them to work harder.

For students who have been there however one advantage towers over all the rest. Many students feel that in college they are in a holding pattern between adolescence and adulthood. An internship puts students over the top, for professionals on the job usually treat students as contributing colleagues who must be mature if they are to fulfill job requirements. Perhaps, more than the internship itself this new vision of themselves as adults becomes the lasting benefit of internships for students.

Writing Practice 1

Choose one of the following topics and write a short essay on it. (See Chapters 19–22 if you need help with writing an essay.) Remember, as you write, concentrate first on what you want to say. Then as you go back over your writing, concentrate on grammar and punctuation.

A. This writer believes that many college students are treated sometimes as adolescents and sometimes as adults. From your own experience, list situations that illustrate being treated as an adolescent, then situations that illustrate being treated as an adult. Finally write two paragraphs, one about each kind of treatment, including two or three specific examples in your essay.

B. How and why did you ultimately choose your major? List the different careers you thought about pursuing, starting from the ambitions you had when you were very young, through high school as your ideas changed, until now when your college preparation has begun. Then in a story form (organized in sequence according to time), write a short essay.

C. What advice would you give someone on how to get along with people at work? Jot down some tips you have learned, and then choose which you would like to write about. In your essay, explain the advice, why it is important, and how you learned its importance.

Essay Editing Practice 2

Read straight through the following essay. Then edit it, watching for and correcting any kind of error. Watch for misused words.

Copyright © 1992 by Harcourt Brace Jovanovich, Inc. All rights reserved.

Why Is the College Bowl System Better?

Many college football fans look with envy at the NCAA basketball tournament. With a football tournament, fans would no longer have to pay **homage** to the newspaper writers or face the excruciating trauma of split polls, for a tournament crowns one clear victor. Furthermore, a tournament would pit the best teams against each other, Brigham Young or Miami would never need to defend its national championship against the accusation of a second-rate schedule. Most enticing of all, however, are the drama and excitement of a championship game. Instead of March Madness. The country could indulge in December Delirium.

For these reasons, college football fans beg for a tournament, yet each year, the bowl system continues. Detractors claim that the system is entrenched, that with their guaranteed revenues the Rose Bowl and the Cotton Bowl would change only after an act of Congress, and that the newspaper sportswriters like their power to much to let go. In fact, the bowl system for college football remains because for many reasons it satisfies.

Unlike the NCAA basketball tournament, the football season ends with many winners, a victorious team for each bowl. Who cares whether Hicksville played Podunk or that the game was televised only on a two-county network? Who cares about anything except victory? In complete contrast the NCAA tournament leaves only one winner, and after the NCAA tournament, few people remember the second place team. No one, not even the basketball players themselves, remember the games they won getting to the final game, defeat is so durable and its memory so lasting! The sight of dull eyes on the sideline lingers, the tears falling freely down faces of young athletes the hunched shoulders the shaking hands. If anything, the longer the string of victories stretches, the more painfully the final defeat hurts the NCAA players.

With the bowl system, not only do more teams win, but also, without inflated dreams and pressing expectations, the defeats bruise the players' hearts more lightly.

The bowl system satisfies as well with its brief season. Basketball's March Madness requires three weekends to accommodate sixty-four teams, and winners play two games per weekend. Football players usually need a week to recuperate from the physical abuse of a football game, so a football tournament would require at least four weekends to accommodate only sixteen teams. Consider as well that these four weekends would occur during the year's busy holiday season. Between Thanksgiving and New Year's. Because the current system requires teams to play only one game, almost all the bowl games occur around Christmas and New Year's Day.

At least one other advantage accompanies the present system. With only one bowl game per team, the bowl system limits injuries. As brutally abusive as one game can be for football players, requiring them to take a week to recuperate, imagine how many injuries a tournament would inflict upon college players. Whichever team could limp through the last game intact would crawl away with the prize, the victorious survivor rather than winner.

So the bowl system, for all its obvious flaws, clearly satisfies in three ways. It multiplies the post-season winners, it takes little time in an already overloaded season, it causes fewer injuries to the players. The clincher for football fans, however, is the affect of a tournament on the vastly lucrative and enormously satisfying pro-football play-offs and Super Bowl. As soon as fans remember that a college tournament would **encroach** on their beloved professional football, even the most **avid** tournament supporters will settle in happily for the New Year's Day extravaganza of bowl games.

Writing Practice 2

Choose one of the following topics and write a short essay. (See Chapters 19–22 if you need help with writing an essay.)

A. One advantage of a tournament is its excitement. List aspects of a tournament, such as the NCAA basketball tournament, that are exciting. Use specific examples as you write an essay about three of these exciting aspects.

B. Not everyone likes sports. If you are such a person, list ways that a major sports event, such as the Super Bowl or the NCAA basketball tournament, affects society. Feel free to take a negative stance on our society's reaction to these events. Use examples from your own life, the media, friends, or family in your essay.

C. List ways that being involved in a team sport can build a person's character. Choose three ways and write a short essay. (Be sure not to be sexist in your language. Sports can build women's characters, too.)

Misused Words: suppose/supposed

When using the words *supposed to*, remember to include the *d* at the end of *suppose*.

>You were *supposed to* drive the car, not push it.

Insert *suppose* or *supposed* in the following sentences:

1. When do you _____ we will finish?
2. I _____ we'll be finished when we're done.
3. They said we were _____ to be finished by suppertime.
4. If we work this late, aren't they _____ to buy us supper?
5. Aren't you _____ to be working instead of complaining?
6. Well, who are you _____ to be—the boss?
7. I _____ it is too much to hope that you two would quiet down?

Review Exercises

Identify each of the following with either F for sentence fragment, CS for comma splice, RO for run-on, or OK for correct.

_____ 1. Androcles, a Roman slave who dreamed of freedom.

_____ 2. One day, as Androcles worked in the fields, his master fell asleep, Androcles ran away.

_____ 3. His fellow slaves shouted after him that a beast would eat him.

_____ 4. Androcles didn't care, it was better to be eaten than owned.

_____ 5. Much later, when he was completely worn out from running so far and too hungry to care about anything anymore.

_____ 6. He fell down and slept, the next morning he awoke to a terrible roar.

_____ 7. A lion stood over him, however, rather than attacking, the lion held out his paw so that Androcles could see the thorn stuck in it.

_____ 8. Androcles gently pulled the thorn out in return the lion allowed him to escape.

_____ 9. Much later, after Androcles had been found, as punishment his master sent him to an arena where Androcles would be thrown to a wild beast.

_____ 10. Rather than eating Androcles, the beast, his old friend the lion, recognized Androcles, came to him, and rubbed against his legs.

_____ 11. The emperor, amazed at this outcome, released both Androcles and the lion they vanished forever into the forest.

Now go back and correct each sentence.

Dictionary Practice

Match the following words with their brief definitions.

_____	1. antagonist (p. 154)	a. cheerful and charming
_____	2. avid (p. 159)	b. adversary; opponent
_____	3. destitute (p. 155)	c. extremely needy
_____	4. encroach (p. 159)	d. honor or respect shown or given
_____	5. homage (p. 158)	e. eager and enthusiastic
_____	6. notorious (p. 155)	f. to trespass
_____	7. winsome (p. 155)	g. well-known, usually unfavorably

CHAPTER 9

Comma Errors

▣ Too Many Commas

This paragraph includes commas that do not belong. Which would you remove?

> Psychologists sometimes suggest, that nervous people get in a small room, and scream. For me, making bread, offers the equivalent of these scream sessions. I get to punch and batter and pound, the bread dough for a full ten minutes, as I knead. After that, I feel great.

At some point in our lives, in second or third grade perhaps, all of us have heard a teacher say, "Put a comma wherever you want your reader to pause." Wanting to make things simple, this teacher has caused most of us to use too many commas. Forget that third-grade rule. Here in college, avoid commas unless you know a specific rule that requires a comma.

Chapters 7 and 8 describe places where you need a comma. In this chapter we point out four situations in which you might use commas that do not belong.

Practice 1

Review sentence structure in the following exercises by underlining subjects once and their verbs twice and then circling the dependent signals.

1. My aunt and uncle, who were college sweethearts, told me once about a time the campus police caught them kissing in my uncle's Chevy.

2. They had enjoyed relative privacy all during the fall semester, but when the colder winter weather arrived they forgot the effect their hot breathing would have on the car windows.

3. Laughing, the policewoman asked them to look up and down the row of cars that were parked in the dorm lot and then explained.
4. "All the other cars have crystal clear windows, but yours are as steamy as a sauna! Those windows will give you away every time."

Subject, Verb

Sometimes you might incorrectly place a comma between a subject and a verb, perhaps because the subject is a long one, and you feel that a break is needed.

Incorrect	Correct
The shiny, slippery, sugary mass in the saucepan, became rich, silky-smooth fudge after we stirred it.	The shiny, slippery, sugary mass in the saucepan became rich, silky-smooth fudge after we stirred it.
The professor standing by the door, is the one whose class I dropped.	The professor standing by the door is the one whose class I dropped.

You can edit these sentences by removing the comma.

Occasionally you can have a comma directly before a verb, but only if it is one of a pair, with another one earlier in the sentence. In the following sentences, the verb is underlined. Note that a comma comes directly before the verb, but that in each case, another comma appears earlier in the sentence.

My mother, the greatest cook in the world, spoiled me for cafeteria food.

Football, that gritty, grimy, grind-it-out game, has moments of incredible grace.

So if you have only one comma directly before the verb, either find its mate or remove it.

Copyright © 1992 by Harcourt Brace Jovanovich, Inc. All rights reserved.

Practice 2

Combine the following sentences into one sentence, using a long, descriptive subject.

1. There are rich, home-cooked meals with chicken-fried steak, mashed potatoes, gravy, and biscuits.
   These meals taste wonderful but linger too long.

   _____

   _____

Verb, Object

You might sometimes incorrectly insert a comma between the verb and its *object*, the thing that a verb acts upon or that receives the effect of the verb.

In the following sentences, the direct object is underlined. It is not important that you learn to identify the object. What's important is that you avoid the comma that separates the verb from the object.

Incorrect	Correct
My dear roommate broke, my glasses yet again.	My dear roommate broke my glasses yet again.
Gita tenderly carried, the wounded dog into the apartment.	Gita tenderly carried the wounded dog into the apartment.

Practice 3

Combine the following sentences into one sentence.

1. Janelle spilled something on her paper.
   It was expensive perfume.

   _____

   _____

Dependent Clauses That End the Sentence

Dependent clauses can come at the beginning of a sentence or at the end.

[Before I spoke, I tried to get my temper under control.

I tried to get my temper under control [before I spoke].

Notice that when the dependent clause begins the sentence, a comma follows. However, the reverse does not hold true.

> **When the dependent clause comes after the independent clause, you don't need a comma.**
>
> Jack refused to declare himself even though he loved Kate.
>
> The prodigal son had not even reached the driveway when his father ran out to welcome him.
>
> I refuse to carry out the trash unless you promise to wash the dishes.

Watch especially for a tendency to insert a comma before *that*, another word that signals a dependent clause.

> The coach promised me that I would have a spot on the team.
>
> As clearly as if he had spoken, my dog told me that I should have been home hours ago.

Practice 4

Write three sentences with dependent clauses at the end of each.

1. _____

2. _____

3. _____

Separating Only Two Items

In your writing, you might sometimes incorrectly put commas when comparing, listing, or describing only two objects. You can create many different kinds of pairs:

> salt or pepper
> coming home and staying there
> happiest and best
> unethical or immoral

These pairs—because they have only two items—should never be separated with commas. You can also create pairs with longer parts of sentences, such as when sentences have one subject and two verbs.

> Cara always dropped everything and rushed to answer the phone.
>
> She wanted a date but lacked the courage to ask a man out herself.

Neither of these sentences needs a comma because Cara only did two things. Yet you might be tempted to insert a comma before these joining words: *and, but, or, nor,* and *yet.* Perhaps you believe this is a good place to pause. Or perhaps you are thinking of the rule to use a comma when joining two independent clauses. Or perhaps you are remembering that a series of three or more items requires commas. The following sentence requires commas because it has a series of three items:

> I like scrambled eggs seasoned with *salt, pepper, and ketchup.*

Practice 5

Insert commas as needed in sentences 1–8.

1. Jules came to America and promptly gained ten pounds.
2. Robinson neither watched the final game nor cared who won.
3. For graduation, I would like a Rolex watch or a plastic Swatch.
4. We will never know exactly what happened to the dinosaurs but we keep guessing.
5. My uncle will either drink the punch bowl dry or die trying.
6. He will also either wipe out the chips or wipe out himself.
7. The food service claims its food is healthy yet all the cooks eat elsewhere.
8. My favorite New Year's Days include lots of football and lots of snacks.
9. Write a sentence in which a single subject does two separate things.

_____

_____

10. Write a sentence in which a person cannot choose between two things.

Combine the following sentences into one sentence.

11. The massive toad threw himself across the pond.
    He landed on a lily pad.

Exercises

Each sentence in this set has one incorrect comma that shows one of the following kinds of errors. Write A, B, C, or D to identify the error, and then correct each sentence.

A   *Subject, verb:* Remove any single comma that comes between the subject and the verb.
B   *Verb, object:* Remove any single comma that comes between the verb and its object.
C   *Dependent clause that ends the sentence:* Remove any comma that comes between the independent clause and a dependent clause following it.
D   *Separating only two items:* Remove any comma that precedes *and, but, or, nor,* or *yet* if you are discussing only two items. Remove any comma that precedes a conjunction *if* what comes after this word cannot stand alone as a sentence.

1. Amanda took the turn too wide and crashed, her dirt bike into an unforgiving blackberry patch.

2. Ward took one look at the dishwasher spots on his fine crystal, and hurriedly gave each goblet a spit bath before calling his guests in to dinner.

3. I never listen to heavy metal music anymore, because my roommate waited until I left for fall break and donated all my cassette disks to the dumpster.

_____ 4. All the colors of the rainbow, are woven into the fur of Alicia's stuffed Cheshire cat.

_____ 5. Anyone who has ever gone to school at a big university, knows how hard it is to get from one class to another on time.

_____ 6. We lost our family farm last November, so I am living and eating at home, and commuting to classes.

_____ 7. The prince began to climb to Rapunzel's rescue, after she let down her golden hair.

_____ 8. He encountered a wasps' nest, and fell forty feet.

_____ 9. Fortunately unhurt, he donned a beekeeper's outfit, and began again.

_____ 10. While they were dancing, Juanita politely removed, the clod's foot from her aching toe.

_____ 11. The brilliant light of the setting sun, blinded my eyes to the approaching motorcycle.

_____ 12. For the people who live in Taos Pueblo in New Mexico, their phrase, "We are in one nest," describes a long tradition, and sense of communal spirit and responsibility.

_____ 13. My twelve-year-old son stands 5'5", just as I do, yet even when we stand face to face, we still, don't see eye to eye.

_____ 14. I am never quite sure what I am going to say, until I open my mouth and say it.

_____ 15. Delphane hopes one day to become a circus clown or maybe a rodeo clown, but for now she enjoys, just being the class clown.

_____ 16. The woman with wild, bushy, flaming red hair and chalky white skin, grabbed the microphone and impersonated Ronald McDonald until the security guards dragged her off the stage.

Sentence Combining

Combine each set of sentences into one sentence, making sure to punctuate correctly.

1. I lost everything I had on my disk.
   My husband turned off my computer.
   (Use *when*.)

2. My boyfriend could not decide what to get me for my birthday.
   My sister could not decide either.
   Why didn't they ask me for ideas?
   (Combine the first two sentences, starting the sentence with *Neither*.)

3. The executives could never wear shorts to work.
   They could not wear sandals either.
   (Use only one independent clause—one subject and verb that belong together.)

4. The donut man created delicious new confections.
   He gained twenty pounds in the process.
   (Use only one subject and a *but*.)

5. The cat rubbed against the refrigerator door.
   It did this whenever it wanted some caviar.

6. This happens on Christmas Island.
   This island is west of Australia.
   Land crabs cross the island by the millions.
   They do this when the rainy season begins.
   They turn the land red.

Paragraph Editing Practice

Read through each paragraph. Then edit them, watching carefully for comma errors.

A. The term "confidence man" was coined in the last century, and refers to the original offender, an **impeccably** groomed, expensively dressed, and well-spoken male. In short, he appeared to be a trustworthy gent. He made his living on the streets of New York City, approaching pedestrians, and asking them in a well-bred manner, "Do you have enough confidence in me, a total stranger, to lend me five dollars for an hour or two?" Five dollars in those days, could equal a week's pay. Amazingly, enough people trusted him to make him a rich man, for he never returned their loans. He became known as the confidence man, because he would first gain his victims' trust and then **sting** them.

This man's features appear in the faces of modern confidence artists. The contemporary con-artist looks for "suckers" who want something so badly they will trust anyone to get it, risking money in the process. Rather than ask for loans, today's con-artists offer goods, and services in return for cold cash. They entice with a proposition, that sounds too good to be true and usually is. In real estate offices, they sell "affordable" condos in Hawaii, urging people to buy now and look later. From behind television pulpits, they offer "limited time only" shares in heaven. Within magazine pages, they promise to reveal how to make millions of dollars without ever leaving the home, or how to build a full bustline in thirty days without pills or exercise. Although a person can learn to recognize these con-artists' come-ons, no one can avoid, these confidence artists entirely. After all, there is one born every minute.

Copyright © 1992 by Harcourt Brace Jovanovich, Inc. All rights reserved.

Essay Editing Practice 1

Read straight through this essay, and then edit it, watching especially for comma errors.

My Wife, the Scientist

Doctors and plumbers get called out at odd hours, teachers don't earn much, farmers contend with the **vagaries** of weather, and factory mechanics get laid off. Many occupations offer troubles to the families of the worker. At first, my wife's job would seem free of these problems. She has a nice, steady job as a research chemist, she earns a good salary, and she never gets called out late at night. Still, I wonder if anyone begins to understand how difficult it is to be married to a scientist. Don't get me wrong. She has yet to blow up the basement or stink out the house, except perhaps once when she attempted to make, taffy for our son's sixth birthday. It's her attitude to scientific issues, that gives me fits.

For one thing, she refuses simple solutions to society's scientific dilemmas. Take acid rain. Back in the seventies, communities began complaining about local pollution from smokestacks, so Congress required higher stacks. These chimneys spewed smoke higher into the atmosphere, where it was picked up by winds, carried away, and deposited through rain. Acid rain, therefore, resulted from a poorly thought-out solution to another environmental problem. Easy solutions like that, my wife says, give birth to new problems and hard consequences. The best and most lasting changes, she says, will come when individuals change their habits and their requirements for comfort.

Besides being so practical, she turns a surprisingly skeptical eye on scientific conclusions. Watching a special on the origins of early humans, I was fascinated by the paleontologists' reconstruction of entire skeletons, from prehistoric bones. Ceramicists then used computer programs to reconstruct the flesh, giving me the chance to look face to face with a far-distant ancestor. My wife was less than impressed. "Stop taking this stuff so much on faith," she said to me. "On conclusions like these that can't be verified, scientists take the available facts, and make a calculated guess, a **plausible** explanation. They never claim to offer ultimate answers. When better or more complete data come along that contradict their hypothesis, they will change their minds." In spite of this apparently necessary skepticism, she pursues her research anyway, confident that while knowledge leads to new questions, old puzzles will disappear. Sometimes this balance between skepticism and confidence, which she maintains so well, confuses me.

Finally, my wife insists on facing the complete truth about scientific problems. A while back, the news was full of the danger of developing cancer from pesticides. News reporters seemed to be saying that, rather than keeping the doctor away, an apple a day would put the mortician on call. My wife sat back, and shook her head. "Sam," she said to me, "don't you realize, that we eat natural pesticides every day? The Food and Drug Administration calculates, that an average American consumes about 45 micrograms a day of synthetic **carcinogenic** pesticides. That sounds awful until you realize that one leaf of the basil in this spaghetti sauce, has 760 micrograms of a natural carcinogen." Because of her balanced outlook, through the whole pesticide scare, our kids went right on drinking their juice, and munching their Winesaps. Of course, while other people could think they had solved their pesticide problems by eliminating fresh fruits, I had to confront the inevitability of carcinogens in all foods.

So because of my wife, no scientific issue is easily resolved for us. Before we can denounce acid rain, attempt no-milk diets, preach vitamin B$_{12}$ as a **panacea**, or **agitate** against nuclear power, we have to weigh the entire issue. That means trying to falsify the latest media claims, offering a **feasible** alternative, and in the end somehow adjusting to the **paradoxes** of modern American life. All of that is just as hard as it sounds. Why couldn't I have married a plumber?

Copyright © 1992 by Harcourt Brace Jovanovich, Inc. All rights reserved.

Writing Practice 1

Almost every issue has two sides, each with legitimate arguments. Choose one of the following topics and write an essay with at least two well-developed paragraphs, one paragraph in favor and the other against the idea. Give at least three reasons in each paragraph. (You'll have an easier time writing if you list these reasons before you begin writing.)

A. A person should spend at least a year overseas.

B. Children should watch television.

C. The government should spend more money preserving the environment.

D. People should use public transit to get to work.

Essay Editing Practice 2

Read straight through the following essay. Then go back through it, inserting commas as needed. This essay gives you practice with all kinds of comma uses.

A Castle in the Clouds

Ralph and Marie Heyer wanted to build a dream house, but they did not want it built by the Slapdash and Haphazard Construction Company. Because they wanted fine quality and construction they decided to build their house themselves. The Heyers, though clever, had never tinkered with anything more elaborate than model airplanes, swing-sets for their children, and bookshelves for the family room. After much research, they discovered that many companies sell unassembled, prefabricated homebuilding kits. To their dismay, they learned that the walls in some of these homes were thin poorly insulated and put together like the sides of a shoebox so they rejected many of these kits outright because of poor materials and construction.

Were they merely building castles in the clouds, or did they stand a chance in the real world of homebuilding? Without experience or an income in six figures, and with only their dreams **tempered** with a whole lot of common sense, the couple may have floundered in the cement foundation of a dream house turned nightmare. Then Ralph and Marie discovered timber frame homes.

Timber frame homes are constructed of excellent materials by skilled artisans and in many cases can be easily assembled. Timber frame designers erect the skeleton of the house out of good strong wood, such as oak or pine. Then builders "fill in the gaps" so to speak with stress panels which are rigid foam sandwiched between plywood sheets. These stress panels serve two important functions. First, the foam acts as a super-insulator, cutting fuel costs and creating a comfortable environment that is cool in the warm months and cozy in the winter—rather like living in a thermos bottle. Also, the panels serve as both the interior and exterior walls of the building.

The beauty of these panels lies in their function, not in their appearance. Some homebuilders choose to cover the interior walls with wood paneling, and others content themselves with painting the walls giving an illusion of added space. The beams are left uncovered. Many people cover the exterior stress-skin panels with wood siding or shingles, beautiful but costly. Ralph and Marie opted for cedar shakes which are shingles split from a log. Besides being less expensive than some forms of siding, the shakes give the Heyers' home the "old-fashioned cottage" look they have long admired.

Actually, timber frame homes are nothing new. In fact, American settlers built them as they pioneered the land from east to west two hundred years ago, making use of the free virgin timber that was then an abundant resource in most new territories. Fortunately, today's homebuilders may still select lumber as a primary building material. Even though the Heyers, unlike the early settlers, will have to pay for their lumber wood still costs less, insulates better, and lasts longer than many other building materials. In addition, wood can now be treated to resist rot, termites, and even fire, so the economy-minded Heyers made an excellent evaluative choice.

The practical Heyers chose to live in a timber frame home because their budget called for moderation and their bodies wanted comfort. What they had not anticipated though was the strong emotional response that they would have to their new home. Their former split-level ranch house, although built with cheap materials and poor insulation, had been adequate for most of their living requirements. When they finally moved into their timber frame, they realized that their souls had long been craving beauty and security and like the ancient Greeks, their lives had needed balance and order. They have found all this in their timber frame. Exposed beams **bestow** a sense of permanence, reminding them of their home's enduring craftsmanship and structural strength. The grace and beauty of the wood comfort and sustain them. The large open space, high ceilings, well-placed skylights, and many large, well-insulated windows designed for optimum light create a spacious airy environment where the Heyers have finally found peace.

Had they been looking for a castle in the clouds? Now that the Heyers have firmly grounded their castle to the earth, they are busily living happily ever after and are dreaming of a gazebo.

Writing Practice 2

Choose one of the following topics and write a short essay.

A. Choose three rooms in a house, and make a list of extras that you would like in each (such as a whirlpool in the bathroom or a butcher-block island in the kitchen). Then write a short essay with a paragraph describing each room.

B. Compare the relative advantages of spending money on a car versus a house. Begin by making a list of advantages and disadvantages for each. Then write a short essay with a paragraph comparing the advantages of one versus the other, a paragraph comparing the disadvantages of one versus the other, and finally a paragraph explaining why at your stage in life you would prefer a car or a house.

Essay Editing Practice 3

Read straight through the following essay. Then go back and edit, watching for any kind of corrections or improvements. Watch for misused words.

Wasted on the Young?

My mother tells me that education is wasted on the young, I often have to agree. I wonder sometimes if I should have waited a year or two after high school before beginning college. Given all the pressures, questions, adjustments, and fears that I am dealing with as an eighteen-year-old college student. My classwork often gets **slighted**. In fact, twenty seems like a better age than eighteen to begin college.

Most people would say that students my age are blessed with freedom. Few of us are married, have children, or even have our own apartment. Could anything be less **encumbering** than dorm life as a single? What others see as an absence of burdens however I see as an absence of anchors. After years of Mom around to wake me up, teachers to remind me of assignments, and principals to haul me in for truancy, I now have complete freedom to do as I please. What hope does a rubber raft have in high seas? Five weeks into the quarter, I'm staying up to late, missing my early-morning classes, skipping breakfast and often lunch, forgetting to show up for required lectures, and generally acting the typical, irresponsible college frosh. Though no one will see it on my transcript, I'm taking an extra course this semester called "Acting Like an Adult," and until I begin to pass a few exams in it, I'm afraid my whole college career is going the way of my ruined chemistry experiments.

More than just a lack of discipline, though, eighteen-year-old students lack focus. Besides having clothes and sports to take our minds off studies there's that wonderful distraction called dating. For many of us, the question deep down is which person we'll end up with. This girl might actually watch *Monday Night Football* with me every week would this one scold me for drinking coffee every morning? This girl's red hair might mean all our kids would be called "Carrots" but she certainly makes me laugh. This one's poetry is beautiful, but what would my dad say about her job prospects? With all these distracting questions, my second unlisted course would have to be "Choosing a Mate." How comforting it must be to have all this settled. Perhaps thirty is the best time to start college.

More seriously, we must decide who we actually want to be. During these crucial years from eighteen to twenty-two, we confront issues of politics, religion, philosophy, lifestyle. And so much more. How shocking it is for someone from a family of Republicans to discover that Democrats can be genuinely caring people. How much more shocking to discover that a Democratic roommate is facing the same dilemma about Republicans! People tell me that similar prejudices occur between Baptists, Muslims, Catholics, and Mormons; gays, straights, and celibates; farmers, businesspeople, and lawyers—and the list goes on and on. All these people, whatever their distinction, can be caring people. As a young person, I haven't met enough people yet. To learn from experience what my teachers keep telling me: that individuals almost always **confound** stereotypes. When we think at all, then, we have to spend a lot of effort on a third unlisted course "Discovering Our Biases." Forty is sounding better and better.

Still, we have reasons for being here. Our parents want us to come, for example, and most are willing to help us pay. For all it's traumas, college certainly beats the drive-through window at Wendy's. And as poorly as we master our nursing, accounting, biochemistry, or political science classes, the eventual degree will help us get the jobs we want.

Copyright © 1992 by Harcourt Brace Jovanovich, Inc. All rights reserved.

I just wonder if older students realize that college for us requires more than just indulging in midmorning naps and endorsing checks from home.

Writing Practice 3

Choose one of the following and write a short essay.

A. This essayist mentions some possible priorities a person can consider when choosing a spouse. List some priorities of your own, and then choose three to write about. For each priority, list reasons why this characteristic, ability, or attribute would be important in a marriage. Then write a short essay.

B. Do individuals really confound stereotypes? Begin by listing common stereotypes you have heard about members of either your own sex or the opposite sex. Then look over your list and choose three for which you know an individual that goes against the stereotype (for example, your brother's girlfriend who was incredibly competitive, your father who loves babies). Write a short essay using these examples.

C. How can you recognize prejudice, whether in yourself or in others? Jot down some ideas on what prejudice is. Then try to list at least three characteristic behaviors that will help you recognize it (for example, a tendency to judge on appearance, a tendency to rely on labels). Add examples of each—stories or illustrations that you know of or create. Then write a short essay on recognizing prejudice.

Misused Words: a lot

Remember that *a lot*, meaning more than *a little*, always requires two words. *Alot* should look as incorrect to you as *alittle*. For practice, write *a lot* in the following sentences.

1. Buying a used car was a sour experience; I saw _____ of lemons.

2. In June, a little rain can make _____ of people unhappy.

Copyright © 1992 by Harcourt Brace Jovanovich, Inc. All rights reserved.

Review Exercises

Insert commas as needed in the following sentences.

1. On a cross-country trip that my family took when I was in seventh grade we happened to break down outside a little town that I will call Wrecker Nevada.
2. It was late at night and my mother was driving our old beat-up station wagon scolding my father almost every mile for not stopping at a motel in the last town.
3. Just when the lights of another town appeared however the car spluttered coughed and died.
4. You will have to imagine my mother's comment.
5. To make things even worse for my poor wife-weary father the only establishment anywhere within walking distance looked a little suspicious.
6. In a moment of rare indecision my mother didn't know whether to send my father in to call the wrecker or to go in herself.
7. "If someone has to go in there we're going in together" she finally declared and even my normally fearless older brother didn't suggest that any of us children go with them.
8. When they came out my mother's face was redder than the neon lights over the establishment's door and my father couldn't even begin to stifle his grin.
9. She still blushes when we tease her about the night she took my father into a Nevada bordello.

Dictionary Practice

Look up the words in bold print and provide a brief definition for each word as it appears in the sentence.

1. That means trying to falsify the latest media claims, offering a feasible alternative, and in the end somehow adjusting to the **paradoxes** of modern American life.

    paradox: _____

2. Doctors and plumbers get called out at odd hours, teachers don't earn much, farmers contend with the **vagaries** of weather, and factory mechanics get laid off.

    vagary: _____

Match the following words with their brief definitions.

_____	3. agitate (p. 173)	a.	to arouse the public's emotion
_____	4. bestow (p. 176)	b.	possible
_____	5. carcinogen (p. 173)	c.	appearing fair, reasonable, or true
_____	6. confound (p. 178)	d.	flawless
_____	7. encumber (p. 177)	e.	to destroy; to confuse
_____	8. feasible (p. 173)	f.	to burden; to hinder
_____	9. impeccable (p. 171)	g.	to cheat
_____	10. panacea (p. 173)	h.	something that causes cancer
_____	11. plausible (p. 173)	i.	cure-all
_____	12. slight (verb, p. 177)	j.	to neglect; to treat with carelessness or disdain
_____	13. sting (p. 171)	k.	to counterbalance; to moderate; to blend
_____	14. temper (verb, p. 175)	l.	to give or present something

Copyright © 1992 by Harcourt Brace Jovanovich, Inc. All rights reserved.

CHAPTER **10**

Apostrophes

Look at the apostrophes in the following paragraph. Can you see the two most common ways to use apostrophes?

> During summer's sweltering days, I can't help but dream of winter's coldness. As I try vainly to stir up July's heavy air, December's chilly days and frostier nights seem so appealing. Seen through a veil of many months, winter's pleasures include afternoons spent sledding, deep breaths of cocoa's steaminess, and long, quiet evenings spent before the fire's warming blazes. It's winter now, though, and I've begun dreaming instead of July's unclad feet, lazy picnics, and leaf-green trees. Whoever called contentment a prize more precious than gold must have been thinking of the weather.

Most commonly, you use apostrophes to show two things. Based on this paragraph, what are the two most common reasons that you might use an apostrophe? List them, and give examples from the paragraph above.

1. _____

_____

2. _____

_____

Unfortunately, even though you know that apostrophes can be used to show possession and to create contractions, you still might forget to insert these apostrophes where they belong. This chapter will describe the rules for using apostrophes to show possession, to make contractions, and (less often) to form plurals, but only by your choice will these rules be transferred to your own writing.

Copyright © 1992 by Harcourt Brace Jovanovich, Inc. All rights reserved.   **183**

■ Apostrophes to Show Possession

As you read over an essay, possessives *sound* the same with or without apostrophes. Only with diligence and determination can you begin to realize that possessives *look* incorrect without apostrophes. From now on, many of the essays for editing practice at the end of each chapter will include possessives that lack apostrophes. Be alert to this mistake so that as you read over your own writing, you will catch any places where apostrophes are missing.

As you come to a word that you want to make possessive, use the following series of questions to help you decide how to write it.

1. Write the word without any indication of possession.
2. Decide if the word is singular (only one thing) or plural (more than one thing).
3. If the word is singular, add 's.
4. If the word is plural and ends in -s (most plurals do end in -s), add only an apostrophe.
5. If the word is plural but does not end in -s, add 's.

This series of questions might look like this:

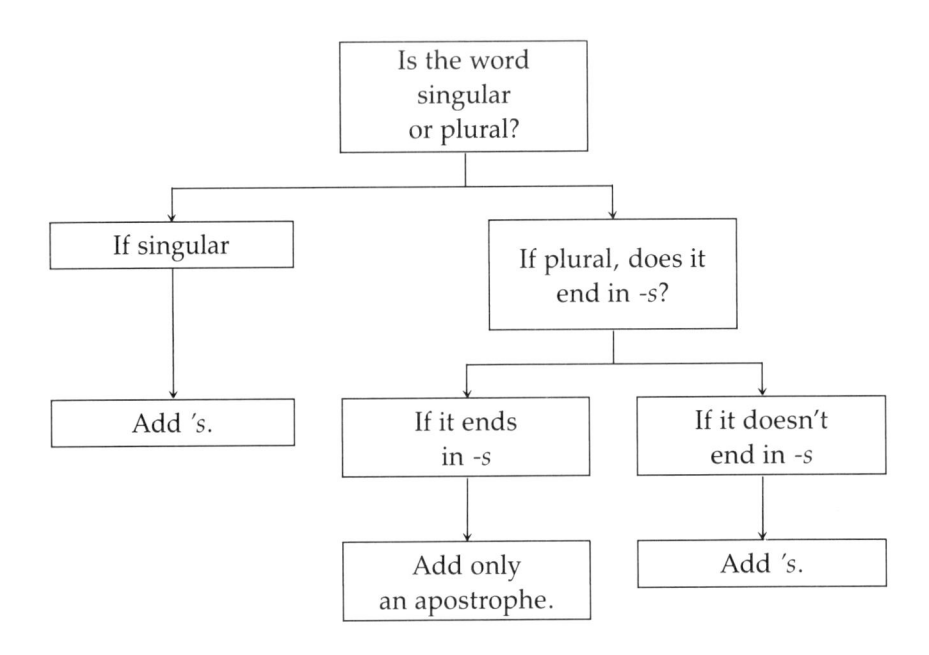

```
              Is the word
               singular
              or plural?
              /         \
     If singular      If plural, does it
         |              end in -s?
         |              /         \
      Add 's.    If it ends    If it doesn't
                  in -s         end in -s
                    |               |
                Add only          Add 's.
              an apostrophe.
```

Copyright © 1992 by Harcourt Brace Jovanovich, Inc. All rights reserved.

The following examples show how you might decide how to write a possessive correctly.

1. No man should underestimate a *roses* power of persuasion.
   Is the word singular or plural? Singular.
   If singular, add 's. Therefore: a *rose's* power of persuasion.

2. Where are the *mens* suspenders?
   Is the word singular or plural? Plural.
   If plural, does the word end in -s? No.
   If no, add 's. Therefore: the *men's* suspenders.

3. Do you have any *dogs* leashes made of patent leather?
   Is the word singular or plural? Plural.
   If plural, does the word end in -s? Yes.
   If yes, add only an apostrophe. Therefore: *dogs'* leashes.

Please watch out for this tendency, though: Some people, wanting to make a word possessive, hear an -s on the end of the word and simply make the word plural rather than adding the necessary apostrophe. This tendency often shows up with words that end in -*y*.

In the examples below, each of the phrases should be written with the *possessive* (not plural) form of the singular word.

Incorrect as plural	Correct as singular possessive
the Communist parties victory	the Communist party's victory
the gray ponies saddle	the gray pony's saddle
the locked diaries secrets	the locked diary's secrets

If you notice this tendency in your writing, be especially careful to correct it, because it can cause a lot of confusion for your readers.

Practice 1

Write the underlined words from each sentence as a possessive.

1. Would you ever wear the insanely impractical styles of Paris designers?

   _____

2. Who can understand the impulses of men?

   _____

Copyright © 1992 by Harcourt Brace Jovanovich, Inc. All rights reserved.

186 Chapter 10 Apostrophes

3. Pity the poor dog, suffering under the tormenting bite of a single flea.

_____

4. Fayetta longed for the danger and romance of a mythic quest.

_____

5. Beware of the graceful but deadly leap of a spotted leopard.

_____

6. The excitement of the holiday season too often goes unrealized.

_____

7. Perhaps this is why January is often the busiest month of psychologists.

_____

8. Could we temporarily remove the teeth of the puppy?

_____

☐ Some Special Cases

For the following special cases, read the rules and the completed examples. Then rewrite the remaining examples, using apostrophes to show possession.

1. Indefinite pronouns: *someone, everybody, anyone*. Just as for singular nouns, add *'s*.

   a. the sighs of someone   someone's sighs

   b. the energy of everybody _____

   c. the ambitions of anyone _____

2. Expressions with more than one word: *mother-in-law, police chief*. Add *'s* to the last word only.

   a. the help of my mother-in-law

      my mother-in-law's help

   b. the challenges of the police chief

      _____

   c. the efforts of the chairman of the board

      _____

Copyright © 1992 by Harcourt Brace Jovanovich, Inc. All rights reserved.

Some Special Cases   187

3. **Joint possession:** When something belongs to two people or things *together*, add *'s* to the second one only.

   a. the dreams of my mother and father for me

   my mother and father's dreams for me

   b. the escape of Jason and Medea from Colchis

   Jason and Medea's escape from Colchis

   c. the wedding of Roger and Rose

   _____

   d. the relationship of King Arthur and Mordred

   _____

   e. the parents of the brother and sister

   _____

4. **Separate possession:** When two different things belong to two different people or things, add *'s* after each one.

   a. the boyfriends of Susie and Stephanie (fortunately for their friendship, this refers to two *different* boyfriends)

   Susie's and Stephanie's boyfriends

   b. the running abilities of the plowhorse and the thoroughbred

   the plowhorse's and the thoroughbred's running abilities

   c. the nightmares of Jeff and Joshua

   _____

   d. the holiday plans of the president and the vice-president

   _____

Practice 2

Rewrite the sentences so that the underlined words show possession with an apostrophe. Then identify each sentence with A, B, C, or D to show which of the rules it illustrates.

   A   *Indefinite pronouns:* everyone's mistakes
   B   *Expressions with more than one word:* the father-in-law's objections
   C   *Separate possession:* my sister's and my brother's clothes
   D   *Joint possession:* Ben and Jerry's ice cream

188   Chapter 10   Apostrophes

_____ 1. The knowing smile of the man-in-the-moon mocked the young lovers.

_____ 2. The notebooks of somebody had been left in the cafeteria.

_____ 3. The project of Carlie and Antonio made their instructor wish for winter break.

_____ 4. The slimy syrup at the waffle shop added the finishing touch to his tie.

_____ 5. In the most bizarre expectations of no one would the multi-millionaire win the grand prize in the lottery.

_____ 6. The culinary wonders of Julia Child and Craig Claiborne would be wasted on my finicky children.

_____ 7. The pride of the Apache men and women showed in their native dress and unflinching posture.

Copyright © 1992 by Harcourt Brace Jovanovich, Inc. All rights reserved.

▢ Apostrophes to Make Contractions

Do not use contractions in formal writing, which includes college writing, unless you know *for certain* that you are permitted to do so. If you may use contractions, insert the apostrophe in place of the letter or letters you remove. To combine *I* and *am*, for example, you must remove the letter *a* and insert the apostrophe in its place:

> I am → I'm

Practice 3
Make contractions of the following words.

1. they are _____
2. she will _____
3. Kerry is _____
4. of the clock _____
5. should not _____

▢ Apostrophes to Form Plurals

A less common use of apostrophes is to create certain kinds of plurals.

> Plurals of letters: *A*'s, *B*'s, *C*'s; *X*'s and *O*'s.
>
> Plurals of words used as words (which must also be underlined or italicized): I shoot too many *no*'s at my teenager and not enough *I love you*'s.

Practice 4
Rewrite the following three sentences, making the underlined words and letters plural.

1. I have two suggestions for getting an <u>A</u> or <u>B</u> on your composition papers.

   _____

   _____

2. In your writing, replace <u>is</u> and <u>were</u> with more active verbs.

   _____

   _____

Copyright © 1992 by Harcourt Brace Jovanovich, Inc. All rights reserved.

3. Try to avoid any negative forms, including <u>not</u>.

Sentence Combining

Combine each set of sentences into one sentence, using apostrophes whenever you can.

1. This happens at our neighborhood potluck.
   The spaghetti casserole never fails to be eaten.
   It is rich with meat sauce, sour cream, and cheese.
   Miss Mavis brings it.
   (Write this sentence with only one subject and one verb.)

2. People scrape up every dab of the black-eyed peas.
   These people never eat black-eyed peas at home.
   Joe Harmon brings the black-eyed pea dish.
   (Use a *who* in this sentence.)

3. Children race to do something.
   They want to grab the brownies.
   Nita Rodriguez brings brownies.
   Sue Ellen Williams also brings brownies.

4. This is the usual result.
   Only one dish doesn't get eaten.
   It belongs to my brother-in-law.
   It is chili.
   He insists on making it hot enough to burn the mouth of a dragon.
   (Use a *because* in this sentence.)

5. This is odd.
Whatever anyone else brings, the chicken goes first.
The chicken belongs to the Colonel.

Paragraph Editing Practice

First, read straight through the following paragraphs. Then reread them, inserting apostrophes as needed.

A. Niccolò Machiavelli (1469–1527), an Italian statesman whose name is synonymous with crafty and **unscrupulous** plotting, is best known as the author of *The Prince*. He intended this book, *The Prince*, as an ethical "how-to" manual for gaining political power, although during the thirteen years that Machiavelli spent as a well-respected Florentine statesman, he never aspired to a tyrants ultimate power. Machiavelli wrote *The Prince* only after the Medici family had regained power and forced him into exile. Ironically, then, the most **notorious** work ever written about acquiring and increasing power was conceived during its authors political impotence and disgrace.

B. I would fail miserably in choir except that all my fellow baritones voices keep me on key and in passable harmony. Actually, I would never have signed up for choir if a certain female someones hints hadnt been so sweetly blatant. Does Jan, the choirs prettiest alto, still feel the same about me after hearing Mike and Adam, two handsome choir members, serenade under her window last night? Undoubtedly, Mikes and Adams girlfriends have had a change of heart since they—along with the entire womens dorm—were awakened by these noisy, two-timing tenors. Mike and Adam hit their high Cs and Fs, but they sure didnt mind their ps and qs! My ever-moral alto minded their manners for them, sending them packing with one of her famous *shame-on-you*s. Moon-

Copyright © 1992 by Harcourt Brace Jovanovich, Inc. All rights reserved.

light serenades arent all theyre cracked up to be. Maybe Mike and Adam should have changed their tune. Yesterday Jan winked at me and said she had already picked out her maid of honors dress. I guess that Id better give her a ring, and I dont mean on the telephone!

C. Before 1910, movie fans never knew their favorite screen actors and actresses names. Strange as it may seem today, movie producers stubbornly refused to reveal the names of their players, for if these players became movie idols, they could rightfully demand high salaries. One might guess that Mary Pickfords or Charlie Chaplins name would have been the first one widely known to movie audiences. Surprisingly, the first movie star born to the publics imagination was Florence Lawrence, known simply as "The Biograph Girl" until she joined an independent studio.

Essay Editing Practice 1

Read straight through the following essay. Then edit it, inserting apostrophes as necessary. (You need only watch for apostrophe errors.)

No Lunch Boxes for Jason

On any school day that he chooses, ten-year-old Jason can go to his front picture window and watch the neighborhood children going to school, knapsacks slung over their shoulders, lunch boxes at their sides. Jason will never go with them. With two sisters and a preschool brother to keep him company, Jason figures his fractions, scrawls out his compositions, and masters his science at home, all under the watchful eye of his mother. Jason is a homeschooler. Even though parents who teach their children at home will readily acknowledge that they have taken on a challenge, they believe they have good reasons for doing so.

Some parents homeschool their children for religious reasons. While accepting that a **pluralistic** society like Americas must guard against school-enforced religious **dogma**, many parents still want their children to get more exposure to the Bible (or the **Qur'an**, as the case may be) than children can get during out-of-school hours. So Jasons mother, for example, teaches spelling by dictating favorite verses from the Psalms and teaches reading with Bible stories. Even without such **overt** use of religious materials, other homeschooling parents seek a religious perspective on childrens lessons, especially lessons devoted to discipline, persistence, kindness, and other character traits.

Asked about the best part of homeschooling, though, Jason will say its the freedom he has. Even in fourth grade, his formal lessons take only three hours. During the morning, he does arithmetic, science, history, writing, spelling, and the other "hard" subjects. These out of the way, Jason spends his afternoons as he chooses, preparing for his families weekly art lessons, building an electronic robot, delving into his hobby of designing paper airplanes, or just reading his Edward Eager books. Without time for attendance records, lining up for lunchtime, or waiting for other students to finish their lessons, homeschooling is much more efficient than formal schooling.

With their extra time, children can pursue their own educational challenges, learning not what a teacher tells them to learn, but what their heart chooses for them. Many parents without religious loyalties homeschool for this educational reason. They believe that these child-selected, child-directed activities result in more effective learning. Jasons mother knows just when Jasons heart is engaged. "He learns so quickly then," she says, "devouring information, asking questions right and left, jumping ahead of me onto new, related subjects. Its a wonder to behold. Encouraging that magical, impatient, active curiosity is the most important reason why I teach my children at home."

Copyright © 1992 by Harcourt Brace Jovanovich, Inc. All rights reserved.

Cautious about such a radical move, however, homeschoolers families and friends often ask about the childrens social skills. Dont homeschoolers need to be with children their own age to learn acceptable social behavior? Homeschooling families respond that schoolchildren learn social *habits* from their classmates, not social *skills*. From their peers, school children are more likely to learn selfishness than generosity, bullying than kindness, swearing than polite speech. Children learn social skills from caring teachers, and who could be more caring than a parent who is willing to homeschool? To ensure that homeschoolers spend time with other children, though, most parents enroll them in childrens clubs, community activities, and athletic teams. Jason, who won a role in the park-district production of *Toby Tyler*, will be rehearsing with community children for the next six months.

Even with social skills covered, questions inevitably remain. Sometimes Jasons mother can give at least a hundred reasons why she shouldnt be homeschooling. The responsibility can be overwhelming, the childrens demands taxing, and on the worst days their constant companionship oppressive. "But all the reasons against homeschooling relate to *me*," she says. "When I can come up with even one good reason against homeschooling for the childrens sake, Ill consider stopping, but not until then."

Writing Practice 1

Choose one of the following topics and write a short essay as instructed.

A. The author of this essay says homeschoolers believe that children in school are more likely to learn selfishness than generosity, bullying than kindness, and swearing than polite speech. What positive social skills did you learn through your schooling, and how? List three social skills, add some descriptive experiences or stories to show why these positive skills developed, and then write an essay (three internal paragraphs on one skill, or one paragraph on each of three skills).

B. Alternatively, write about three negative social experiences or skills, using the same format as the one specified for positive social skills.

C. What was the best part of school for you? What would you have regretted missing if you had been schooled differently? List three good memories, add some descriptive experiences or stories for each, and write your essay.

Essay Editing Practice 2

Read straight through the following essay. Then edit it, watching for all kinds of errors, correcting and improving as necessary. Watch for misused words as well.

"But I Studied!"

The shock is frightening, perhaps not on the magnitude of a San Francisco earthquake, but certainly big enough to cause internal tremors. After years of breezing through tests in high school, students take their first big college exam and fail. What could have gone wrong how could the old study methods have failed so miserably? Regrettably, college courses expect more from students than high school courses did. College students must learn more material, and harder material, in fewer time. To make the best use of study time, students may want to consider three suggestions.

First, students should never study with a pillow under their head. Sad to say, but it seems that when the head goes back against the pillow the brain begins a gradual shift into neutral. Perhaps, when students prop a book up on their stomach, the gentle motion of the book rising and falling with each breath lulls them to sleep. Or perhaps like the eyelids of a child's doll an inner mechanism somewhere causes a student's eyelids to slowly slip shut whenever the body falls into a horizontal position. Most likely, the content of college textbooks, too often serious dull and difficult makes any escape appealing, and when students are lying down anyway, sleep is to close a temptation to resist.

Once students have lifted their drooping body off the bed, the second suggestion becomes important, students should never study with an empty hand. Whatever they are studying, be it linear algebra, the history of the Persian rug, or the procreation of crustaceans, students should pick up the nearest pencil. And begin to take notes. Some genius somewhere with a photographic memory might be able to remember everything he or she reads, but most students are not of that breed. If students can see the words and make their hands shape the words onto paper. They will be pulling the information through the brain in two ways, and any path walked twice is more easily remembered. For really difficult material, students can say the gritty details out loud, hoping, of course, that their roommates will not object. Then the material will have gone through the brain four times: through the eyes with reading, the hand with writing, the mouth with speaking, and the ear with listening. Without at least a pencil however, students cannot claim to be studying. They are only reading. Besides, when students take the time to write down the important information, they will have a shortened version to study from the night before the test.

Finally, when studying, students should never listen to music with words. Studying inevitably involves information, and most college information involves words. Like a Pied Piper, music with words will pull the students thoughts away from their wordy studies. Without doubt, Whitney Houston, Phil Collins or any other popular singer has more appeal than the intricacies of the American political system. Anyone who doubts that can check out the relative earnings of Van Halen with those of textbook writers. The difference will almost certainly be **exponential**. True, some students need background sound to drown out the sounds of their roommate munching corn chips or typing a paper or sobbing over a Dear

Copyright © 1992 by Harcourt Brace Jovanovich, Inc. All rights reserved.

John letter. If, when confronted with this necessity, students choose music without words, then the efforts of the brain will not be torn in two directions.

These three suggestions will help students successfully make the transition from studying in high school. To studying in college. Students should sit up to study, always take notes as they study, and listen to music without words. While these guidelines cannot guarantee good grades, they will help students get more from the time they do spend studying.

Writing Practice 2

Choose one of the following topics and write a short essay, as instructed.

A. List study tips other than the three given in this essay. Choose the three best and write an essay with an internal paragraph on each, describing the tip and explaining why it is important.

B. Do you agree with the essay writer's suggestions? If not, choose one to disagree with and explain three reasons why you disagree, writing an essay with an internal paragraph about each reason.

C. Compare how a person should study for two different types of courses: one that requires mostly reading (literature or history, for example) and one that requires problem solving (math or chemistry). List study tips for each type of course and then write a short essay explaining the different ways to study.

Misused Words: passed/past

Passed is what the quarterback did in the game, what your angry roommate did without even saying "Hi," what even the worst day did. *Passed* is something a person, place, or thing does.

>Our room *passed* inspection—barely.

>The elevator *passed* our floor again.

Past relates to a period of time and is part of the phrase *past, present, and future.*

> The *past* looks quite attractive until I remember polio and smallpox.

Past also describes where something went and, for this use, can be replaced with the word *by.*

> The balloon sailed serenely *past* the airplane window.

Write either *passed* or *past* in the following sentences.

1. In the _____, we have counted our professor saying "Let's see now" sixty-four times in one lecture.

2. Then someone _____ this record onto the college newspaper.

3. Walking _____ her office the day the paper came out, I heard her listening to a tape of her lecture, counting for herself.

4. She must have decided to bury this trait in the _____.

5. Today, the entire lecture _____ without the professor saying these words even once.

Review Exercises

1. Describe three uses for apostrophes and give two examples of each.

   a. _____

   b. _____

   c. _____

2. Why do you think writers forget to insert apostrophes to form possessives?

   _____

   _____

3. Look at these examples:

   > my mother and father's ambitions for me

   > my mother's and father's completely different hobbies

Apostrophes to Form Plurals   199

Write the rule that applies to showing joint versus separate possession.

_____

_____

In the following sentences, mark the subjects with a single underline, the verbs with a double underline, and the dependent signals with a circle.

4. When England ruled India, it controlled the sale of salt, one of the most basic and common flavorings that the Indians used in their cooking.

5. The English sold salt to the Indians at extremely high prices and refused to allow the Indians to make their own salt.

6. To protest this injustice and many others, Mahatma Gandhi walked 200 miles across India to the ocean so that he could make his own salt.

7. This gentle, peace-loving leader of the Indians went to jail willingly, knowing that eventually world sentiment and the English people themselves would force the English out of India.

8. Today India honors Gandhi, for it owes its freedom chiefly to this man.

Dictionary Practice

Look up the words in bold print and provide a brief definition for each as it appears in the sentence.

1. While accepting that a **pluralistic** society like America's must guard against school-enforced religious dogma, many parents still want their children to get more exposure to the Bible (or the **Qur'an**, as the case may be) than children can get out of school.

   pluralistic: _____

   _____

   Qur'an (or Koran): _____

   _____

Copyright © 1992 by Harcourt Brace Jovanovich, Inc. All rights reserved.

Match the following words with their brief definitions.

_____ 2. dogma (p. 193)   a. doctrine; that which one believes is true

_____ 3. exponential (p. 196) b. without moral integrity or conscience

_____ 4. notorious (p. 191)   c. easily perceived; obvious

_____ 5. overt (p. 193)   d. dramatically larger

_____ 6. unscrupulous (p. 191) e. widely known, usually unfavorably

CHAPTER 11

Subject-Verb Agreement

◼ Subject and Verb Endings

All of the following short sentences demonstrate subject-verb agreement—a singular noun requires a singular verb.

    A cat pounces.   A dog barks.

    A car starts.   A horn honks.

    A gymnast flips.   A runner races.

Look carefully at the pattern of these words, especially the endings of the subjects and verbs. What would you say is the regular pattern for the endings of a singular subject–singular verb combination?

_____

_____

Now consider the same sentences rewritten with plural subjects.

    Cats pounce.   Dogs bark.

    Cars start.   Horns honk.

    Gymnasts flip.   Runners race.

How would you describe the regular pattern for the endings of plural subject–plural verb combinations?

_____

_____

Copyright © 1992 by Harcourt Brace Jovanovich, Inc. All rights reserved.   **201**

Not all verbs follow a regular pattern, of course. For example:

> The cat *has* yellow fur.
>
> The cats *have* yellow fur.
>
> The dog *is* a champion breed.
>
> The dogs *are* champion breeds.

Under regular conditions, however, subjects and verbs do follow a pattern. Singular subjects, which have no ending, are used with singular verbs that end in -*s* or -*es*.

> The bird screeches.

Plural subjects, which usually end in -*s* or -*es*, are used with plural verbs, which have no ending.

> The donkeys bray.

Practice 1
Circle the correct verb form in the following sentences.

1. June (wear, **wears**) only Chanel No. 5 perfume.
2. Every morning, Ramona (wake, **wakes**) up to her kid sister's scratchy, blaring 45's.
3. Victorian Christmas trees (was, **were**) often ablaze with dozens of candles.
4. More and more parents (is, **are**) concerned that their children may be learning violence and aggression from television.
5. Somehow, Raoul (**has**, have) managed to avoid talking on the telephone for five years.
6. The leaves (has, **have**) been raked into a pile in front of the swing-set.
7. Kristin's pet chameleons (was, **were**) surprisingly chipper and affectionate.

Copyright © 1992 by Harcourt Brace Jovanovich, Inc. All rights reserved.

8. Many (think, thinks) tarantulas (is, are) deadly poisonous to people, but tarantulas (is, are) really just big, slow, hairy spiders with a mean bite.

9. Look out! The angrier I (is, am, are) at you, the sweeter I will behave.

In Chapter 3, we state that subject-verb combinations must live in the same sentence. Now we're adding a new idea to that: They must also be matched carefully so that the subjects and verbs will live together harmoniously. In other words:

> **Singular subjects require singular verbs, and plural subjects require plural verbs.**

Unfortunately, knowing this rule is not enough. To apply this basic rule you have to be able to recognize which subjects are singular and which are plural, which is not always easy.

This chapter will describe the rules that relate to the many different kinds of subjects that you might use. While lists of rules rarely entertain, this chapter does have one saving grace for many people: These rules have few exceptions. Once you master the rules of this chapter, then you can look over what you have written, find the rule that applies to the kind of subject you are using, and apply a fail-safe combination (now, if only finding a compatible roommate were this easy).

◼ Questions Related to Sentence Structure

What About Compound Subjects?

> **As long as you have two different things or people in your subject, you have a plural subject and need a plural verb.**

Together, the owl and the pussycat in the following sentence equal more than one and so require a plural verb.

> The <u>owl</u> and the <u>pussycat</u> <u>have</u> strange-looking children.

Do Compound Subjects Ever Take a Singular Verb?

Some compound subjects actually refer to one object or entity and thus are singular subjects.

In the following sentence, because *red beans and rice* refers to a single dish, the sentence requires a singular verb.

> Red beans and rice tingles my tongue.

Compare that to this sentence:

> Ham and eggs both threaten my cholesterol level, so I eat oat bran for breakfast.

If this confuses you, try inserting *both* after the compound subject. If the sentence makes sense, you need a plural verb. If the insertion sounds odd, then you probably have a singular subject.

What About *or, either/or,* and *neither/nor*?

Unlike the sentence about the owl and the pussycat, sentences with the word *or* or *nor* offer two separate options, not both combined.

> Either my abscessed tooth or my sanity has to go.
> (Both subjects are singular.)

> The violinist or the viola players are missing their cue.
> (One subject is singular and the other plural.)

> Neither my friends nor my parents are going to believe that I passed linear algebra. (Both subjects are plural.)

For sentences that include such options, remember this rule:

Make your verb agree with the subject closer to the verb. If this closer subject is singular, make the verb singular; if the closer subject is plural, make the verb plural.

> Neither my son nor my daughter admits to eating the last piece of triple chocolate cheesecake.

> Either a red pen or a green pen stands out on a page of type.

> Neither my parents nor my brother is willing to back down.

> Greens or blues go well with my red hair.

Copyright © 1992 by Harcourt Brace Jovanovich, Inc. All rights reserved.

Practice 2

Combine the sentence pairs in exercises 1–4.

1. Thelma plays professional tennis.
   Her sister does, too.
   (Use the S+S+V pattern.)
   Thelma and her sister play professional tennis

2. My felt-tip pen has no ink.
   Neither does my ballpoint pen.
   (Use *neither/nor*.)
   Neither my felt-tip pen has no ink nor my ballpoint pen.

3. The camping trip to Big Bend does not appeal to my wife.
   The four days in Paloduro Canyon do not appeal either.
   (Use *neither/nor*.)
   Neither four days in Paloduro Canyon nor a camping trip to Big Bend appeals to my wife.

4. Seven days in Hawaii sound good to my wife.
   Alternatively, five days on a cruise sound good.
   (Use *either/or*.)
   Either five days on a cruise or seven days in Hawaii sound good to my wife.

Complete the following sentences.

5. Abercrombie and Fitch (a retail store) _are in malls all over the country._

6. Packing up and moving to a new place _sound good to me._

What About Inverted Sentences?

By now, you probably realize that the first word in a sentence is not necessarily the subject. Often the subject can actually follow the verb, such as in questions or in sentences that start with *There are* (also *There's*) or *Here is* (also *Here's*). For an inverted sentence, you must first find the subject, and then make certain that the verb agrees.

> Here <u>are</u> the <u>sweaters</u> I borrowed. I am sorry they all shrank.
>
> There <u>is</u> a chill <u>wind</u> blowing through the steeple tonight, moving the bell to a ghostly rhythm.

Practice 3

Rewrite the following sentences as indicated.

1. I had some notes for my comparison of George Herbert and John Donne. I cannot find them.
   (Write a single question beginning with *where*.)

   Where are my notes for my comparison of George Herbert and John Donne?

2. Three things excite me about the summer: sun, fun, and a chance to earn some money.
   (Begin this sentence with *there*.)

   There are three things that excite me about the summer; sun, fun, and a chance to earn some money.

What About Words That Separate the Subject and Verb?

As we saw in Chapter 4, words and phrases that describe or add extra information often follow the subject of a sentence. Their appearance can cause confusion as you try for subject-verb agreement.

Prepositional phrases: Prepositions include words that show relationship to an object (see pages 16–17 for a more complete discussion of prepositions).

> *of* the furniture   *behind* the drapes
> *around* the coffee table   *beside* the television
> *except* the armchairs   *inside* the fireplace

Prepositional phrases can make subject-verb agreement difficult when they come between the subject and the verb. The subject might be singular, but if the object of the preposition is plural, you might be tempted to make the verb plural as well. In the following sentences with prepositional phrases, underline subjects once and verbs twice.

Questions Related to Sentence Structure   **207**

The <u>detail</u> in the walls and ceilings <u><u>shows</u></u> the architect's sense of humor.

The <u>author</u> of these incredibly difficult riddles <u><u>has</u></u> a sadistic bent.

The <u>hopes</u> of the marathon runner <u><u>were</u></u> dashed on Sunday.

If you read these subject-verb combinations together (*detail shows, author has,* and *hopes were*), they agree more clearly. As you edit, isolate the subjects and the verbs this way before you decide they agree.

Practice 4
Combine the sentences in each set.

1. There is a mouse.
   The mouse is inside the Lucky Charms.
   Eating all the marshmallows is the mouse's activity.
   (Begin this sentence with *The mouse.*)

   The mouse inside the Lucky Charms is eating all the marshmallows.

2. There are a boy and a girl.
   They are behind the bookshelves.
   The bookshelves are in the library.
   Kissing each other is their activity.
   (Begin this sentence with *A boy and a girl.*)

   A boy and a girl in their activity are in the library behind the bookshelves kissing each other.

Phrases with participles: Like prepositions, participles can begin phrases that come between the subject and the verb (for a description of participles, see pages 8–9.) When a noun in such a phrase is close to the verb, you might think the verb should agree with that noun instead of the subject.

In the following sentences, underline subjects once and verbs twice.

The <u>clown</u> entertaining the children <u><u>is</u></u> really my great-aunt.

The <u>fudge</u> handed out during the holidays <u><u>was</u></u> donated by the local sugar processing plant.

The <u>symptoms</u> causing such problems for my neighbor <u><u>mystify</u></u> her doctors.

Copyright © 1992 by Harcourt Brace Jovanovich, Inc. All rights reserved.

208 Chapter 11 Subject-Verb Agreement

As you can see, the participles *entertaining, handed,* and *causing* begin phrases that separate the subject from the verb. If we leave out these phrases, *clown is, fudge was,* and *symptoms mystify* sound correct.

Practice 5
Combine the sentences in each set, using a phrase that begins with a participle. Place that phrase between the subject and the verb.

1. There are the grandmother and two parents.
   They sit in the audience.
   They hold their breath through the little girl's recital piece.

   The grandmother and two parents sitting in the audience holds their breath through the little girl's recital piece.

2. There is the student.
   She is dressed in Gypsy clothes.
   She is draped in gaudy jewels.
   She is the professor's wife.

   There is a student dressing in Gypsy clothes and draped gaudy jewels and is the professor's wife.

Phrases that add extra information: In some sentences you may want to insert extra information, set off by commas, between the subject and the verb. In the following sentences, underline subjects once and verbs twice.

> A prize-winning photograph, as well as many other art objects, is offered for purchase at the auction.
>
> The auctioneer, in addition to her many assistants, stands waiting for the starting time.

Notice that if you ignore the extra information, *photograph is* and *auctioneer stands* sound correct.

Practice 6
Combine the sentences in each set, using *as well as* to set off the extra information between the subject and the verb.

1. This happens whenever we watch *Jeopardy*.
   My wife says I should become a contestant.
   My three children say so as well.

   Whenever we watch Jeopardy, my wife as well as my three children say I should be a contestant.

2. I always refuse.
   I do this because the science categories scare me.
   Being in the spotlight also scares me.

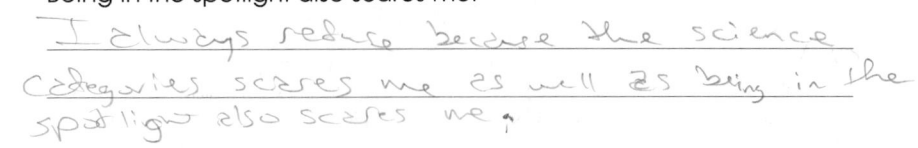

   I always refuse because the science categories scares me as well as being in the spotlight also scares me.

Exercises

Read each sentence, underline the subject that belongs with the verb in question, and circle the correct verb form. Then identify each entry as A, B, or C to show which sentence pattern it demonstrates.

    A   "Or" or "nor": He or she paints. Neither the singer nor the drummers wear shirts.
    B   *Subject follows the verb:* There are three wishes.
    C   *Something separates the subject and the verb:* Sal, the mother of twins, skates.

_C_ 1. The sand at Utah's Coral Pink Sand Dunes (is, are) not really pink until the sunset casts a rosy glow over everything.

_C_ 2. The spirit of the holidays (gets, get) lost under all the overspending and debts and depression.

_A_ 3. Neither July's drought nor September's hailstorms (has, have) made Joshua bitter about farming his land.

_C_ 4. Why (wasn't, weren't) Leigh, the lead's understudy, invited to the cast party?

_B_ 5. The combination of newly fallen snow and the end of finals (causes, cause) me to head for my favorite sledding hill.

_C_ 6. The students playing canasta (has, have) been there all night.

_B_ 7. What (is, are) the names of the musicians in the Guarneri Quartet?

_C_ 8. The jockey who races both Lady Luck and Silverflash (has, have) never been injured on the racetrack.

_B_ 9. The ants that cover my lunch bag (doesn't, don't) know they signed up for a quick game of squash.

Chapter 11 Subject-Verb Agreement

B 10. What good (is, are) a house in the suburbs, a German Shepherd, and a security system when my own mother has sticky fingers?

A 11. Either ability or ambition (was, were) missing from her character.

B 12. How (does, do) that flimsy, ticky-tacky beach house resist Oregon's coastal storms year after year?

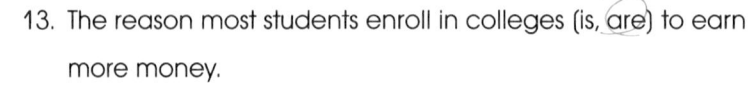

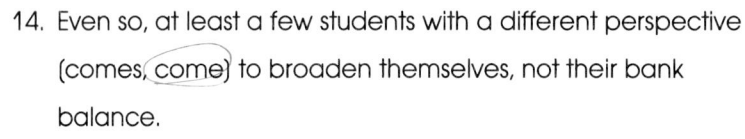

C 13. The reason most students enroll in colleges (is, are) to earn more money.

C 14. Even so, at least a few students with a different perspective (comes, come) to broaden themselves, not their bank balance.

B 15. Where (is, are) all those safety pins when you need them?

Pronoun Problems

Some writers have trouble with subject-verb agreement when the subject of a sentence is a pronoun. Pronouns are words that take the place of nouns.

Practice 7

The following pronouns can be used as the subject of a sentence:

>   Singular: *I, you, he, she, it, this, that*
>   Plural: *we, you, they, these, those*

In exercises 1–8, write the pronoun you would use in place of these words and phrases as subjects of sentences. The first one has been done as an example.

1. My sister and I We
2. Karen _____
3. The computer _____

4. Yourself _____

5. James _____

6. The toys _____

7. Myself _____

8. The parents _____

Three special types of pronouns occasionally cause problems, because you may find it hard to tell if they are singular or plural. These problems arise with *indefinite pronouns* (both with and without a modifier) and *relative pronouns.*

Indefinite Pronouns

Indefinite pronouns include words that end with *-one, -body,* or *-thing.*

anyone	anybody	anything
everyone	everybody	everything
someone	somebody	something
no one	nobody	nothing
none		

Each, either, and *neither* are also indefinite pronouns.

Indefinite pronouns that do not require a modifier are singular and therefore require singular verbs.

As long as you remember that these words refer to only one person, body, or thing—that is, they are all singular—then the singular verb will seem correct.

> Everyone needs to see *Romeo and Juliet* at least once.
>
> Does anything on the sale rack fit you?
>
> Nobody loves me. Everybody hates me. I'm going to go eat a pound of red hots.
>
> None of us has ever seen Bigfoot, but at one time or another each of us has imagined seeing him under the bed.

Practice 8

Combine the pair of sentences in exercise 1.

1. I have many cats.
   They do not know where the litter box is.
   (Begin this sentence with *none*.)

___

___

Complete the unfinished sentence.

2. Some people like chocolate ice cream.
   Some people like vanilla ice cream.
   Whatever the flavor, everyone _____

___

Indefinite Pronouns That Appear with a Modifier

Some indefinite pronouns may be either singular or plural, depending on the words—or modifiers—they appear with. Examples include *all, any, more, most, some.*

In the following sentences, *most* and *all* are followed by modifiers. The modifiers determine whether the pronoun is singular or plural.

> *Most of my days* begin with a long jog and a short cold shower. (a plural number)
>
> *Most of the cookie dough* gets eaten uncooked. (a singular amount)
>
> *All of the water* in the lake has been poisoned by agricultural runoff. (a singular amount)
>
> Therefore *all of the resort owners* have had to close down. (a plural number)

When pronouns appear with modifiers, the modifier determines whether the pronoun is singular or plural. A singular modifier means that the pronoun requires a singular

verb; a plural modifier means that the pronoun requires a plural verb.

Practice 9
Write answers to the following questions.

1. Did I spill paint on my chin? (Begin your answer with *Some of the paint.*)

   _____

   _____

2. Did I spill any sequins under the table? (Begin your sentence with *Most of the sequins.*)

   _____

   _____

Relative pronouns

Relative pronouns include *who, which,* and *that.* As pronouns, they always refer to an object or person somewhere else in the sentence. Sometimes, as in the examples that follow, these pronouns form the subject of a dependent clause that describes the subject of the main sentence. (See pages 28–29 for another description of these "double-duty dependent signals.")

> **With relative pronouns (*who, which, that*), the word that the pronoun refers to determines whether the pronoun requires a singular or plural verb.**

In the following sentences, identify with brackets the dependent clause that follows the subject of the main sentence.

> Stephanie, *who* has more energy than a heavy-duty battery, bounds across our hardwood floors with the spring of a gazelle and the tread of an elephant.
>
> Bicycles *that* have an aerodynamic shape reduce wind resistance to increase speed.

In the first sentence, *who* requires a singular verb because it refers to a singular subject, *Stephanie.* In the second sentence, *that* requires a plural verb because it refers to a plural subject, *bicycles*. Here are some other examples:

>My sister, *who* is gorgeous, looks just like me. (singular)
>
>My friends, *who* are numerous, have great taste. (plural)
>
>The car *that* is green looks like a pickle. (singular)
>
>Cars *that* are yellow look like lemons. (plural)

Practice 10

Combine the sentences in each set. (Do you remember when to use commas around the clause and when not to? Refer to pages 145–147 to refresh your memory before completing this exercise.)

1. I have learned never to give the soft drinks to my roommate.
   He jostles and jiggles everything he carries.
   (Use *who* as the relative pronoun.)

   _____

   _____

2. At college, I avoid late-night walks.
   The walks are scary.
   They could be dangerous.
   (Use *which* as the relative pronoun.)

   _____

   _____

Exercises

Read each sentence, underline the subject that belongs with the verb in question, and circle the correct verb form. Then write A, B, or C to identify the type of pronoun that determines the verb form in each case. Finally, correct each sentence as necessary.

>A *Indefinite pronouns: each, either, neither,* and pronouns ending in *-one, -body,* or *-thing.* These require singular verbs.
>
>B *Pronouns with modifiers: all, more, some, any, most.* These take verbs that agree with the word that modifies them.
>
>C *Relative pronouns that serve as subject to a dependent clause: who, which, that.* These take verbs that agree with the nouns they represent.

Copyright © 1992 by Harcourt Brace Jovanovich, Inc. All rights reserved.

Questions Related to Sentence Structure   215

1. As a first-year student, joining a sorority or fraternity is tempting, because after all, almost everybody (needs, need) friends.

2. Toward the end of spring, all of my female friends (discusses, discuss) what sort of swimsuit will hide their figure flaws.

3. I do not care what anybody (says, say). Swimsuits have not hidden figure flaws since the days when a calf-length dress and thick stockings served as a "bathing costume."

4. Either of the local newspapers (is, are) fine for me, since I only look at "The Far Side" and the grocery circulars.

5. Yesterday, I bought my first real leather boots, which even my father thinks (looks, look) great on me.

6. All of my memories of my old boyfriend Jack (waits, wait) until a certain song brings them rushing and tumbling through willing tear ducts.

7. Fortunately, once each of these tears (has, have) been shed, I forget all about him again.

8. Everyone in basic composition classes (is, are) expected to learn word processing.

9. All of our spare change (gets, get) stashed in a mason jar behind my husband's never-opened copy of *The Hidden Joys of Saving Money*.

10. Each of Jessica's fingernails (is, are) painted a different shade of purple.

11. Most of the state (votes, vote) conservatively on economic and environmental issues.

12. Neither of them (is, are) fit to drive home, so since I cannot drive, I am taking a taxi, thank you.

Copyright © 1992 by Harcourt Brace Jovanovich, Inc. All rights reserved.

☐ Other Special Cases

Collective Nouns

Nouns that are singular in form and refer to groups of people or things, such as *family, team,* or *quartet,* are called collective nouns. The same word may have a singular meaning in some cases and a plural meaning in others. For example:

>The quartet sounds off key.

In this case, the quartet is seen as a single unit, so it takes a singular verb. Of course, a quartet contains more than one person, and when they are referred to as separate people, these four quartet members require a plural verb.

>The quartet wear dark suits or dresses for evening performances.

Crowd is another collective noun. Although a crowd includes many people, it is only one group and thus often takes a singular verb:

>Each Fourth of July, a crowd forms on the park green to watch fireworks.

Sometimes *crowd* refers to the individual people in it; then a plural verb may be needed.

>As the night grows cooler, the crowd begin to pull on their jackets and sweaters.

>**When referred to as a singular group, a collective noun requires a singular verb. When the individual members are meant, a collective noun requires a plural verb.**

Quantities

>**A word that refers to a single quantity as a whole requires a singular verb, even if that quantity has many individual parts. It takes a plural verb only if the separate parts are thought of individually.**

Look at the following examples:

> <u>Seven football games</u> <u>are</u> telecast on New Year's Day.
>
> <u>Seven football games</u> on New Year's Day <u>is</u> more than I can sit through.

In the first sentence, the seven games, individually, are telecast. But in the next sentence, the quantity of seven games collectively becomes too much, not the seven games individually. Any one of the games on its own may be fine, but all the games together put the person to sleep. Following are some more sentences with subjects that look plural but are used in a singular sense:

> A thousand chocolate chips manages to appease my craving for chocolate—barely.
>
> "Three broken dates is too many," Daryl told Samantha, and then went ahead and bought tickets to go with her to hear Amy Grant. Won't he ever learn?
>
> A thousand dollars sounds like a lot of money until I go into an electronics store.
>
> Seventy degrees is my favorite temperature.

Titles

> **A title requires a singular verb even if the word or words in the title are plural.**

The following sentences require singular verbs:

> *Highlights* is my children's favorite magazine.
>
> Better Homes and Gardens' *All Time Favorite Recipes* includes a towering vanilla and sour cream cake.

Singular Nouns with Plural Forms

Words like *mathematics, economics, news,* and *aerobics* appear to be plural, but their meaning is always singular.

> **Singular nouns with plural forms (ending in *-s*) require singular verbs.**

> Aerobics is good for my heart but I do it for my hips.

Chapter 11 Subject-Verb Agreement

Practice 11

Combine the pair of sentences in exercise 1.

1. Certain people are considering "A Moment in Time" as the theme for homecoming.
   The people considering this are the Homecoming Committee.

   _____

   _____

Complete the following sentences.

2. How much is too much at Thanksgiving? Three platefuls _____

   _____

3. The television show *Cheers* _____

   _____

4. Good news _____

   _____

Exercises

Read each sentence, underline the subject that belongs with the verb in question, and circle the correct verb. Then write A, B, C, or D to identify which kind of subject each sentence illustrates.

- A *Collective nouns:* Groups seen as a unit require singular verbs; seen as individuals, they require plural verbs.
- B *Quantities:* Quantities seen as whole amounts require singular verbs; if the separate parts are emphasized, the verb should be plural.
- C *Titles:* Single titles, even with plural words, require singular verbs.
- D *Singular nouns with plural forms:* Singular nouns require singular verbs.

_____ 1. Cleveland High's rowdiest gang (was, were) dismissed from the principal's office with a mock warning and a wink because the gang's leader was the school superintendent's son.

_____ 2. I am told that Eudora Welty's *Thirteen Stories* (is, are) still my old American literature professor's favorite.

Copyright © 1992 by Harcourt Brace Jovanovich, Inc. All rights reserved.

Other Special Cases   219

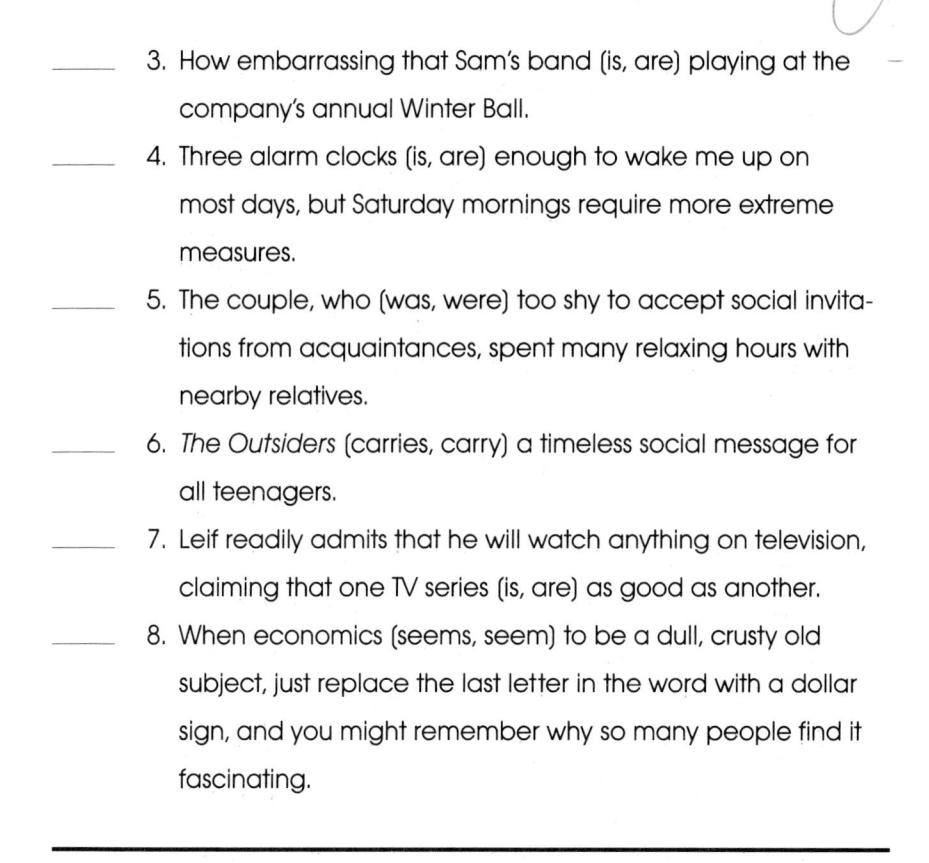

_____ 3. How embarrassing that Sam's band (is, are) playing at the company's annual Winter Ball.

_____ 4. Three alarm clocks (is, are) enough to wake me up on most days, but Saturday mornings require more extreme measures.

_____ 5. The couple, who (was, were) too shy to accept social invitations from acquaintances, spent many relaxing hours with nearby relatives.

_____ 6. *The Outsiders* (carries, carry) a timeless social message for all teenagers.

_____ 7. Leif readily admits that he will watch anything on television, claiming that one TV series (is, are) as good as another.

_____ 8. When economics (seems, seem) to be a dull, crusty old subject, just replace the last letter in the word with a dollar sign, and you might remember why so many people find it fascinating.

Paragraph Editing Practice

Read straight through the following paragraphs (they belong together). Then go back through them, marking subject-verb combinations in each sentence and correcting any agreement errors that you find. Be careful. These are tricky.

A. Campers, who are healthy, robust, outdoorsy types, swear on their camper's manuals that camping entertains them. Not only is camping fun, claims these **irrepressible masochists**, but also exciting and exhilarating. They exaggerate. Contrary to these ridiculous claims, camping are exasperating and exhausting.

About once a year, my husband, aided by my children, pack up the van, and we are off for another camping disaster. At each meal, all of us tries to forget that we have left a comfortable, orderly existence to eat food that back home would be fed to our dog. At night, mosquitoes and at least one pesky fly dive-bombs us all night. None of my family want to tackle outhouses unfit for anything that *breathe*, but who among us want to use the unaccommodating **terra firma**, either? Everyone spend the long, lumpy night alternately sweating and freezing inside a goosedown **shroud**. Then, just as the last of the tired campers are falling off to sleep, the fretful sound of raindrops are heard on the permeable nylon roof that we left optimistically uncovered. We all wake up, of course. Under the increasing torrent, the entire family debate whether we should fumble for an hour in the drenching darkness assembling the waterproof "storm fly" or continue sloshing about in a puddle for eight hours. Then, ah yes, joy cometh in the morning. At last, each of the weary campers emerge from the womb stiff-limbed, sore-backed, into the damp and dewy dawn. None of us want to wake up, but each of us are glad to see the morning, for this particular sunrise **heralds** the sweetest of days. Today, the unpacked will be packed and the everlasting campfire extinguished. Today, our brood of angels look homeward.

Essay Editing Practice 1

Read all the way through the following essay, and then go back through the essay editing any subject-verb agreement problems that you find.

Painted Faces

How much makeup is enough? How much is too much? Many women concern themselves with these questions on a daily basis. Of course, where one woman might prefer to leave her face **au naturel**, another has mastered the art and never needs to check whether her foundation and eye shadow shows in streaks or her lipstick has bled halfway down her chin. Each of these women looks perfect for any occasion. But many women are not blessed with cosmetic confidence. These women spend a fortune (no exaggeration) trying to balance their act somewhere between the Gerber Baby and the Joker.

Take Krista, a young accounting firm receptionist who realize that her smiling face presents her company's first impression. During her first month, she spends her first six months' paychecks (thanks to Master-Card) on every fashion magazine available, national and international. She diligently searches through glossy pages for guidance but soon becomes burdened with conflicting advice. Neither a "spring" color scheme nor a "winter" color scheme look quite right on her. None of the magazines agree on whether she should wear eye liner to work or not. One says that iris petals make the best moisturizer, and another says that aloe does. As for the magazine models, they provide little guidance. Krista suspects that they would look good bald, with green cold cream over their faces.

So Krista abandons the magazines and heads for the department stores' cosmetic counters. Salespeople, zeroing in on an easy mark, sell her bottles, brushes, jars, tubes, pencils, clippers, and a terrifying assortment of other paraphernalia. The multitude of methods for applying color astound her. She buys blushers, lotions, sticks, and crayons, and even then wonders if she has everything she needs. Each passion pink, sexy scarlet, and ravishing rose look more enticing than the last. Smiling **beneficently**, the goddesses behind the counter assure Krista that just a small dab of *this* and just a light stroke of *that* will make Krista look so good that she can herself become a cosmetics goddess.

Finally, desperately confused by her priceless collection of cosmetics, which on her dresser tower so high that she cannot see herself, Krista seeks the aid of a makeup consultant. Calling himself Pygmalion, this gentleman scolds and cajoles Krista until she feels ready to scream.

Copyright © 1992 by Harcourt Brace Jovanovich, Inc. All rights reserved.

Nevertheless, the marvel of contemporary cosmetics, as well as the consultant's individual attention, help Krista to finally apply her makeup correctly.

Thanks to her excessive purchases and the consultant's exorbitant fees, Krista now skips breakfast and lunch. Pork and beans has become her dietary staple. She rents a room above a garage, sleeps on a beanbag chair, and listens to a Sony Walkman for stereo sound. This sacrifice of physical and aesthetic comforts are worth it, however. Krista has achieved her goal: She blends perfectly with the decor in her employers' reception area, painted walls with painted cheeks, and plastic fixtures with a plastic face. She now feels she has job security.

Unfortunately, she feels less secure with her boyfriend, Ryan, who thinks only dolls should have painted faces.

Writing Practice 1

Choose one of the following topics and write an essay.

A. This writer describes how one woman uses makeup to create a certain impression of herself. Make a list of ways people in our society try to create a certain impression about themselves. Include methods related to looks (including figure, makeup, and clothes), manners, and possessions. Then choose three specific ways of creating an impression in all three categories. Write an essay with a paragraph on each, describing each category or method, the stereotypes related to each, and your reaction to this stereotype.

B. Write a narrative account of a hobby that you have pursued, focusing especially on how this hobby ended up costing a great deal of money. In your first internal paragraph, you could describe how you got into the hobby. In your second, you could describe the basic equipment, materials, or supplies that you had to buy as you began your hobby. Then, in the third internal paragraph, you could describe the extra, unsuspected items that you ended up having to purchase (or refusing to purchase, as the case may be).

Copyright © 1992 by Harcourt Brace Jovanovich, Inc. All rights reserved.

C. Having the right appearance seems to be important to the self-esteem of the character in this essay. What is the difference between self-esteem and pride? List some distinctions and some ways to explain each distinction. Then write an essay with internal paragraphs on three of your distinctions between self-esteem and pride.

Essay Editing Practice 2

Read through the following essay. Then edit it for any error you have studied so far, but watch *especially* for apostrophe errors.

Supper's Ready!

Sociologists and psychologists and all the other **multisyllabic** men and women who comment on modern society frequently feel led to lament America's lack of dinnertime ritual. America needs more family togetherness, they say, America needs more family communication. In spite of these professionals moans, however, families in America do have rituals and especially at dinner. The routine of each of these families is unique, and therefore hard to detect in the surveys that this group of learned sociologists and psychologists always uses.

Some families still have the old-fashioned, supper-is-ready, come-sit-down-and-eat routine. The family of one of my roommates did. Her mother worked only in the morning. So had time to make meat, potatoes, vegetables, and homemade desserts every night. She even made her own mayonnaise from scratch. Every night, her family ate dinner around the table, sometimes spending over an hour together.

My other roommate's family also always sat down around a table to eat. They just never sat down at home. Her mom would say, "Okay, kids, it's time to eat," and everyone would run to jump in the car. They ate out four or five times a week, but they still had family togetherness. They spent time together in the car, kept the kitchen clean, and rarely complained about their mothers' cooking. Who could complain when she so seldom cooked? Think of all the hurt feelings this spared my roommates mother.

My family, on the other hand, never sat down in one place to eat. Most nights, we would just grab a plate of whatever was in the fridge, sometimes eating my dads lasagna and other nights eating my moms fried chicken. Actually, most nights we ate Le Menu or Stouffers. (Hey, they're pretty good!) We would zap the food in the microwave and go on about our business. My brother who was in college majoring in pre-med ate his food at his desk upstairs studying. Dad and I ate in front of the TV (no pre-med for me), and as for Mom, she usually got home too late for dinner. As a pediatrician, she often had to fit extra patients in. Our family consistently ate together at only two times: Sunday breakfasts and Thursday nights when *Star Trek* came on at 6 o'clock.

Three completely different routines my roommates and I had at home, but routines they were. In fact, each family everywhere has its own rituals, each moves and breathes and relates to its own rhythm. As different as families are, however, I bet none of these families have a dinner routine where it sends a daughter alone to a cafeteria to line up with people she hardly knows, to pick out food that is only half edible, and then to walk into a cavernous dining room and find someone—anyone—she knows to eat with. No wonder my roommates and I feel most homesick at dinnertime.

I have just one question. If dinner routines at the college cafeteria are so awful. Why are we all putting on so much weight?

Copyright © 1992 by Harcourt Brace Jovanovich, Inc. All rights reserved.

Writing Practice 2

Choose one of the following topics and write three paragraphs.

A. Make a list of five to ten different kinds of meals that your family has, including everyday meals, holiday meals, meals with guests, and so forth. Choose three of these categories, write down how each kind is different from the others (the distinctive conversations, foods, purposes, behaviors, and so forth), and then write an essay that describes how these kinds of meals are distinctive.

B. Make a list of dinner habits your family has. Put these into three categories, write a list of information about each category of habit, how you think it got started, its effect on your family, and whether you like or dislike the habit and why. Then write a short essay.

C. What is Sunday morning like at your house? List details about a typical Sunday morning, either in your family setting, on your own, or what you anticipate for the future. Your details might relate to food, clothes, atmosphere (pressured or nonpressured), and so forth. Then write a short essay that incorporates these details.

Misused Words: set/sit

Set is something a person does to something else. When you use the word *set*, you need an object to go with it—the thing that gets set down, whether that is a book or a baseball glove, a plate of food or pillow.

>Please *set* the plate of rumaki beside me.

>*Set* your pillow down beside me, you gorgeous creature.

Sit is something a person, place, or thing does itself; *sit* requires no object because the subject of the sentence is doing the sitting.

>(You) *Sit* down beside me.

>The rest of my family *sits* across the field from me.

Insert the correct form of either *sit* or *set* in the following sentences.

1. Always under control, Lyle ____set____ the offensive letter gently into the trash can.

226 Chapter 11 Subject-Verb Agreement

2. Did the new father get a chance to __sit__ down even once during the Super Bowl?

3. Sometimes Thad __set__ the trash bag too far out onto the street.

4. Did Tatiana remember to __set__ some food out for the birds?

5. Betsy and Brad __sat__ beside each other everywhere except in class.

Review Exercises

Write the rule for each of the following subject-verb applications.

1. Neither my sister nor my parents know that I am taking skydiving lessons.

   _____
   _____

2. All of my cousins have been allowed to pursue dangerous hobbies.

   _____
   _____

3. My grandmother, as well as my aunt and uncle, has a pilot's license.

   _____
   _____

4. Unfortunately, my pair of petrified parents is a throwback to a more cowardly generation.

   _____
   _____

5. However, three chickens in a family is more than enough.

   _____
   _____

6. Therefore, I will continue learning to fold my parachute.

   _____
   _____

Copyright © 1992 by Harcourt Brace Jovanovich, Inc. All rights reserved.

Dictionary Practice

Look up the words in bold print and provide a brief definition for each word as it appears in the sentence.

1. Smiling **beneficently**, the goddesses behind the counter assure Krista that just a small dab of *this* and just a light stroke of *that* will make Krista look so good that she can herself become a cosmetics goddess.
   beneficent: _____

   _____

2. Not only is camping fun, claim these **irrepressible masochists**, but also exciting and exhilarating.
   irrepressible: _____

   _____

   masochist: _____

   _____

Match the following words with their brief definitions:

_____ 3. *au naturel* (p. 220) a. burial garment or covering

_____ 4. herald (verb, p. 220) b. natural; nude

_____ 5. multisyllabic (p. 223) c. to announce; to greet

_____ 6. shroud (p. 220) d. having more than three syllables

_____ 7. *terra firma* (p. 220) e. solid ground

Copyright © 1992 by Harcourt Brace Jovanovich, Inc. All rights reserved.

CHAPTER 12

Pronoun Agreement

Different Pronouns for Different Uses

Pronouns are words used in place of nouns. Each pronoun may take several different forms, as the chart shows. The form you use in any particular case depends on its job in the sentence.

	Subject pronouns	Object pronouns (receive the action)	Pronouns that show possession	Pronouns that refer to the subject
Singular				
First-person	I	me	my, mine	myself
Second-person	you	you	your(s)	yourself
Third-person	she	her	her(s)	herself
	he	him	his	himself
	it	it	its	itself
	who	whom	whose	
Plural				
First-person	we	us	our(s)	ourselves
Second-person	you	you	your(s)	yourselves
Third-person	they	them	their(s)	themselves

Subject Pronouns

The pronouns in the first column of the chart are the ones we would use as a subject.

> *I* came home.
>
> *They* threw tomatoes.
>
> *We* hope for greatness.

The other team and *we* arrived at the same time.

Since we were both trying to quit, *he* and *I* agreed to call each other when we felt tempted to drink.

When you are using two pronouns together in a compound subject (as in the clause starting "*he* and *I* . . ."), how can you decide which pronoun to use second? Mentally ignore the first pronoun and see how the second pronoun alone sounds. For example, the sentence "The other team and us arrived" might possibly sound okay, but "Us arrived" sounds wrong.

Practice 1
Write a sentence using "He and (a pronoun)" as the subject.

_____

_____

Another confusing use of subject pronouns is in comparative sentences. Note the pronoun at the end of this sentence:

That TV-mother has more time than I.

How can a pronoun at the *end* of a sentence be a subject pronoun? The verb that goes with the subject pronoun is "understood," or left unsaid. The full sentence would read like this:

That TV-mother has more time than I do.

Also use this form of pronoun after any form of *to be* (*is, are, was, were, will be*):

It is *I* who have been accused.

It was *they* who swam through the flood.

Object Pronouns

The pronouns in the second column of the chart can receive an action.

The movie amused *us*.

The ball hit *her*.

The bus almost hit *them*.

Rodrigo worried his mother and *me*.

These pronouns can also work with prepositions (see pages 16–17 for a discussion of prepositions).

>   There is little difference between *her* and *us*.
>
>   Is my banana under *him*?

Again, when you have a compound object, decide which pronoun to use second by ignoring the first noun or pronoun. In the following sentence, should you end the sentence with *me* or *I*?

>   My aunt forgot to invite my sister and _____ .

Try saying the sentence without *my sister and*.

>   My aunt forgot to invite _____ .

I sounds incorrect now; in fact, *me* is the correct pronoun. You could also remember that *me* is the pronoun form that receives the action of your aunt's forgetting.

Practice 2
Write a sentence using a pronoun that receives the action.

_____

_____

Pronouns That Show Possession

The pronouns in the third column of the chart show possession.

>   *Our* chili won the cook-off.
>
>   Where is *my* wallet?
>
>   Which is *their* car?

Practice 3
Write a sentence using a possessive pronoun.

_____

_____

Copyright © 1992 by Harcourt Brace Jovanovich, Inc. All rights reserved.

Pronouns That Refer to the Subject

The pronouns in the last column of the chart always refer back to the subject of the clause.

> I can do it *myself*.
>
> She made the dress *herself*.
>
> They praised *themselves*.

Practice 4

Write a sentence using a pronoun that refers to the subject of the clause.

Exercises

Circle the correct pronoun(s) in the following sentences.

1. My sister and I are identical twins. Can you tell the difference between (she, her, herself) and (I, me, myself)?
2. Shavale and (I, me, myself) belong to the same sorority.
3. Jenn-Huei watches more golf on TV than (I, me, myself).
4. Who would like a re-test for this impossibly difficult grammar final? The other students and (I, me, myself) do.
5. When the librarian was asked who had been making all the noise, she pointed at Denise and (I, me, myself).
6. Don't bother reminding (we, us, ourselves) about the all-night pep rally. We hate football.
7. Thekla and (we, us, ourselves) worried so much over the auditions that (we, us, ourselves) were too sick to show up.
8. It may be (we, us, ourselves) who win the dorm contest, but it will be (they, them, themselves) who had the most fun competing.

9. Akiko is as passionately daring as (I, me, myself), so watch out when you see (we, us, ourselves) coming.
10. Have the council and (your, yourselves, you) agreed yet?
11. No words of discord ever passed between my boss and (I, myself, me).
12. Actually, no word at all passed between (we, ourselves, us).
13. Do (you, yourself) see that meek-looking fellow over there?
14. None of (we, us, ourselves) should ever judge by appearances.
15. (He, Him, Himself) and (I, me, myself) spent all last Saturday hang-gliding off the Indiana dunes.

■ Pronoun-Reference Problems

A pronoun usually refers to a person or an object that has been named somewhere else in the sentence or an earlier sentence. This person or object that the pronoun refers to is called the *antecedent*. When readers cannot know for certain which person or object the pronoun refers to, they become confused.

> Mary and Matilda drove together to the costume ball. The police pulled her over for speeding, but when the officer saw her dressed as Wonder Woman, he laughed. "I know, I know," he said. "You're racing off to save the world. Well, Wonder Woman, unless you have police escort, go a little more slowly." And he let her off.

Looking back over the paragraph, can you tell whether Mary or Matilda had the lucky break? Pronoun confusion occurs when two objects or people precede the pronoun, and you fail to make clear which object or person the pronoun refers to. You can avoid this mistake by restating the antecedent (the person or object that the pronoun refers to):

> The police pulled Mary over for speeding . . . .

Copyright © 1992 by Harcourt Brace Jovanovich, Inc. All rights reserved.

234 Chapter 12 Pronoun Agreement

Pronoun confusion can also occur when you fail to make certain that your pronouns agree with your antecedents. Notice how the circled pronouns refer back to the underlined antecedents:

> The woman hugged (her) daughter.
>
> The men started (their) hike.
>
> The elephant lifted (its) trunk.
>
> The giraffes craned (their) necks.
>
> Nick says that kids in grade school teased (him) about being Santa Claus.
>
> The stockbroker was offended when we didn't take (her) advice.

All those sentences demonstrate pronoun-antecedent agreement. Look at them again. They demonstrate the most basic rules about pronoun-antecedent agreement. A pronoun has to agree with its antecedent in two ways. Can you detect what those two ways are?

1. _____
2. _____

After learning to recognize exactly what the antecedent actually is, the trick is learning how to recognize the number and the gender of that antecedent.

The rules in this chapter are much like the rules in the previous chapter on subject-verb agreement. To make it easier for you to see the parallels, we follow the same outline as in the last chapter. But we first cover a problem that relates only to pronoun-antecedent questions.

☐ Sexist Language

Looking for gender agreement between pronouns and their antecedents raises the question of what to do about sexist language. Many years ago, writers could use male pronouns exclusively for any unknown singular person.

> A student should always read (his) notes right after class to refresh (his) memory.

Copyright © 1992 by Harcourt Brace Jovanovich, Inc. All rights reserved.

You should no longer use only the "generic" male pronoun. Unless you are speaking about antecedents that clearly must be one sex (as in "The father bounced his baby on his knee," or "The patient had her baby at midnight"), avoid using either male or female pronouns exclusively. If this is the standard, what pronouns should you use in the following sentence?

> A student should rewrite (his, her) notes before the test, especially if the professor tests from (his, her) lectures.

You can solve this dilemma in three ways. First, you may use the often awkward *his or her.*

> A student should rewrite (his or her) notes before the test, especially if the professor tests from (his or her) lectures.

As you can see, this less-than-ideal solution can quickly begin to sound repetitious. Some writers use *his/her* or *s/he*, but we recommend that you avoid these nonstandard usages.

Your second option is to alternate the pronouns, trying to use both masculine and feminine pronouns equally.

> A student should rewrite (his) notes before the test, especially if a professor tests from (her) lectures.

This is a slightly better solution than the awkward *he or she*, but to work well, it requires a series of statements where the reader can discern that you are balancing the usage.

In our opinion, the best solution is to eliminate the pronouns wherever possible and to make your antecedents plural everywhere else.

> Students should rewrite (their) notes before the test, especially if the professors test from lectures.

As you sort through this problem, try to remember that this is not just another whim of the grammar royalty. This is an issue of justice. For too long, using the so-called "generic" male pronoun has helped to keep women from seeing themselves in certain roles. Women can be and are professors. They are also students and scientists and athletes and Supreme Court justices and almost every other title we use to describe ourselves. Using nonsexist language allows women to see themselves in these roles.

Copyright © 1992 by Harcourt Brace Jovanovich, Inc. All rights reserved.

Questions Related to Sentence Structure

What About a Compound Antecedent?

A compound antecedent has two or more different objects or people. In this sentence, *owl* and *pussycat* form a compound antecedent:

> The owl and the pussycat cause quite a stir when (they) take their children out walking.

As long as you have two different things or people, you need a plural pronoun, for together these things or people equal more than one.

Practice 5

Combine the following sentences, using a compound subject.

1. The newscaster garbled her lines last night.
   The sportscaster garbled his lines last night.

Do Compound Antecedents Ever Take a Singular Pronoun?

> **When compound antecedents actually refer to one object or entity and thus are considered singular, these antecedents require singular pronouns.**

Look at this sentence:

> Without cayenne pepper, red beans and rice would lack (its) zing.

Because this sentence refers to a single dish (red beans and rice), the antecedent requires a singular pronoun. Compare that to the following sentence:

> Without salsa, nachos and refried beans would lack (their) zing.

Copyright © 1992 by Harcourt Brace Jovanovich, Inc. All rights reserved.

If this confuses you, try inserting *both* after the compound antecedent. If the sentence makes sense, you need a plural pronoun. If the insertion sounds odd, then you probably have a singular antecedent.

Other compound, yet singular, antecedents include the underlined portions of these sentences:

> My boss and friend knows how to make (her) innovative ideas work.
>
> On my birthday, my husband makes me bacon and eggs. (It) is my favorite breakfast.

What About *or, either/or,* and *neither/nor*?

In some sentences you will have two nouns linked by *or* or *nor*, but only one pronoun. If the nouns differ in number or gender, you have to know how to make the pronoun agree. Here's the rule:

> **Make your pronoun agree with the antecedent closer to the pronoun. If this closer antecedent is singular, make your pronoun singular; if plural, make your pronoun plural. The same rule applies to gender.**
>
> Either the cat or the dog has left (its) mark on my Persian carpet.
>
> Neither my father nor my brother spends (his) weekends watching football.
>
> Iris or Sue has forgotten to finish (her) experiment.
>
> Either the Martins or the Washingtons will share (their) produce with us.
>
> Neither my brother nor my parents are willing to change (their) mind.
>
> Neither my parents nor my brother is willing to change (his) mind.

From these last two examples, you can see that this construction can be awkward and misleading. Probably the brother's parents would be quite happy to change the brother's mind! Watch carefully for this confusion and rewrite the sentence. If possible, make the antecedent plural:

Clumsy	**Better**
Either the *fans* or the *band* will have to lower its volume.	Either the *fans* or the *band members* will have to lower their volume.

Because gender and number in these either/or constructions can cause confusion, be cautious. The best solution might be rewriting the sentence another way.

Clumsy	**Better**
If either Jack or Jill had been more careful, she would have gotten her water home safely.	If either Jack or Jill had been more careful, one of them would have gotten the water home safely.
Neither you nor I have gotten my license renewed.	You and I still need to get our licenses renewed.

Practice 6

Combine the sentences in each set as instructed.

1. Samantha will share her notes with Candace, who is sick.
   Alternatively, Angelita will do so.
   (Use *or*.)

2. Did the Harpers spend their vacation in Hawaii?
   Perhaps it was Ms. Delpino who did.
   (Use *or*.)

3. My grandparents did not help their children pay for college.
   My parents did not either.
   I will, however.
   (Use *neither/nor*.)

What About a Pronoun That Comes Before the Antecedent?

Look at the following sentences:

> (This) is my mother's prize <u>Pomeranian</u>.
> (They) are among the best rock <u>musicians</u> performing now.
> (Those) are the <u>tapes</u>, <u>disks</u>, and <u>records</u> that were stolen.

In each case, the pronoun is the first word and the antecedents come later. You must first find the antecedent, and then make certain that the pronoun agrees.

Practice 7

Complete the following sentences, providing nouns that agree with the pronouns (and the verbs).

1. They are _____

2. It is _____

Exercises

Read each sentence, underline the noun or nouns that the pronoun in question refers to, and circle the correct pronoun. Then identify each sentence with A, B, C, or D to show which pattern it illustrates. Finally, rewrite any sentence that sounds clumsy when written correctly.

- A *Compound antecedents:* Joe and Mary waved their banners.
- B *"Or" or "nor" with singular antecedents:* Jack or Jim forgot his backpack.
- C *"Or" or "nor" that refer to different antecedents* (male or female, singular or plural): Tony or his parents forgot their keys.
- D *Subject follows the verb* (V + S): These are the times when the bus stops here.

_____ 1. Either the class members or the professor will have to change (their, his or her) attitude if the class is to end the semester on a good note.

Copyright © 1992 by Harcourt Brace Jovanovich, Inc. All rights reserved.

240 Chapter 12 Pronoun Agreement

_____ 2. Anne Shirley of Green Gables fame and Laura Ingalls of the prairie (has, have) worked (her, their) way into my select group of favorite heroines.

_____ 3. Either Zane's overalls or Jim's shirt lost (its, their) buttons in the wash.

_____ 4. (That, Those) (is, are) the three most expensive sports cars on the market today.

_____ 5. Either my electric sleeping bag or the generator burned (itself, themselves) out last night because I woke up as stiff and cold as a flounder on ice.

_____ 6. (That, Those) (is, are) the highest hamburger, the frothiest milkshake, and the best-looking uniform I have ever seen.

_____ 7. Neither the fans nor the coach could hide (his, their) true feelings when the quarterback fumbled for the fifth time.

_____ 8. Either the Franklins or Mrs. Lu will have to lend me (her, their) car if I am going to make it to work tonight.

_____ 9. Every morning without fail, Egbert reminds Albertina that his jam or honey loses (its, their) flavor when spread over butter.

_____ 10. The dim lights and soft music outdid (itself, themselves)— Delora dozed off almost immediately.

▢ Pronoun Problems

Certain kinds of pronouns themselves may become the antecedent of another pronoun. In these cases agreement problems may come up.

Indefinite Pronouns

Indefinite pronouns include words that end with *-one, -body,* or *-thing. Each, neither,* and *either* are also indefinite pronouns.

anyone	anybody	anything
everyone	everybody	everything
someone	somebody	something
no one	nobody	nothing
none		

Indefinite pronouns that refer to only one person, body, or thing are considered singular and therefore require singular pronouns.

As long as you remember that these words refer to only one person, body, or thing—that is, they are all singular antecedents—then the singular pronoun will seem correct.

<u>Something</u> left ⟨its⟩ spiky paw prints all over the hood of my Alfa Romeo.

Again, when people (and thus gender) are involved, this construction seems awkward. When this happens, rewrite the sentence.

Clumsy	**Better**
Nobody loves me. Everybody hates me. I wish he or she would go eat worms.	Nobody loves me. Everybody hates me. I wish everyone would go eat worms.
Someone left his or her coat.	Someone left a coat.
How could he or she have forgotten it in this cold weather?	How could anyone forget a coat in this cold weather?

Practice 8

Combine the sentences in exercises 1 and 2, using possessive pronouns.

1. Each tree lost something in the fall.
   The something was leaves.
   The leaves belonged to the trees.

Copyright © 1992 by Harcourt Brace Jovanovich, Inc. All rights reserved.

2. Everybody needs to do something.
   They need to take off their shoes.
   (Begin this sentence with *Everybody*.)

   _____

   _____

Complete the following sentences, using a possessive pronoun in each.

3. Everyone should carry _____

   _____

4. Somebody didn't eat _____

   _____

5. Everything has lost _____

   _____

Indefinite Pronouns That Appear with a Modifier

Some indefinite pronouns may be either singular or plural, depending on the words—or modifiers—they appear with. Examples of such pronouns include *all, any, more, most, some*.

> **When pronouns appear with a modifier, the word they modify determines whether the pronoun requires singular or plural pronouns.**

In the following sentences, notice that *most* and *all* are followed by modifiers. The modifiers determine whether the pronoun is singular or plural.

> Most of the fans wave (their) hands when they see the TV monitor pointed toward them.
>
> Most of the crowd showed (its) appreciation for the speaker.
>
> All of the winter chill waited outside, biding (its) time until I emerged.
>
> All of the winter winds held (themselves) still, knowing I would have to come out.

Copyright © 1992 by Harcourt Brace Jovanovich, Inc. All rights reserved.

Practice 9

Combine the sentences in each set as instructed.

1. The team sacrificed something for the win.
   All the players sacrificed themselves.
   (Start this sentence with *All of the team.*)

   _____

   _____

2. The team members sacrificed something for the win.
   Each sacrificed herself.
   (Start this sentence with *All of the team members.*)

   _____

   _____

Relative Pronouns

Relative pronouns include *who, which,* and *that.* Sometimes these pronouns are the subject of a dependent clause. They may be either singular or plural. (See pages 28–29 for another description of these "double-duty dependent signals.")

For relative pronouns, singular antecedents require singular pronouns, and plural antecedents require plural pronouns.

In the following sentences, identify with brackets the dependent clause that follows the main subject of the sentence.

Stephanie, who spends (her) energy by noon, takes a long nap after lunch.

Cars that have colorful designs on (them) usually belong to flamboyant people.

In the first sentence, *who* requires a singular pronoun because *Stephanie* is a singular antecedent. In the second, *that* requires a plural pronoun because *cars* is a plural antecedent.

Copyright © 1992 by Harcourt Brace Jovanovich, Inc. All rights reserved.

Practice 10

The following sentences all have two pronouns. Draw an arrow from each pronoun—both the relative pronoun and the other pronoun—to its antecedent.

1. Carrie, who carries herself like a princess, began ballet lessons at age three.
2. The Patels, who bought their house only last year, had a fire last night.
3. The cat that has black tips on its ears is my neighbor's.
4. The cats that have brown tips on their ears are mine.

Combine the following sentences as instructed.

5. Mustafa had to walk home last night.
   He couldn't start a car.
   The car belonged to him.
   (Use a *who* clause.)

_____

_____

Exercises

Read each sentence, underline the noun or nouns that the pronoun in question refers to, and circle the correct verbs and pronouns. Then write A, B, or C to show the type of pronoun that is the antecedent in each case.

A	Indefinite pronouns: anyone, somebody, everything (and the like).
B	Indefinite pronouns that appear with a modifier: all, more, any, some, most.
C	Relative pronouns that serve as subject to a dependent clause: who, which, that.

_____ 1. None of the writing professors (has, have) had (his or her, their) own work published this year.

_____ 2. Lenore, who gained (her, their) fame in Edgar Allan Poe's poem, would have likely perished from a rejection note if her name had been Prunella.

_____ 3. Either of our fathers would be fantastic if (he, they) actually kept (his, their) promises.

4. Everybody (remembers, remember) a time when (his or her, their) parents had to break a promise, and everyone who has children knows who felt worse.

5. Most of the parade watchers forgot (his or her, their) cold hands and feet when the floats went by.

6. None of your papers (has, have) to be typed for me to accept (it, them), but (it, they) (has, have) to be legible.

7. All of the summer sunshine seemed to spill into my bedroom, spreading (its, their) golden glow like butter on my bed.

8. Anyone who (go, goes) to see Inspector Clouseau in the Pink Panther movies will be giving (his or her, their) humor a workout.

9. Niota spilled some of the pancake batter on her dress, and (it, they) stayed there all day.

10. Everything on my roommate's side of the room (is, are) in (its, their) own place—jammed under the bed, spilling out of the drawers, and lying all over the floor.

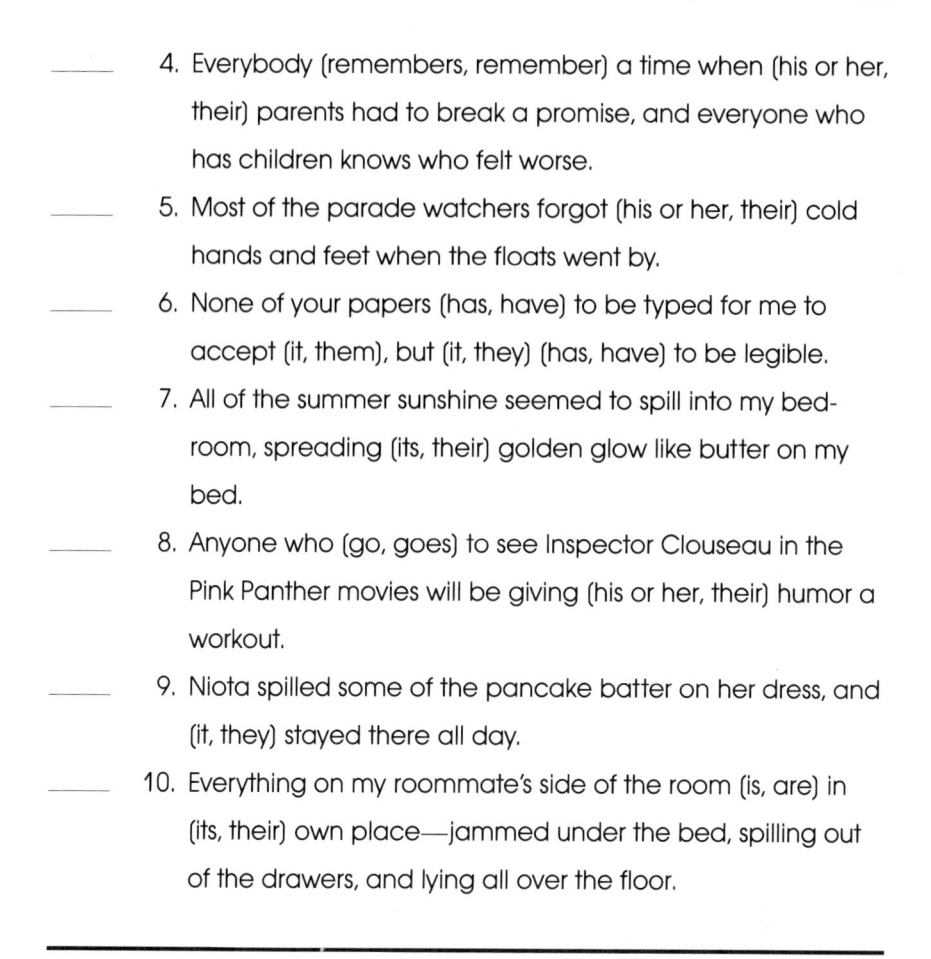

■ Other Special Cases

Collective Nouns As Antecedents

Collective nouns refer to groups of people or things, such as *family*, *team*, or *quartet*.

> **When collective nouns refer to a single entity as a whole, they require singular pronouns. When the emphasis is on the individual members, the pronoun may be plural.**

Only one <u>family</u> on our block puts (its) trash out in colored bags.

Copyright © 1992 by Harcourt Brace Jovanovich, Inc. All rights reserved.

The family draped their wet clothes on bushes in the sun.

Each team insisted its chances for winning exceeded the other team's.

The team carried their gloves, bats, and balls on the bus.

Quantities As Antecedents

When a word refers to a single quantity, even if the quantity has many parts, it requires a singular pronoun. It may require a plural pronoun if the separate parts are seen individually.

You can see the difference in these sentences:

The dozen eggs fell and spread their goopy slop all over my clean kitchen floor.

The second dozen eggs hung over the counter's edge; it threatened to follow the first.

The teacher gave the class two days extra to study for its test. This seemed generous to her.

Titles As Antecedents

A title requires a singular pronoun even if the word or words in the title are plural.

Look at the following examples:

The poem "The Bells," by Edgar Allan Poe, sounds like the objects it describes.

Many readers avoid The Brothers Karamazov because of its length and because of its unfamiliar Russian names.

Singular Nouns with Plural Forms

Words like *mathematics, economics, news,* and *aerobics* look plural but in fact are singular.

Words that have plural forms (ending in -s) but refer to singular entities require singular pronouns.

Copyright © 1992 by Harcourt Brace Jovanovich, Inc. All rights reserved.

Other Special Cases   247

I seldom watch the news. Its many stories of violence and death upset me too much.

Fiona refuses to do aerobics. She thinks it will be sweaty, strenuous, and dull.

Practice 11

Combine the sentences in each set.

1. The committee could not even agree on one thing.
   That one thing was a name.
   The name belonged to the committee.

   _____

   _____

2. The hundred dollars lost something.
   That something was appeal.
   The appeal belonged to the money.
   This happened when Ammon discovered that the money was stolen.

   _____

   _____

Exercises

Read each sentence, underline the noun or nouns that the pronoun in question refers to, and circle the correct pronoun. Then write A, B, C, or D to show the type of antecedent that determined your choice of pronoun.

  A *Collective nouns:* Groups seen as a unit require singular pronouns; seen as individuals, they may take plural pronouns.
  B *Quantities:* Single quantities require singular pronouns, unless their parts are seen individually.
  C *Titles:* Titles, even if plural in form, require singular pronouns.
  D *Singular words with -s at the end:* Singular nouns, even those ending in -s, require singular pronouns.

_____ 1. The jury couldn't come to any decision, so (it, they) had to be dismissed.

_____ 2. The family prides (itself, themselves) on dreaming up creative, low-cost vacations.

_____ 3. Cora hated mathematics last year, but she now finds that (it, they) (fascinates, fascinate) her.

Copyright © 1992 by Harcourt Brace Jovanovich, Inc. All rights reserved.

248 Chapter 12 Pronoun Agreement

_____ 4. The baseball team won (its, their) game last night, but with only one win all season, (it, they) probably won't win the championship.

_____ 5. Salinger's *Franny and Zooey* never achieved the acclaim of (its, their) author's earlier book, *The Catcher in the Rye*.

_____ 6. The ten dollars I made baby-sitting didn't last very long. (It, They) (wasn't, weren't) even enough to buy a large pizza.

_____ 7. The trio wore different colored sashes, but (it, they) all sang in the same dreadful monotone.

Paragraph Editing Practice

When editing your own paragraphs and essays, make sure that your readers can know, *without any doubt,* who or what each pronoun refers to. That is your first task: Can you tell for certain what each pronoun refers to? If not, use the antecedent again, rather than the pronoun, to make the sentence clearer.

Next, try to eliminate sexist language. Remember, it is usually better to make the antecedent plural than to use the awkward *he or she, his or her.*

Read through the following paragraphs, and then edit them, especially for pronoun-reference agreement, but also for subject-verb agreement, confusing construction, and sexist language.

A. At one time, a scientist or mathematician based their measurement standards on physical **artifacts** rather than on something that occurs naturally. The meter was defined by a piece of platinum shaped to be a meter long. When anyone wanted to have an accurate meter, they would have to take a stick and measure them against the platinum standard, which was stored in Paris, hoping as they did so they would not chip or wear down during travel. With this method, no one could be certain they had a precise meter. In the same way, a second of time was defined as a certain fraction of the solar year, another unreliable comparison because when the length of the year varied, the

Copyright © 1992 by Harcourt Brace Jovanovich, Inc. All rights reserved.

length of the second also varied. To improve on this system, the scientific community has recently changed their methods. Scientists now base most measurement standards on naturally occurring **phenomena** that can be determined in any location. They define the second as the time of transition between two levels of a cesium-133 atom, a measurement that remains standard the world over. They define the meter by how far light travels in a vacuum within a given time period. Because mass measures the amount of matter, however, and all matter is itself a physical artifact, the standard for the kilogram, the unit of mass, still depends on a physical artifact, another bar of platinum metal.

B. Most of the illegal drugs sold and consumed in the United States are first grown and manufactured in other countries, and then it is smuggled illegally across United States borders. While national outrage is justified, a broader historical perspective on international drug trafficking may encourage them. In the nineteenth century, the Chinese had similar drug problems, though with **opium**, not the currently more common cocaine, marijuana, or heroin. At that time, British merchants from the East India Company brought it from India to China, selling it openly. Chinese addicts, who flocked to opium dens, used the drug in ever-increasing numbers. The Chinese government responded by trying to halt the East India Company's drug shipments, but backed by England's superior military strength they refused to stop. The angry, frustrated Chinese waged war with England in 1839 but lost. The Chinese had to continue to allow the sale of opium. Neither the opium traffic nor the opium addiction stopped having their terrible effect on China. Like nineteenth-century China, the United States cannot stop drugs from crossing their borders. Unlike China, though, the United States does not have to allow drugs to be sold legally because of the source country's superior military strength.

Essay Editing Practice 1

Read through the following essay, and then edit it, watching especially for pronoun-reference problems (pronouns that do not agree with the words they stand for).

College Reasons

Eventually, every high school lecture on term papers reaches the same rule: "Always footnote what you take from another author." Hearing teachers equate **plagiarism** with stealing, students readily vow to give credit where credit is due. After all, who would seriously want to waste a **transgression** by stealing some stuffy author's ideas? In college, students should have better reasons for identifying sources than just to avoid the charge of plagiarism.

First, documentation gives a student's paper **credibility**. If first-year college students writing on **deforestation** claim that part of the Brazilian rain forest has lots of plant and animal life, who would pay attention? If instead she cites a *Time* article from September 1989 that says a four-square-mile plot of the Brazilian rain forest has 750 different kinds of trees, 125 kinds of mammals, 400 kinds of birds, 100 kinds of reptiles, and 60 kinds of amphibians, readers will not only believe her but will also begin to comprehend how much Earth's ecosystem loses with deforestation. Whatever students are arguing, whether the topic is AIDS or how to clean burned oatmeal off a cooking pot, they should try to find experts to support their case because these experts will help readers accept the argument. This added credibility is an important reason for college students to document sources.

When students document their sources, they are also helping their readers to pursue their own research. Anyone doing research on Toni Morrison's *Beloved* will benefit from using the reference list in one article to find other articles on Morrison that they can use. This reader might see an interesting fact about Morrison's background, become curious, check out where the author got the fact, and follow up by finding the original source, a book they may not have realized existed until reading the article. Students should therefore make it clear where they found their information, in order to help readers pursue their own research.

Given these reasons, what should students document? A student should document everything he gets from another writer, every idea, every fact, every statistic, every quote, every claim, everything. It might seem that almost every sentence in a student's research paper should be documented, but teachers expect this in their students' papers. Only a person writing on their own original research can write without documenting: the chemist reporting her **chromatography** studies, the English scholar explaining a new approach to George Herbert's *Temple*, and, yes, the college student describing his struggles to date the school's most glamorous cheerleader. Only one other kind of information needs no documentation: information that is such common knowledge that everyone knows it. If a definition is widely used, if a claim is widely accepted, if a statistic is widely known, then students may use the information without documenting it. No one needs a reference to believe that Golda Meir was prime minister of Israel, or that the sun is 93 million miles away, or that for every two marriages in America each year one divorce occurs.

Nevertheless, if someone gains this or any other information from a book, article, interview, video, or any reference material other than their own common knowledge, they must always proceed with caution. By not citing a source, they not only risk the charge of plagiarism, but they also lose credibility and block from readers an avenue for further research.

Writing Practice 1

Choose one of the following articles to read, and then follow the directions for writing an essay. Somewhere in your paper you will need to cite the article, including title, author, magazine, date of issue, and page numbers. Show clearly when you are taking information from someone else. Use tags such as, "The reviewer said" or "According to the authors of this article."

A. Find the *Time* cover story on deforestation cited in this paper ("Torching the Amazon," September 18, 1989, pp. 76–85). Take notes on these questions: What is deforestation, why is it a problem, and what are some examples of what people are trying to do about it? Then write an essay with an internal paragraph that answers each question. Make sure to show somewhere in your paper where you are getting your information. Remember to use quotation marks anytime you use more than four words in succession from another writer and to add the page number after every quotation.

B. Find the *Newsweek* review of Morrison's *Beloved* (Walter Clemons, "A Gravestone of Memories," September 28, 1987, p. 75). Using the review, take notes on the reviewer's summary of the novel and the reasons (at least according to the reviewer) why Morrison wrote the novel—her motives, inspirations, hopes for the novel. Then report whether the reviewer finds value in the novel (whether the reviewer thinks it is "good" or "bad"). Remember to use quotation marks anytime you use more than four words in succession and to add the page number after every quotation.

Essay Editing Practice 2

Read through the following essay, and then edit it, looking for both subject-verb agreement and pronoun-reference problems.

Who Are the Greatest?

They are all great. That needs to be said first. The issue here is relative greatness not absolute greatness. Who could fail to recognize that Magic Johnson, Marcus Allen, or Nolan Ryan excel? All sports, however, do not require the same level of athleticism. They are all great athletes, just not equally great.

Consider baseball first. The tip-off here is that baseball teams play two games in a row. If baseball were all that strenuous, how could players possibly do that? Apparently, the only team member who gets a workout is the pitcher, who plays one game every four days. The rest of the team sit around the dugout half the game, then stand around the field the other half. No wonder doubleheaders seem to require as much effort of these men as a double-dip ice-cream cone requires of a child. Surely no one, except perhaps their most ardent fans, believe that baseball players are the greatest of professional athletes.

So what about football? Again, the players sit around half the game, or at least they do if the teams are evenly matched. On some teams, the offensive squad has the productivity of a sterile chicken, which means it stays on the field for three quick downs and then leaves. If, in their turn, the defensive squad presents a wall of wet noodles to the opposition, the offense will sit out even longer than half the game. Even when the players are on the field, what do they do? The majority of the players grunt and shove and pull each other down, then jump on the **ensuing** pile. Strength, perhaps, these players need. But if anyone believes these men need stamina, he or she need to watch the players gasp into their oxygen masks after they run a measly eighty yards. To give their bruises and cracked ribs a chance to mend, these men rest for an entire week between games. After watching the players chug down the field, however, one could *also* conclude the football league schedule their games so far apart because the players' lungs need a chance to mend as well.

Of all professional athletes, basketball players demonstrate the most complete **prowess**. Their endurance astounds. One season Larry Bird and his fellow Celtics averaged over forty minutes a game, and he did not spend that time as baseball players would, behind second base watching the dandelions grow. During those forty minutes, the Celtics ran an average of 1,000 yards a quarter, or 4,000 yards a game. Football fans should remember that 4,000 yards equal forty lengths of the field, run almost continuously. That takes endurance. That takes condi-

Copyright © 1992 by Harcourt Brace Jovanovich, Inc. All rights reserved.

tioning. That takes stamina. NBA players have the strength, too. Just watch as Moses Malone or Akeem Olajuwon bully their way into the key or as Spud Webb jumps high enough to shoot the ball over men whose waist he hardly reaches. What about agility? Watch the master, Michael Jordan, make one of his impossible shots. He starts at the top of the key, jumps past all the other team's players and a few of his own men as well, changes direction mid-leap, and tosses the ball from an impossible angle somewhere way off to the left of the basket. To add accuracy to finesse, he even makes the shot.

Fans of another sport probably disagrees. They may explain how fast baseball players need to run or describe the incredible catches a wide receiver must make. In more ways than one, though, basketball players stand taller than anyone else among the giants of professional sports.

Writing Practice 2

Write an essay on one of the following topics.

A. Do you agree with this author? If you do, choose three basketball players that you believe demonstrate outstanding athletic prowess. Write an essay with an internal paragraph describing each player and why you believe that this player demonstrates athletic prowess.

B. If you disagree, choose three reasons why the author is wrong. Write an essay with an internal paragraph for each paragraph. You could alternatively explain in three internal paragraphs why your favorite sport requires more or different athletic skills than basketball does.

C. If you have no interest in sports, write an essay explaining three reasons why you find sports uninteresting, why Americans pay too much attention to spectator sports, or what your pet peeves against sports are.

D. Explain why exercise is better than watching sports. Choose three reasons, and write an essay with an internal paragraph on each.

Essay Editing Practice 3

Read through the following essay, and then edit it for any errors studied so far.

Genius by Design

Students don't necessarily have to study for good grades, at least not if students are willing to make certain adjustments in their lives. In the never-ending quest for an easy way to make good grades, statistics offer three suggestions. Any one of these could boost grades, but taken together, these would surely elevate ones grades to curve-breaking status. Imagine that!

First, because an "only" child does better academically than a child from a large family, statistics suggest that students eliminate their siblings. Because of certain laws of the land, however, and a basic tendency toward decency, students may feel uncomfortable eliminating their siblings permanently. Therefore, students could instead arrange privately for childless couples to adopt their siblings. A student who has so many brothers and sisters that the cost becomes prohibitive. This student could find one preferably rich couple to adopt him or her. An adoption costs a lot, of course, it seems only fair that the student seeking better grades should pay for them. This student will find it a small price to pay for the dramatically better grades they will receive.

Students could also boost their grades by learning to use both their left and right hands. Statistics now suggest that ambidextrous people are more creative and adaptable, two traits which will certainly come in handy when creating answers to unknown test questions. To become ambidextrous, students must simply deny themselves the use of their dominant hand. They could put an arm in a sling, or attach a hand to a belt. A student, who prefers more realism, could fall out of a tree or skid across the ice at the top of some stairs. However students do it, their grades will almost inevitably take an initial dip, due to the physical difficulty in writing with a strange hand. Nevertheless, unless statistics lie, in the long run grades will climb.

Finally, because people who wear glasses get better grades, the appearance of **myopia** will also give student's grades a boost. The more shortsighted students appear, the better, therefore, students should get themselves an extremely thick pair of glasses. Usually, teachers assume, that these students have harmed their eyes reading too many books. Teachers favor them, on many questionable answers, and without fail, these students' grades go up.

So if genius in fact seems increasingly impossible, statistics offer genius by design. Students need only become an only child, use both hands, and wear glasses. With these correct characteristics, students will be on their way toward the highest grades they can imagine. Of course, if all of these suggestions fails. The older methods of studying consistently and getting enough sleep have also been known to raise grades.

Writing Practice 3

Choose one of the following topics and write an essay with three internal paragraphs.

A. Make a list comparing small families and large families, including about five advantages and five disadvantages under each heading. Write an essay with an internal paragraph describing the advantages and disadvantages of small families, then a similar paragraph about large families, and finally a paragraph describing which kind of family you would choose for yourself and why.

B. How would your life change if you were suddenly deprived of a physical ability (walking or speaking, for example), a physical sense (hearing or seeing, for example), or the use of one hand, arm, or leg? Make a list of what would change and a list of what would not change. Then write an essay with three internal paragraphs: one on what would change, one on what would not change, and one on how you would want people to treat you.

Copyright © 1992 by Harcourt Brace Jovanovich, Inc. All rights reserved.

C. Why does a person read? List things a person might read in a typical day and then group these items into three categories (for example, for personal information, entertainment, education, job advancement, and so forth). Choose three reasons for reading and write an essay with three internal paragraphs explaining why a person reads.

Misused Words: who/whom

Use *who* as the subject of a clause, the thing in a sentence that does something.

> *Who* wants to come with me?
>
> The little girl, *who* looks like Shirley Temple, probably has a perm.

Use *whom* as the object; it receives the action of a sentence and is also used with prepositions.

> You buried *whom* in the chocolate pudding?
>
> I saw the dancers, each one of *whom* had a sleek shape.

In brief, *who* does the action, and *whom* receives the action. Insert either *who* or *whom* in the following sentences, asking yourself for each sentence, Does this person or thing *do* the action (use *who*) or receive the action (use *whom*)?

1. The house was full of students _____ Yusuf had invited.
2. The house was full of students _____ ate like weight lifters.
3. They auditioned forty people, _____ hoped to get parts.
4. They auditioned forty people, only two of _____ will receive parts.
5. Lionel knows _____ the professor will pass.
6. Lionel knows _____ deserves to pass.
7. _____ did the golf ball hit?
8. _____ hit the ball?

Copyright © 1992 by Harcourt Brace Jovanovich, Inc. All rights reserved.

9. _____ kissed the little girl?
10. _____ did the Santa pick up?

Review Exercises

Complete the following sentences with the correct pronoun.

1. In spite of working hard, the wrestling team has lost all _____ matches.
2. Neither of the two men has ever gotten over losing _____ car in the accident.
3. Luther and Joel carried _____ furniture up four flights of stairs.
4. Celeste, Golene, or Linda has left _____ paper on the printer.
5. My sister and _____ wish _____ mother would stop wearing a punk hairdo.
6. None of the women will admit that _____ dropped _____ hairnet in the potato soup.
7. That little girl put on her makeup more artistically than _____ usually do.
8. Judging from our waistlines, my mother cooked too well for my brother and _____ .
9. The second squad won _____ scrimmage today against the starters.
10. Every student should rewrite _____ first draft.
11. Either the ginger jar or the porcelain vase will find _____ on my mantle tomorrow.
12. The rose lost _____ last petal yesterday.

Other Special Cases   259

Dictionary Practice

Look up the words in bold print and provide a brief definition for each word as it appears in the sentence.

1. Finally, because people who wear glasses get better grades, the appearance of **myopia** will also give students' grades a boost.

    myopia: _____

2. Scientists now base most measurement standards on naturally occurring **phenomena** that can be determined in any location.

    phenomenon: _____

3. Hearing teachers equate **plagiarism** with stealing, students readily vow to give credit where credit is due.

    plagiarism: _____

Match the following words with their brief definitions.

_____   4. artifact (p. 248)   a. addictive narcotic drug

_____   5. credible (p. 250)   b. exceptional ability

_____   6. chromatography (p. 251)   c. object or tool made by humans

_____   7. deforest (p. 250)   d. to result or follow from something

_____   8. ensue (p. 253)   e. believable

_____   9. opium (p. 249)   f. to sin; to go over a limit

_____ 10. prowess (p. 253)   g. a way of separating mixtures for scientific study

_____ 11. transgress (p. 250)   h. to clear away forests

Copyright © 1992 by Harcourt Brace Jovanovich, Inc. All rights reserved.

CHAPTER **13**

Shift in Person

When we write we can choose any of three different ways to speak about the things and people in our writing. If we want to be personal and include ourselves in our writing, using "I" frequently, we can use the *first person*. If we want to speak directly to our readers, calling them "you," we can use the *second person*. If we want to speak impersonally, as an objective bystander removed from the action, we can use the *third person*.

What do these "first," "second," and "third persons" refer to? To understand this, think of yourself standing in a wide plaza with imaginary circles surrounding you. You are in the middle, standing in the first circle. Your perspective begins with yourself. When you speak about yourself, you are using first person. The next circle out, the second circle, includes your friend standing beside you. When you speak *to* this person, you are using second person. Then you look out toward the classmates sitting on the grass at the far edge of the plaza, in the third circle. When you speak *about* those people, you are using third person. In summary:

First person Pronouns	Talking about yourself *I, me, my, myself* *we, our, ourselves*
Second person Pronouns	Talking to someone *you, your, yourself*
Third person Pronouns	Talking about someone *she, her, hers, herself* *he, him, his, himself* *it, its, itself* *they, them, their, themselves*

Which "person" you use will depend on the type of writing you are doing. What's important is to keep the same perspective throughout a piece of writing. When you make mistakes in this area, you will probably do so by shifting from speaking *about* other people ("They did"), to speaking *to* other people ("You did"), to speaking about yourself ("I did").

> **Try to maintain your perspective as you write, not shifting from one person to another.**

This chapter describes the three "persons" that we use in writing and offers some practice in maintaining the same person.

☐ First-Person Perspective

First-person perspective, remember, means talking about yourself or from your own point of view. First-person perspective can make writing personal, so it is a useful quality for some kinds of writing. Letters are written using the first person, and so are some personal essays.

Practice 1

1. Which of the following pronouns might you use when talking about yourself? Circle them.

   I   me   them   you   its   their   we   your   our   my   they

For sentences 2–5, put a check by those that are written from a first-person perspective.

_____ 2. My father wears the most outlandish slippers.

_____ 3. California electric rays deliver powerful electrical shocks to anything that touches them.

_____ 4. Unlike us, robots cannot decipher the meanings behind our words.

_____ 5. The rat-a-tat of a snare drum makes me want to march.

Rewrite sentences 6–10 using a first-person perspective.

6. Djemma had never been to a horse race or ridden a horse.

_____

_____

Copyright © 1992 by Harcourt Brace Jovanovich, Inc. All rights reserved.

7. One day she picked up a book by Dick Francis.

8. It was one of the most exciting and clever mysteries she had read.

9. Now she owns all the books by this retired jockey.

10. What is more, Djemma never misses a Grand National steeplechase on TV.

11. Write two sentences using the first-person perspective.
    a. _____
    b. _____

The following paragraph has been written as if the writer is speaking to you, the reader. Rewrite it using the first person, so that the writer is speaking about himself or herself.

12. Some dreams you would like to have over and over again. For instance, sometimes you dream that you are hungry and suddenly find yourself at a banquet, in your honor, of course. Table after table is piled high with every imaginable delicacy. Floating to a table, you eat and eat, without the least twinge of shame or embarrassment. It's no coincidence that you wake to the smell of Dad's famous blueberry pancakes or bacon and eggs. Encouraged by the dream, the food tastes better than ever, and you let yourself have seconds.

☐ Second-Person Perspective

Second-person perspective means you are talking to someone, so it can be very helpful for instruction or explanation. However, the single most common "person problem" that you will probably have is using "you" when you are speaking about people generally. Use "you" *only* when you are actually speaking to your readers, instructing them, advising them, or proposing as an example an experience they may have had.

In the following sentences, the writer is not talking *to* the reader. The writer is talking about people in general—and only some people at that. Notice the underlined pronouns:

> Almost all high school students have had someone offer them drugs. You go to school one day, speak to someone you thought you knew, and unexpectedly that person pulls out a quarter-gram of cocaine or a bag of marijuana.

If this is part of a college composition, imagine how this sounds to the teacher. No, the teacher does not go to school one day, the teacher does not have this friend, and the teacher is not offered cocaine. The writer here is speaking about high school students in general, not the reader of the essay. The writer should have continued talking about students, using the third person.

> Almost all high school students have had someone offer them drugs. They go to school one day, speak to someone they thought they knew, and unexpectedly that person pulls out a quarter-gram of cocaine or a bag of marijuana.

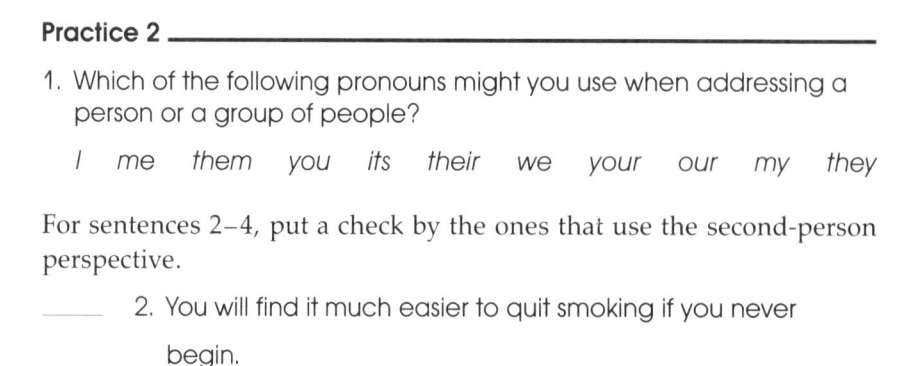

Practice 2

1. Which of the following pronouns might you use when addressing a person or a group of people?

    I   me   them   you   its   their   we   your   our   my   they

For sentences 2–4, put a check by the ones that use the second-person perspective.

_____ 2. You will find it much easier to quit smoking if you never begin.

Second-Person Perspective   265

_____ 3. Scandinavian furniture conveys a grace through its gently curving lines and elegantly pale wood.

_____ 4. Come dance the Locomotion with me.

5. Write two sentences using the second-person perspective.

   a. _____

   b. _____

In sentences 6–8, replace the generalized "you" with the person or people the writer actually means (what word describes people who go home from college?) and with appropriate pronouns.

6. When you go home from college, you often find that your parents want you to revert back to being a high-schooler.

7. Your father still wants to know where you are going all the time.

8. Your mother expects to keep up on your homework assignments.

Edit the following paragraph, changing it from third person (speaking *about* the person who should train his or her cat) to second person (speaking directly *to* the person).

9.   When a person buys a cat, the first task is to decide what rules the cat will have to follow. These might include staying off the kitchen counters, using the litter box, sleeping in its own bed, and avoiding a date. To train a cat, the owner must begin a system of rewards and punishment. For a reward, cats love the juice of a can of tuna, a gentle scratch on the back or under the chin, or a five-minute free spree in the refrigerator. For punishment, cats hate hugs and kisses, big pink bows, and most of all having to watch Morris eat all the cat food. Timely delivery of these rewards and punishments has been known to have a momentary effect on cats. Unfortunately, because cats will purposely forget everything their owners teach them, owners must resign themselves to carrying this training on indefinitely. Owners could alternatively give in and let the cats train *them*.

Copyright © 1992 by Harcourt Brace Jovanovich, Inc. All rights reserved.

▢ Third-Person Perspective

In any formal writing, which includes most of the papers you write in college, you should maintain a third-person perspective. This can be hard to do.

Shifting from first-person to third-person requires seeing events from a general perspective—from outside those events rather than from inside them. If you have trouble understanding this, perhaps it would help to imagine yourself watching a video of yourself, your family life, your experiences in high school, your volunteer work. Then, in your writing, you can refer to the person on the imaginary video rather than to yourself.

Following are some tactics you can use when changing your perspective from first to third person.

Use general terms:

I	some people, college students, or whatever description applies to the situation (athletes, writers, dorm residents, and so on)
my family	families, some families
I can never find a pen when I need one.	Some people can never find a pen when they need one.

Use names:

my dad	Mr. Beeghly, Joe Beeghly
my family	the Beeghlys
My father is a building supervisor.	Ruth's father (or Mr. Beeghly) is a building supervisor.

Repeat antecedents to avoid pronoun confusion:

When my brother and I go home, he eats and I sleep.	When he and his brother go home, he sleeps and his brother eats.

Copyright © 1992 by Harcourt Brace Jovanovich, Inc. All rights reserved.

Restate opinions as questions or conclusions:

I am surprised anyone could eat that.	Who could eat that?
I find this incredible.	This is incredible.

As for the practice of accomplishing this shift from first- to third-person perspective by replacing "I" with "one," we don't recommend it. Using "one" becomes an awkward and ineffective way to sidestep the problem, an ugly bandage that hides nothing. Who ever talks that way? More than that, how many people even write that way?

Practice 3

1. Which of the following pronouns would you use when talking *about* other people or things?

    I   me   them   you   its   their   we   your   our   my   they

For sentences 2–7, put a check mark by the ones that use a third-person perspective. Rewrite the first- or second-person sentences using the third person.

_____ 2. By the time Mozart was five, at an age when most children feel proud to color in the lines, he had begun composing music.

_____ 3. Like so many child stars, though, as Mozart grew older fewer people came to hear him play.

_____ 4. I think his *A Little Night Music* shows his lighter side.

_____ 5. In *Requiem Mass,* though, with its sad and noble character, you can hear his serious side.

268 Chapter 13 Shift in Person

_____ 6. I am most surprised at how quickly he wrote music.

_____ 7. He wrote the overture to *Don Giovanni* only two days before this opera was first performed.

For practice in switching from first- to third-person, change sentences 8–11 from first-person to third-person perspective. To do so, you may have to change the verb tense as well as the subject.

8. My children like to use stickers to decorate my cans.

9. I have collected a whole row of colorful canisters with holiday themes.

10. After high school, I took two years off for military service.

11. I believe that Halloween has become too dangerous to celebrate.

Edit the following paragraph, changing it from the first-person perspective to a more formal third-person perspective. As you do so, make sure your reader will be able to keep the women straight.

12.   My mother, Clara, who always regretted our last name Stubbs, insisted I be named Celeste. She never told my father, who was very proud of our family name, that she didn't like Stubbs, but she would happily have remained Clara Carrol for life. In those days, that would have meant staying single, so my mother made the ultimate marital sacrifice and became Clara Stubbs. When my sister

Copyright © 1992 by Harcourt Brace Jovanovich, Inc. All rights reserved.

and I were born, however, hoping to compensate for the unfortunate surname, she fought my father's simple tastes and named us Adrienne and Celeste. Someday, she hoped, we would marry into a beautiful name. Poor Mother—I married a handsome Frenchman with a name to match, Philippe Cecile, yet out of principle and because, like Dad, I see nothing wrong with Stubbs, I have proudly kept my maiden name. Adrienne, too, has disappointed our mother by finally marrying her tax accountant, Herman Schweklesburger. Dashing Mother's last hope, my **wayward** sister has become Ms. Adrienne Stubbs-Schweklesburger. Although Mother **bemoans** our terrible fate, loudly and often, we know she has become as loyal to her own name as the man who once asked her to share it. After all, Dad died ten years ago, and she is still Clara Stubbs.

Paragraph Editing Practice

The following paragraphs contain inappropriate shifts from one person to another. First read the paragraphs; then write in the blank which perspective you think each paragraph should be written from, and edit to eliminate the shifts.

> *First-person:* Talking about yourself, using *I, me, we, our,* and so forth.
> *Second-person:* Talking to someone else, using *you, your, yourself.*
> *Third-person:* Talking about someone else, using *she, they, it, his,* and so forth.

A. Perspective: _____

Humans can dive less than 100 feet down before they run out of oxygen. Without a fresh supply of oxygen our brains stop, and when your brain stops, you stop. Weddell seals, which live beneath the Antarctic ice, sometimes go down as deep as 2,000 feet. You might wonder how they can do this. First, they have a smaller brain, about a third as big as ours. Second, they have ten times more blood than humans do. With a brain that needs less blood and a body that has more blood, these seals can maintain their supply of usable oxygen much longer. This allows them to stay underwater and go much deeper than we can.

B. Perspective: _____

To improve your textbook reading, take a few minutes before beginning a chapter to preview it so that you can have some idea where the chapter is heading. As you look ahead through the chapter, jot down the main headings. Since most textbooks put major division headings in bold print, these divisions should be fairly easy for students to detect. Next, jot down a few preliminary questions that you might have, anything you might be wondering about. This may pique students' curiosity and motivate them to read with more interest. These two steps take only a few moments but can make a big difference in what students get out of their reading.

C. Perspective: _____

In the Middle Ages, diners ate their plates. You were given a large slab of thick bread, called a trencher, on which you could put pieces of meat or vegetables. The bread soaked up the juices and gave a place for diners to cut their food. Sometimes the bread was so stale that you could not eat it without breaking your teeth. Maybe that sensation of biting into rock gave someone the idea of making plates out of more permanent materials, such as wood or crockery.

D. Perspective: _____

My family loves to play Pit, the card game about a grain exchange. In this game, you try to corner a market on barley, corn, or other commodities. The game gets frantic as players trade cards. Although some people allow the winner to yell "Pit" when he or she has collected all of a set, we always play with spoons instead. You put a spoon for every person except one in the middle of the table. When one of us corners the market, he or she secretly grabs a spoon and

Copyright © 1992 by Harcourt Brace Jovanovich, Inc. All rights reserved.

continues trading. Eventually you realize a spoon is missing and grab one. Soon everyone is pouncing. Whoever is left without a spoon (usually my father) loses the round.

E. Perspective: _____

At a time when we marvel at Bo Jackson for excelling at both pro-football and pro-baseball, we sports fans should remember another amazing athlete. In college this athlete was an All-American basketball player for three years, and then, in the 1932 Olympics, set world records in the 80-meter hurdles and the javelin throw. This athlete also excelled in baseball, football, tennis, and swimming, and even tried boxing. Later this athlete won lasting fame as a champion golfer, winning seventeen major tournaments in a row. Do you recognize this athlete? She was Associated Press's Woman Athlete of the first half of the twentieth century, Babe Didrickson.

F. Perspective: _____

Few people realize how very small the solid part of Saturn is. They hear about its rings, but no one tells you that most of what you see in pictures of Saturn is really hydrogen and helium. In pictures, viewers actually see Saturn's atmosphere, not its mass. Tiny amounts of other substances in Saturn's atmosphere form clouds of many colors, the yellows and tans and golds that we see. The solid core, much smaller than we realize, hides under these vivid clouds.

G. Perspective: _____

I spent my early years living in a small village in central India. The town clustered around three bends in the road, the district police station sitting high atop a hill at one corner and the town post office and central well nestling into the other one. Around the next bend stood a large open field, quiet most of the week until Thursday, the day of the village bazaar. Early in the morning, before the sun had risen, you could hear a caravan of **bullock** carts creaking down the road in front of our house, about a mile out of town, heading toward the bazaar grounds. If you were lucky, you could convince your mother to let you follow them later that morning, hopping onto a passing bullock cart and riding into town in humble, but lazy fashion. I loved to wander among the tents, gazing at the brightly colored Indian garments called *saris,* gawking at the scorpion keepers, fingering the glistening glass bracelets, and drooling at the *jalabies, samosas,* and spicy chick-pea snacks. The whole extravaganza would be gone by the next day, the vendors packing up that evening and traveling by night to the next village or township down the road. Your only **consolation** was knowing they would be back again, and maybe next week your mother would slip some Indian money into your hand to spend.

Essay Editing Practice 1

As you will see, the following essay offers advice to would-be baby-sitters, so it probably works best with a second-person perspective. Edit the essay to make the perspective consistent. Remember that with the second person, writers often use commands (with the subject understood) rather than "you should." Watch for misused words.

Money in the Bank

Everyone needs money, especially college students, and baby-sitting offers an easy way to earn it. Or, rather, baby-sitting *can* offer an easy way. Baby-sitting can also make *Friday the 13th* sound like a dull movie. If you want to baby-sit, consider a few tactics to make the job easier.

First, choose your hours wisely: Baby-sit when the children aren't home. As strange as it sounds, parents whom are out of town sometimes want someone around the house in case the school calls with an emergency. These jobs are few indeed, but you can always hope. Grab such a job, if offered. The next best choice is to sit when the children are sleeping during their afternoon nap or late at night. Sitters should always demand extra pay if the parents stay out passed eleven. For some reason, parents seem willing to pay this bonus, though any experienced sitter knows it is the hours from six to eight in the evening that really deserve combat pay.

Next, sitters should never listen when children describe their parents' rules. So what if their mother lets them make their own peanut butter and honey sandwiches? Sitters are not their mother and consequently lack the tender heart necessary to clean the honey off the kitchen curtains, cabinets, toaster, microwave, silverware drawer, refrigerator handle, milk jug, and floor. Besides, while sitters are giving one child a bath to clean the honey off that child's hair, they cannot know what the rest of the children are doing.

This brings up the next rule. Never let children out of your sight. To keep track of the children, sitters should require periodic sound-offs, barricade the doors to keep the children in the room with them, or bribe them with candy to tattle if one wanders off. A sitter's motto must always be, "Out of sight is out of control!" Burdened with habitual runaways, sitters can always keep their wee chicks under their wings with this foolproof method: They can make some popcorn. The hot, buttered aroma will waft through the house and invade the farthest hiding hole, drawing the children like ants at a picnic. As long as you hold the popcorn, the children will hold onto you. The method is foolproof.

There they are: three simple rules for baby-sitting. Fortunately, because these baby-sitting jobs abound, sitters can readily forget the hellions they have just left and look forward instead to the next, bound-to-be-perfect baby-sitting job, the one where the child goes to sleep at 6 in the evening and where the parents' last words are, "Help yourself to the Häagen Dazs!"

Copyright © 1992 by Harcourt Brace Jovanovich, Inc. All rights reserved.

Writing Practice 1

Choose one of the following topics to write on.

A. Recount an interesting experience you have had with children, giving the context in the first paragraph and the story in the next two paragraphs. Be complete enough to make the story interesting.

B. Think about the employers you have had, and jot down some ideas about what makes an employer a "good" one. Then, write an essay with three internal paragraphs in which you discuss three characteristics of a good employer. Be sure to include examples, illustrations, and other details.

C. Think about the different types of supervisors a person can have at work, such as friendly, remote, helpful, mean, perfectionist, or practical. Make a list of information for each type, describing how this supervisor acts and how an employee can recognize this type, plus tips on dealing with this type of person. Then write a short essay.

Essay Editing Practice 2

Read through the following essay for content, and then go back through it editing any errors you find.

Different Characters

At first glance, Christopher Columbus and Jacques Marquette seem to have much in common. Both explored new worlds. Columbus sailing across the Atlantic to explore the Caribbean and Marquette sailing down the Mississippi to explore the North American interior. Both showed great courage. Columbus had to contend with stories of fierce monsters waiting at the edge of the world, and Marquette had to face stories of devils with wings. Who could walk on the waters of the Mississippi and kill anyone who came near. Courageous explorers both these men were, but there the similarities end.

Columbus and Marquette differed greatly in their reasons for setting off into the unknown every school child knows that Columbus sought a new route to the rich bounties of the Orient. When the Caribbean Islands and then Mexico itself halted his progress to this wealth greed continued to motivate him, leading him to abuse the people of the new world, sometimes outrageously. Marquette, on the other hand, explored new worlds for a completely different reason. When he set off to explore the Mississippi, he did so in an effort to reach the previously unknown inland tribes, the Illinois, Chickasaw, Arkansas, and others, with the news of his God, the Great Manitou, and with the benefits of his teaching. As a Jesuit priest, he went among the Native Americans so that he could accomplish one great purpose: to serve God by serving the human race.

The two men, therefore differed as well in their religious commitments. Although outwardly religious, Columbus shared little of Marquette's true piety. Unable to return to Queen Isabella and King Ferdinand with the fabled gold, Columbus took hundreds of prisoners and delivered these men and women up as slaves. Revealing his spiritual blindness, he wrote: "Let us in the name of the Holy Trinity go on sending all the slaves that can be sold." Ambition and greed seemed to dominate Columbus's life, and in many ways, it seems that he served gold as his god. Marquette, on the other hand, sustained his devotion to God through years of poverty with uncertain provisions, discouragement from uncommitted converts, and sickness incurred while caring for others. While Marquettes devotion influenced him to live a life of sacrifice, Columbus devotion influenced him to inflict cruelty upon the people he found.

Foiled in his attempts to find the spice route and desperate to make good on his promise of gold, Columbus ordered all persons fourteen and older to deliver up a certain quantity of gold, in return you received a copper coin to wear around your neck. Without this coin, everyone over fourteen had their hands cut off, most bleeding to death. Unable to fight against the Spaniards' superior military strength, many

Copyright © 1992 by Harcourt Brace Jovanovich, Inc. All rights reserved.

natives killed their children and themselves. According to one writer, within two years "half of the 250,000 Indians on Haiti were dead."[1] Even the most distinguished writer on Columbus, Samuel Eliot Morison, admits that Columbus's policies resulted in complete genocide.[2]

So Columbus and Marquette differed sharply in their treatment of the men and women who inhabited the new worlds they explored. Columbus saw them as a commodity to be used for his own gain, but Marquette saw them as individuals, equal in humanity to himself. According to one story told about Marquette, when a traveling companion exclaimed about being one of the first people to explore the Mississippi regions, Marquette scolded him. "My dear friend, have not the Indians come long before us?" So at a time when people considered early Americans to be "savages," at a time when Marquette's own companion excluded them from the company of "people," Marquette stood apart and saw the Americans not only as human, but as worthy of service. Marquette didn't take from the people he found; he gave to them instead—his knowledge of farming health practices and nutrition; his food and other provisions; and even his protection. In return, the people welcomed their Black Robe, as they called him.

Both men have received great honor in the United States, with monuments, universities, and even cities named after each. Only Columbus, however, has a national holiday named for him. Unfortunately, given the greed and materialism that seems to have become acceptable in our country in recent years, it is hardly surprising and probably fitting that Columbus receives the greater honor.

---

[1] Howard Zinn, *A People's History of the United States* (New York: Harper & Row, 1980), p. 2.
[2] Samuel Eliot Morison, *Christopher Columbus, Mariner* (Boston: Little, Brown, 1954).

Copyright © 1992 by Harcourt Brace Jovanovich, Inc. All rights reserved.

Writing Practice 2

Choose one of the following topics to write about.

A. Some people believe that we now live in an extremely materialistic society. Things, possessions, and money mean more to us, these people say, than people and relationships. Do you agree with this? Jot down reasons why you agree or disagree, and then choose three of these reasons. For each, give two or three examples that support your reason. Then use these notes to write an essay with three internal paragraphs on whether we do or do not live in a materialistic society.

B. Marquette and Columbus demonstrated different character traits. Although both men were intelligent and brave, Marquette's traits—service, sacrifice, and generosity—stand at odds with Columbus's—greed, self-service, and selfishness. What character traits do you think mark a "good" person and why? List five or six traits, such as those seen in Marquette or others, and then choose three to write about. Before beginning, however, expand your definition of each trait by listing specific examples of how this trait might be demonstrated in a person's life. Then write a paper describing a "good" person, covering one character trait and its examples in each of three internal paragraphs.

C. Most people now agree that slavery is wrong. List reasons that justify this position (for example, slavery is morally wrong, economically wrong, and politically wrong). Add specific examples or illustrations explaining each reason and write a short essay.

Misused Words: their/there/they're

Use *their* to show that something belongs to *them*. *Their* shows possession.

> Which is *their* scuba equipment?

Use *there* to show direction or to point out something.

> The oxygen tanks are over *there*.
>
> *There* are flippers and face masks, too.

Copyright © 1992 by Harcourt Brace Jovanovich, Inc. All rights reserved.

Use the contraction *they're* to take the place of *they are*.

> Better hide—*they're* coming now.

Insert *their, there,* or *they're* in the following sentences.

1. I have put up with _____ nonsense too long.
2. _____ are a few things a person shouldn't have to take.
3. _____ going to wish they had eased up a lot sooner.
4. In fact, if those cats don't start using _____ litter box soon, it's going to be a cold night in the snow for them.
5. I just wish I could get _____ sad eyes out of my mind.
6. I guess _____ going to be warming my bed one night longer at least.

Review Exercises

Insert commas and apostrophes in sentences 1–6.

1. In years past college cafeterias seemed to operate under one and only one guiding principle.
2. They chose the easiest cheapest menus and then served these menus as often as possible.
3. Students rarely asked "Whats for dinner?"
4. It was always the same old spaghetti casserole chicken à la king or tuna noodle blend.
5. Now however cafeterias have bowed to students tastes for lighter foods.
6. Almost all food services offer a salad bar and many offer other low-calorie options.

Identify sentences 7–13 with either F for sentence fragment, CS for comma splice, RO for run-on, or OK for correct.

_____ 7. At the same time that food services cater to students with lighter tastes.

_____ 8. They also cater to students with fast-food tastes.

_____ 9. Such as for hamburgers, french fries, milk shakes, and other junk fare.

_____ 10. So in today's college cafeterias, some students eat healthier foods than students ten years ago did others eat unhealthier fare.

_____ 11. The food services organizations, however, can at least say they are providing both options.

_____ 12. Food services do many things better now, however, none has managed to duplicate college students' favorite foodstuff.

_____ 13. No food service will ever be able to match the quality of a pizza delivered late at night, piping hot and steaming, I am sure of it.

Dictionary Practice

Match the following words with their brief definitions.

_____ 1. bemoan (p. 269)   a. comfort

_____ 2. bullock (p. 271)   b. to convey grief or displeasure

_____ 3. consolation (p. 272) c. contrary

_____ 4. wayward (p. 269)   d. a young bull; a steer

CHAPTER **14**

Shift in Verb Tense

In English, verbs give us a sense of when something is happening. The problem that you will probably have with verb tense is switching randomly from one tense to another.

Try to maintain a consistent stance toward time without shifting randomly from one tense to another.

The first verb you use in a piece of writing will determine the reference point for all the rest of your verbs. If you write about the past, usually you will use past tense, and if you write about what is happening now, you will use the present tense. Whatever tense you choose, you will need to maintain a consistent stance toward time, using past tense for events in the past, present tense for the present, and so forth. This chapter describes your options.

▣ Present Tense

If you begin writing in the present tense, you should choose your verb tenses to reflect the time in relation to that present tense.

1. *Present, and has been happening for a while:* I have been eating. She has been eating. They have been eating.
2. *Present:* I eat. She eats. They eat.
3. *Present, but only a possibility:* If I am eating . . . If she is eating . . . If they are eating . . .
4. *Present, but contrary to fact:* If I were eating . . . If she were eating . . . If they were eating . . .
5. *Present, and still happening:* I am eating. She is eating. They are eating.

Practice 1

In the following paragraph, the writer uses present tense to communicate her ongoing preference for watching videos at home. Underline the complete verbs and write the number from the list to tell which tense each verb illustrates. The first one has been done as an example.

1. I <u>enjoy</u>² watching most movies at home on my VCR. If I am sitting at home, I can make my own popcorn and stop and start the movie at will. In fact, I have been planning to rent some videos for this weekend. Occasionally, however, a movie comes out that I want to see in the theater. No small screen can do justice to the sweeping landscapes of *The Man from Snowy River* or *Out of Africa*. If I were rich, I would have a real theater in my mansion. Instead, I insist upon watching movies such as these in the theater.

Rewrite sentences 2–7 in the present tense.

2. The student's first speech was an excruciating experience.

3. As he rose, he looked pale green, like watery pea soup.

4. The hand holding his notes shook violently.

5. He had to clear his voice three times before any sound emerged.

6. I was the only person more frightened than he was.

7. I had to go next.

Edit the following paragraph so that it reflects a future-tense perspective.

6. Next week, I go to Chicago to spend the weekend with my sister. We go to the Chicago Symphony on Friday evening and then eat a late-night dinner at Gino's Pizza. The next morning, after sleeping in late, we go down to Michigan Avenue and fantasize about having Cher's bank balance and her figure. To end that dream appropriately, we then eat an enormous Indian lunch at Gaylord's, which has all our favorites on its buffet line. In the afternoon, we visit the Art Institute and ride the Loop back to her apartment. It is a weekend worth remembering.

Some Special Problems

Quotations

Remember that whatever tense you are using for the rest of your writing, when you quote someone, you must always write the words exactly as the person said them or wrote them.

Books, Movies, and Such

Whenever you are discussing printed matter, such as literary works, articles, scripts for plays, or any video, movie, or other preserved performance, use the present tense. This is why: Even though the U.S. Constitution was written long ago, I can go to the document today, and it will still say what it said so long ago. In the same way, even if you saw *E.T.* many years ago, I could rent the video today and still see now exactly what you saw then. Therefore, according to convention, because we can experience them in the present, we write about written material and all preserved performances in the present tense. (If you are describing a certain actress's performance in a play, however, especially one that occurred at a given time in the past, you will need to use the past tense about her performance. You will still use present tense to describe the play itself.)

Copyright © 1992 by Harcourt Brace Jovanovich, Inc. All rights reserved.

288 Chapter 14 Shift in Verb Tense

Practice 4

Edit the following paragraphs to reflect the rule about books and movies.

1. Although she was normally a peace-loving person, my roommate showed a surprising affection for certain violent movies. In *The Terminator,* for example, a human-looking **cyborg** returned from the future to kill the mother of the man who would ultimately defeat his creators. During the course of the movie, the cyborg and the woman's defender blasted Uzis, shotguns, and other heavy firepower at each other, threw bombs, lit fires, and did many other violent acts, killing innocent bystanders in the process. And yet my roommate loved that movie. I think the danger heightened the impact of the movie's romance for her, which for my die-hard romantic roommate redeemed the movie.

2. In *My Ántonia,* by Willa Cather, a wealthy New York lawyer named Jim Burden described his friendship with a **Bohemian** immigrant. He first met Antonia Shimerda when he was eleven and had moved from Virginia to Nebraska to live with his grandparents. After one carefree year during which they ran wild across the prairie, visiting neighbors, inspecting prairie-dog towns, and exploring the nearby **arroyo**, their lives grew apart. Jim attended school, and Antonia worked her family's farm. Looking back from middle age, however, Jim found that as different as their lives turned out they both still shared a deep, abiding love for the land, and that the life of each had been molded by this love.

Paragraph Editing Practice

Read through the following paragraphs, editing any inconsistency in verb tense that you detect.

A. In Greek mythology, Orion was a mighty hunter, large and strong and fearless. In the winter sky, Orion was a mighty constellation, easily recognized by the three apparently linear stars in his belt. As befits a mighty hunter, the constellation Orion has some of the largest and brightest stars in the sky. The red supergiant star called Betelgeuse marked Orion's right shoulder. If placed in our sun's place, Betelgeuse will extend past Earth and beyond the orbit of Mars. The blue supergiant Rigel marks Orion's left leg. Rigel is the seventh brightest star in the sky. Although Betelgeuse and Rigel appear to be in the same plane in the sky, Betelgeuse shone from 520 light years away, which means its light will take 520 years to reach us, and Rigel shines from 900 light years away, 380 light years more distant than Betelgeuse.

B. The names for our planets come primarily from Roman mythology, and a review of the nine planets offers a review of major mythological figures as well. Mercury, moving so fleetly around the sun, reminds early astronomers of the gods' messenger. Thinking that under the swirling clouds of Venus beautiful gardens grew, early astronomers name the planet for the goddess of beauty—although scientists now believe that under the acid clouds a hellish environment lurked. Blood-red, Mars evoked thoughts of the god of war; larger than any other planet, Jupiter naturally deserved to be named for the king of the gods. Saturn, its rings causing a fertile bulge, got its name from the god of reaping, Uranus from the father of both Jupiter and Saturn, and ocean-colored Neptune from the god of the sea. As for Pluto, after Clyde Tombaugh finds this most-distant planet in 1930, an eleven-year-old girl suggests that this dark, gloomy, and bitterly cold place be named for the god of the underworld, and the name stuck.

Essay Editing Practice 1

Read through the following essay, and then edit it for any inconsistent verb tenses that you find. Remember that you must first decide the overall perspective that the writer is using to describe something, whether past, present, or future. Watch for misused words.

Copyright © 1992 by Harcourt Brace Jovanovich, Inc. All rights reserved.

Each Sport in Its Time

A few years ago, a group of businesspeople got together and started the United States Football League. They scheduled they're games during the spring so that the games would not compete with those of the more established National Football League in the fall. This springtime football league fails because, like brightly colored leaves, the beginning of school, and the harvest moon, football belongs in the fall. Actually all three major sports, football, basketball, and baseball, play well only in their proper season.

Football games, for example, offer the perfect date for the fall. They were long enough to let people really get to know each other, slow enough to allow plenty of time to talk, and noisy enough to cover any lack of conversation. Could students ask for a better first date with someone they do not know well? Then, as the season progresses and students become more serious about their dates, the increasingly cold weather offered the perfect excuse for getting really close at football games. In the crisp coolness of later fall, dates can snuggle side by side or cuddle under the cover of a comfy lap robe. Football in the spring would reverse this process. Who wants to begin with snuggling at the chillier beginning of the season and **regress** to distance at the sweatier end? This anti-romantic aspect will always doom springtime football.

Basketball, in its turn, plays best in the winter, for the indoor court beckons as a **bastion** against the icy winds and frosts outside. The speed of the movement, the frequency of scoring, and the almost unbroken continuity of play meant that basketball offers spectators many more opportunities for cheering than either football or baseball. In winter, couples will welcome this additional way to keep warm. They also find the intimacy of a gymnasium inviting. As the team improves and begins winning games, the gymnasium fills up, and people will be crowding in more closely, so closely in fact that they must sit shoulder to shoulder with the fans nearby. Coming in from the cold outdoors, however, fans find no discomfort in this **proximity**. How much more uncomfortable they would find the same proximity in summertime!

Summer is the time for baseball, for sitting outside in spacious ballparks, where even the downdraft from the beer-bellied, sweaty fellow sitting nearby doesn't linger long. Besides, everything in summer, except perhaps the managers' tempers, slows down to the pace of a lazy doubleheader at the ballpark. Students off for the summer had pressed the "Quit" command on their thinking. Businesspeople on vacation had exchanged stress for stretching. Even mothers with small children had chased their charges out the door. For all, what better break than baseball? For vast stretches of time, the field seems paralyzed, with the organ droning in the background, the outfielders standing like statues in the sun, and the pitcher doing nothing but twitching his head, back and forth, back and forth, back and forth. When he finally winds up, and the batter connects, everyone briefly will **rouse**, but even then only for a moment. And that is just as it should be in the lazy, languid days of summer.

Football, basketball, and baseball—each in its own season plays well to its fans. Like being born and dying, like planting and reaping, like laughing and weeping, each sport has its own season and its own time.

Writing Practice 1

Choose one of the following topics and write an essay with three internal paragraphs.

A. Make a list of your memories about a game that you attended in person, either a professional, college, or high school game. Then use the three internal paragraphs to describe the experience. For example, you could write a paragraph describing what happened before the game, during the game, and after the game.

Copyright © 1992 by Harcourt Brace Jovanovich, Inc. All rights reserved.

B. Make a similar list of memories about a special experience you had with one of your parents or with a friend, again dividing the memories into three types for use in three internal paragraphs. Be sure to start with a random list of memories about the experience so that you have plenty to work from as you develop your paragraphs.

C. What is your favorite season and why? Choose a season and compare it to other seasons, listing reasons why you like this season better than the others. For each reason, give two or three specific examples or experiences that illustrate this reason. Then choose your three most important reasons and write a short essay comparing your favorite season to others.

Essay Editing Practice 2

Read straight through the following narrative essay, and then edit it for any errors you find, especially inconsistent verb tense.

Twice-Told Tails

Ajax snuggled deep into the family sofa, a pile of soft paper and cloth scraps in chic rose and gray. Palm-Olive his mother, had a keen eye for interior decorating, she kept **abreast** of fashion trends by faithfully nibbling through the magazines left by the new set of Occupants that rented their Palm Beach condominium. Actually, Palm-Olive had a keen eye for absolutely everything. For instance, just then she was busily chasing out a pesky flea and a curious ant, which have dared to stick their heads in through the open doorhole. If either the flea or the ant had moved one step closer, they would have landed in the stockpot. Luckily for them, Palm-Olive had just added five cups of dust mites to the steaming broth, and everyone knows dust mites clash with other insects.

The soup smelled good. Ajax closed his eyes and burrowed even more deeply into the sofa. Then, unbearably hungry, he rustled out and crept quietly through the doorhole. Maybe he could scavenge some snack crumbs from the condominium's kitchen floor. He slipped between the floorboards, and poked his little pink nose between the hidden gap under the cupboard beneath the kitchen sink. He could hear his father, Clorox II, investigating the fertile fields between the stove and the refrigerator. Then, oh joy, Ajax spots a piece of chocolate cake the size of a Brussels sprout (his favorite vegetable) that a person must have dropped from his or her plate. With a low squeak, Ajax thanked this weeks Occupants for their untidiness and their shared passion for sugar, spice, and everything mice. Now, if only you could reach the cake—oh, and that bunch of green grapes that had fallen over by the butcher block.

That butcher block was new. He craned his short neck to see the top and caught sight of two giant knives with blades glittering from the suns' reflection. **Mesmerized**, Ajax stopped still, whiskers quivering involuntarily. As if in a dream, he hears an Occupant's voice calling "Bill, honey, Jeffrey left his toy back home on the farm, that mouse without eyes or a tail. He raising a fuss, and I think we'd better chop him up another one."

Clorox must have heard because he poked his nose around the refrigerator and caught sight of Ajax. "Scurry, Son," he hissed. "Scurry for your life."

Ajax scrambled back to the safety of his family nest. For the next hour, him and Palm-Olive prayed that their family's husband and father would find his way back unharmed. Finally, just as Ajax was about to go looking for him, they heard a tap-tap-tap, and Clorox stumbled into the living-nest wearing dark glasses and tapping a white tipped cane. He swayed drunkenly, off-balance without his tail. "She got me," he moaned. "She cut off my tail with a carving knife. That was the last sight I saw in my life. Oh, Ajax, Ajax . . ."

Copyright © 1992 by Harcourt Brace Jovanovich, Inc. All rights reserved.

Ajax woke with a start. His father is shaking him gently, quietly telling him to get up for supper. His fathers eyes looked directly into his. Gee whiskers, his father could *see!* Ajax rubbed his eyes and peeped around behind Clorox, gleefully noting his father's fine long tailpiece.

"Come on, Sleepyhead. It was time for supper."

Supper sure smelled wonderful. As Ajax stood on two legs to stretch, the book he had been reading, *13 Tails of Horror*, dropped on its spine and opened to the story entitled, "Wherein Three Sightless Mice Encounter a Farmer's Wife."

"Ajax" Palm-Olive squeaked from the kitchen, "Dad scavenged some especially moist cake and some nice green grapes for tonight's supper."

Writing Practice 2

Choose one of the following topics and write a story with at least five paragraphs.

A. Retell the story of "Goldilocks and the Three Bears," but tell the story from the baby bear's perspective. Use first person in your narrative if you want to.

B. Retell the fable "The Tortoise and the Hare," but tell the story from the hare's perspective.

C. Tell a story you know from your own ethnic background.

Misused Words: lay/lie

Lay requires an object, something that gets set down.

> *Lay* your head on my shoulder.
> The trainer *laid* the injured player's helmet on the bench.

Lie describes what a subject does, whether that subject is a person, place, or thing.

>(You) *Lie* down beside me.

>The book *lies* under the pillow.

Additional confusion comes from *lay* being the past tense of *to lie*.

>After the accident last week, the injured player *lay* down on the bench.

>When an accident happens, the injured players *lie* down on the bench.

If you remember that *to lay* requires an object and *to lie* requires only a subject, you'll be all right. Insert the correct form of either *to lay* or *to lie* in the following sentences.

1. The kittens _____ down on my feet each night.
2. Her roommate _____ the final draft into a puddle of baby oil.
3. Horace patted his dog, who was _____ beside him.
4. Horace patted his dog, who had _____ itself down beside him.
5. The gallant gentleman grabbed the woman's coat and _____ it across the mud.
6. Where did I _____ my keys down this time?
7. Genessee _____ the welcome mat down just inside her room.
8. I would rather sit down than stand, and rather _____ down than sit.

Review Exercises

This is the context for the following exercises:

>Carl's neighbor has had an accident and has broken his leg. Carl makes his neighbor's dinner each night during the week of February 1 through February 8.

Copyright © 1992 by Harcourt Brace Jovanovich, Inc. All rights reserved.

Complete sentences 1–9. Note that some sentences will have several correct options.

1. On Saturday, January 31, Carl tells his girlfriend,

    "I _____ dinner for my neighbor all next week."

2. On Saturday, January 31, Carl tells himself,

    "By next Saturday, I _____ dinner for my neighbor for a whole week."

3. On Sunday, February 1, Carl tells his mother,

    "I _____ dinner for my neighbor this week."

4. On Tuesday, February 3, Carl tells his teacher,

    "I _____ dinner for my neighbor every night this whole week."

5. On Thursday, February 5, Carl tells his friend,

    "I _____ dinner for my neighbor for five days now."

6. On Friday, February 6, in the morning, Carl tells his girlfriend,

    "I _____ dinner for my neighbor again tonight."

7. On Sunday, February 8, Carl tells his sister,

    "I _____ dinner for my neighbor every night last week."

8. On Sunday, February 8, Carl tells himself,

    "By last Wednesday, I _____ dinner for my neighbor for four nights."

9. On Sunday, February 8, Carl tells his mother,

    "By Saturday, I _____ seven dinners."

Dictionary Practice

Look up the words in bold print and provide a brief definition for each word as it appears in the sentence.

Some Special Problems   297

1. Basketball, in its turn, plays best in the winter, for the indoor court beckons as a **bastion** against the icy winds and frosts outside.

   bastion: _____

   _____

2. Who wants to begin with snuggling at the chillier beginning of the season and **regress** to distance at the sweatier end?

   regress: _____

   _____

Match the following words with their brief definitions.

_____ 3. abreast (p. 292)   a. keeping up with the latest developments

_____ 4. arroyo (p. 288)   b. watercourse; gully

_____ 5. Bohemian (p. 288)   c. a human machine

_____ 6. cyborg (p. 288)   d. to awaken; to excite

_____ 7. mesmerize (p. 293)   e. to spellbind; to hypnotize

_____ 8. proximity (p. 291)   f. native of Bohemia; Gypsy; unconventional person or lifestyle

_____ 9. rouse (p. 291)   g. closeness

Copyright © 1992 by Harcourt Brace Jovanovich, Inc. All rights reserved.

CHAPTER **15**

Punctuation

This chapter will describe rules for certain punctuation marks that are used to link or to set off different parts of a sentence. These marks include semicolons, colons, dashes, hyphens, parentheses, and brackets.

◻ Semicolons

The semicolon is a rather formal mark of punctuation that you may use only rarely. It is most useful in two instances.

To Link Two Closely Related Independent Clauses

Occasionally, you may want to attach two independent clauses without using a coordinating conjunction. (Remember FANBOYS? See pages 84–85 for a complete description.) You can link the clauses with a semicolon.

> The woods seemed to be covered in mystery; the branches hovered menacingly over me.
>
> Katie refused to be comforted; she cried the whole time her parents were away.

If this use seems familiar, you are probably remembering the kinds of sentences that caused comma splices. Indeed, semicolons can replace the comma in a comma splice to make the punctuation in that sentence correct.

In much the same way, use a semicolon to link sentences combined with a transition word.

> I know I should be making dinner; however, I would much rather read than cook.
>
> He had forgotten to call ahead for reservations; therefore, he and his date had to wait over an hour for a table.

You can use a semicolon in this way only when the words both before and after it include an independent clause.

Practice 1

Write OK to identify the sentences in which the semicolon has been used correctly. Write X to identify the sentences in which semicolons have been used incorrectly, and then correct these sentences.

_____ 1. I would never want my cremated ashes put in a jar what if someone knocked them off the mantel?

_____ 2. Lili finally found the perfect man; then reluctantly put him back on the shelf with the other Ken dolls.

_____ 3. My husband served his mother's home-canned green beans last Sunday; however, having just studied botulism in biology, I could not make myself eat them.

_____ 4. This is Jason's first morning in preschool, his baby sister misses him already.

_____ 5. No one wants to share a dormitory bathroom with Narcissa O'Hara; who takes half the morning to wash, condition, dry, curl, and tease her waist-length hair.

_____ 6. Please give me more guacamole; and pass the chips.

_____ 7. My sociology professor suggested a good topic in class today; comparing reclusive Howard Hughes to flamboyant Donald Trump.

_____ 8. I think Bertha, my pig, makes a great house pet. She causes quite a stir; however, as she daintily minces close beside me on our walks through Central Park.

To Clarify Lists

Sometimes you may write sentences that include lists—lists that have commas within the items being listed. Using semicolons between these items will help readers understand the sequence.

> This weekend, I need to do a lab, write the lab report, and finish a take-home test for my chemistry class; read a history

assignment, write a brief biography, and begin an annotated bibliography; and go out with my girlfriend, meet her parents, and ask her to marry me. Check on Monday to see if I survive.

Practice 2

Insert semicolons as needed in the following sentences.

1. My parents, who were diplomats in Asia, lived first in Tokyo, Japan, then in Seoul, Korea, Beijing, China and finally ended their career in Hong Kong.
2. Before Haskall can make it to his 8 A.M. class, he has to set two alarms, one on each side of the room, drink the two cups of coffee waiting in the automatic coffee maker by his bed, take an aspirin, a cold shower, and a brisk walk, then eat a Danish and dash to catch the bus.
3. Becky sometimes feels that her life is a cliché: She was captain of her cheerleading squad, she married the football quarterback, she has two kids, a cat, and a hamster, she lives in the suburbs and drives a van, and she presides over the Hopper Valley PTA.

When using semicolons, remember that they should be placed outside of quotation marks and parentheses.

> He said, "I promise I will come to your recital"; however, when he didn't come, I was neither surprised nor disappointed.
>
> He has never come in the past (I have asked him three years in a row); he must not like the bagpipes.

Colons

Colons serve as a jumping-off point to introduce certain elements.

> 1. *A list of items or examples.*
>
>   I will need the following: a map, some honey, and a dash of salt.

2. *An explanation, statistic, supporting fact, example, or other elaboration.*

He has one sustaining goal: to hear his father praise him.

This is the problem: She can't work and also spend as much time as she would like with her new daughter.

3. *A quotation or formal statement.*

On world affairs, Benjamin Franklin said this: "There never was a good war or a bad peace."

When asked why she had moved to the country, my mother repeated Christina Rosetti's words: "One day in the country is worth a month in town."

Colons always follow complete sentences. Notice that in the following example on the left, the words before the colon make only a sentence fragment. The corrected sentence has a complete sentence before the colon.

Incorrect	**Correct**
My favorite things are: sunshine on daisies, beards on goats, dull pewter pitchers, and cool Lycra swimsuits.	These are my favorite things: sunshine on daisies, beards on goats, dull pewter pitchers, and cool Lycra swimsuits.

Colons also separate certain standard items.

1. *Salutations and the letter that follows.*

Dear Ms. Cohen:

2. *Hours and minutes.*

8:30 A.M., 5:15 P.M.

3. *Title and subtitle.*

The Life of Christ: Images from the Metropolitan Museum of Art

4. *Place and publisher.*

Fort Worth: Harcourt Brace Jovanovich

5. *Biblical chapter and verse.*

Psalm 23:6, Romans 8:28

6. *Numbers in a ratio.*

3:5, 100:1

Copyright © 1992 by Harcourt Brace Jovanovich, Inc. All rights reserved.

Practice 3

Insert punctuation (commas, semicolons, and colons) as needed in the following sentences. (See Chapters 7 and 8 for a discussion of comma use.)

1. The manager of the Highway Host in Bemidji Minnesota has a novel way to discourage rowdiness late at night he offers 50 percent discounts to anyone from the local police force.

2. George has a recurring dream as he looks up into the evening sky stars with women's faces wink at him other stars shoot across the sky for his benefit alone and then a rude meteor falls on his head and wakes him.

3. When dancer Isadora Duncan suggested to author George Bernard Shaw that they might have a perfect child by combining her beauty and his brains Shaw said this in reply "Yes my dear but what if the child has my beauty and your brains?"[1]

▢ Parentheses

Use parentheses to set off interruptions from the rest of the sentence.

> I would if I could (and I should), but I can't.
>
> We have several skylights that let in bright (sometimes glaring) noonday sun.
>
> Plants without flowers (such as mushrooms, seaweed, lichen, and moss) reproduce from spores rather than seeds.
>
> Esther Summerson (in Dickens's *Bleak House*) never quite seems realistic.

---

[1] Norman Schur, *1000 Most Important Words* (New York: Ballantine, 1982), p. 4.

Copyright © 1992 by Harcourt Brace Jovanovich, Inc. All rights reserved.

Dashes

Use a dash to replace parentheses or commas when you want a stronger or a more casual break. Using dashes gives the material more emphasis than it would have inside parentheses.

> My son—perish the thought—wants to be just like Rambo.
>
> St. Francis, Gandhi, and Martin Luther King—I would much rather he admired these men of peace.

You may also use a dash to indicate a sudden break in thought.

> Chevahn told me a great story about your roommate—no, that would be gossip.
>
> If I hear one more lecture on getting things done early—well, I'll have to answer to a parole officer.

Hyphens

Some words have been used together so often that they are now spelled as one word. Such compound words include *steamboat, baseball,* and *homesick*. Until they reach this compound status, words that are often used together may be joined with a hyphen: *baby-sitter, grown-up, play-offs*.

You will also use a hyphen to connect two or more words that together describe a word.

> the well-known politician
>
> the light-footed elephant
>
> her blue-black hair
>
> a why-did-I-ever-get-out-of-bed day
>
> one of those can't-seem-to-forget-it songs

To make sure that you need a hyphen, ask yourself: "Do I need both these words, and in this particular order?" If the answer is yes, you probably need a hyphen between the words. These words are only hyphenated when they come *before* the noun, however. If the words follow the noun, they don't need hyphens.

> the politician that was well known
>
> the elephant that was light footed
>
> one of those songs I can't seem to forget

Furthermore, you don't use a hyphen if one of the describing words ends in *-ly*.

> the progressively funnier skit
>
> the hopelessly wild antics

Usually you will need a hyphen to connect *pro-*, *all-*, *ex-*, and *self-* to the beginning of words and *-elect*, *-like*, and *-in* to the end of words.

> pro-Navy   Secretary-elect
>
> all-glorious   pearl-like
>
> ex-wife   stand-in
>
> self-esteem

Use a hyphen to join elements in numbers that you are spelling out.

> thirty-five   three-eighths

Use a hyphen to split words of more than one syllable when you need to break them at the end of a line of type.

> syl-la-ble   el-e-ments   hope-ful-ly

Note: Using hyphens correctly depends on current spelling practices. Checking a dictionary can help you decide when to use a hyphen.

▢ Brackets

Use brackets to interrupt direct quotations with your own comments or explanations, or to insert information into a quotation.

> Charles Lamb said, "Credulity [the ability to believe] is the man's weakness, but the child's strength."

You may also use brackets to identify someone referred to in a quote by a pronoun.

> As my political science professor put it, "He [Gorbachev] is caught between a rock and a hard place."

Sentence Practice

For the following entries, provide necessary punctuation. Remember that often the choice between dashes and parentheses depends on how much emphasis you want on what goes inside them. The sentences may need commas, semicolons, colons, brackets, parentheses, hyphens, dashes, and apostrophes, but in many sentences the choice of what to use depends on you. See Chapters 7 and 8 to review comma use.

1. The surgeon usually so skillful grabbed a knife and hacked at the thigh and leg of the roast turkey.
2. Whenever my sister Carlin visits I pick up these items at the grocery store a pound each of tofu brown rice and adzuki beans five ounces of low salt miso a gallon of soy milk and sixteen ounces of Kefir cheese.
3. Lynda Benglis a highly regarded Modernist sculptor exhibits at Paula Cooper Gallery in Manhattan New York although other galleries also show her work.
4. Another Modernist sculptor John Chamberlain he can also be called an Abstract Expressionist assembles crushed and welded car parts into colorful forms with such whimsical titles as *Tomato Poodle*.
5. Ron picked up the phone and a strange voice he couldnt tell whether the caller was male female or even human told him "I know what you saw and I did what you know."
6. I hope to be at least ninety five before I die.
7. Jan yelled "I never want to see you again, Jasper" nevertheless she called the next day and invited him out to dinner.
8. Since Timmys parents were dieting he left Santa a plate of cookies sugar-free and a glass of milk skim he hoped Santa Claus a bit overweight himself wouldnt take offense.

9. I could not believe my eyes when Cindy ate the squid tentacles and all but then she always was adventurous.
10. Puck the impish spirit who plays mischievous tricks on infatuated lovers in *A Midsummer Night's Dream* has two other names in British folklore Robin Goodfellow and Hobgoblin.
11. In Chaucers medieval *Canterbury Tales* the Parson warns in his tale that "after avarice comth glotonye gluttony."
12. I want only one thing for my birthday a big hug from each of you.
13. Sex drugs and rock n roll were yesterday what wine women and song were the day before today we just say no.
14. Please don't give me that ask me later look I'm not going to ask for a loan.
15. The undercover cop quickly spotted the suspect's well hidden birthmark only because she knew just where to look.

Paragraph Editing Practice

Read straight through each of the following paragraphs. Then go back through them, inserting punctuation. If the paragraphs seem hard to follow, difficult to understand, choppy, and generally confusing, that is not surprising. Without proper punctuation, all but the simplest writing would be extremely difficult to understand.

A. Alexander the Great 356 323 B.C. owned a much treasured volume of Homer. Homer wrote *The Iliad* and *The Odyssey*. Alexander's volume was especially valuable because it contained Aristotle's corrections a fascinating thought what could Aristotle have corrected? After the battle of Arbela a victory for Alexander a jewel studded golden casket just a box, not a coffin! was found in the tent of Darius, king of Persia. When Alexander was asked what should be done with such a wondrous object he replied "There is only one production in the world worthy of so costly a depository" and into the golden casket he placed his edition of Homer. Thereafter the book was called the *Casket Homer*.

Copyright © 1992 by Harcourt Brace Jovanovich, Inc. All rights reserved.

B. Sometimes especially during a heated argument one person might decide to argue a point just to keep the coals hot and the tempers flared. He or she might make baseless claims or accusations or decide to battle for the underdog the motives vary with the situation. Often these **incendiaries** will find themselves likewise accused of playing the devil's advocate a debate strategy with a long history. Few people including those who either play the devil's advocate or accuse another of doing so know that this term has religious roots. When proposals are made to canonize someone to officially recognize a deceased person as a saint the Roman Catholic Church appoints two people one a champion and one an adversary. The champion the *Advocatus Dei* upholds the motion honoring the candidate with praise the adversary the *Advocatus Diaboli* attempts to defame or dishonor the candidates character in every possible way. From this usage it is clear how the term has now come to mean as defined in *Webster's New Collegiate Dictionary* a person who champions the less accepted or approved cause for the sake of argument.[2]

Essay Editing Practice

Read through the following essay, and then edit it, watching for all the errors studied so far.

Of Pizza Smears and Salad Spills

First dates are tough a person has to get through the ordeal somehow without making any major mistakes in conversation appearance and etiquette. For heaven's sake, a person even has to watch his or her grammar! To make everything more difficult, many first date's often include the ritual of dining, so difficult that many people falter and lose

---

[2] *Webster's Ninth New Collegiate Dictionary* (Springfield, MA: Merriam-Webster, 1985), p. 347.

all their etiquette points. Surely every person has made at least one food **faux pas** and disgusted a squeamish date. To survive a first dinner date gracefully, each participant needs to remember three rules.

First, a person should choose the kind of dinner carefully, especially avoiding pizza and Mexican food. Pizza may be casual, but a person never looks casual eating it. The pizza is always too hot to pick up, and who can gracefully maneuver a sagging, dripping triangle without smearing tomato sauce and chasing strings of cheese? If a person attempts to eat it with a fork, he or she look foolish (only the uninitiated eat pizza with utensils) and saws first hopefully, then desperately through the **impenetrable** crust. Spattering sauce and dropping toppings in spite of the effort. As for Mexican food, most dates make the mistake of digging freely into the chips and salsa appetizer, never realizing that they sound like a two-ton giant crushing chips underfoot. Soon the gracious beauty or dignified hunk across the table stops eating entirely, watching as each chip goes whole into the other date's mouth, wincing as each gigantic crunch splinters the chip into a thousand pieces. No matter how delicately I eat the chimichanga that follows, all hope of future romance has died. Who would want to kiss a mouth with such fatal energy?

Having finally chosen a simple, three course dining establishment, a date must still choose carefully from the menu. Given the choice between soup or salad, a person should take the soup, even if it happens to be "Chef's Kitchen Sink" or "Cream of Brussels Sprout," for salad presents a potential minefield of dining disasters. The plate comes loaded with perky leaves already leaning provocatively over the edge, just waiting to fall at the slightest touch of a nervous fork onto a lap or onto the floor for the waiter to swoop up with a flourish. The size of some salad items also present dangers. Dates attempting to eat whole the artfully arranged chunks of tomato, cucumber and cauliflower will almost certainly find themselves **reminiscing** about the days in grade

Copyright © 1992 by Harcourt Brace Jovanovich, Inc. All rights reserved.

school. When they chewed a whole pack of gum on a dare. Only too late do they realize how extremely large these chunks are and alas! a cauliflower will not quickly dissolve. A person should also not forget that those limp sprouts that nestle so lovingly, so lightly among the salad greens cling just as lovingly and lightly to the lip, a location where they cannot be felt, only seen much later in the mirror. By then its too late to save this poor persons reputation. Soup offers its own hazards, such as slurping and dribbling, but of the two, soup's the safer.

   Having negotiated the choice of restaurant and having survived the choice of the first course, a person needs only to choose his or her main course correctly and all will be well. Wise dates avoid hand-held main courses, such as sandwiches, ribs, fried chicken, or heaven forbid!—corn on the cob. Hand-held foods inevitably ascend to the mouth whole so that the bite itself determines the size of the mouthful, and anyone who is nervous can bite off more than they can gracefully chew. A person's date will inevitably choose the moment that a bite goes in to ask a question, leaving the choice of swallowing the bite whole, exposing half-chewed food, or waving an **ineffectual** hand in an effort to stall the answer. Furthermore, most of these hand-held foods leave sauce or butter or bits of coating behind at the corners of the mouth so that a person feels compelled to wipe his or her mouth after each bite. This **doleful** eater ends up looking like a Victorian wind-up doll: bite, wipe, bite, wipe, bite, wipe. A plain chicken cutlet or broiled fillet of sole offer delightful simplicity, a diner merely cuts off a bite so miniscule that even a goldfish could eat it delicately, places it securely into the mouth, and swallows the tiny morsel immediately upon being asked, "So what's your major?"

   If a dater can commit these three rules to memory, he or she can forget about food—or at least enjoy it—and concentrate on the person across the table, who after all is trying just as hard to please.

Copyright © 1992 by Harcourt Brace Jovanovich, Inc. All rights reserved.

Writing Practice

Choose one of the following topics to write about.

A. What advice would you give daters? List some possible suggestions and choose three that belong together (three suggestions on clothes, conversation, manners, choice of person, refusing or accepting, or whatever). For each of these suggestions list examples, dangers, considerations, descriptions, or whatever you could use to develop your suggestion and convince your reader that it is a good one. Then use your lists to write an essay with three internal paragraphs.

B. Unless it is too painful to remember, describe your first date in an essay with three internal paragraphs. (This will be easier if you first list what you remember about this date and then group these memories into three workable paragraphs.) You could alternatively write about your most memorable, most expensive, most humorous, most exciting, or most unusual date.

C. Choose one of the following items related to dates: categories of events (concerts, athletic events, meals); categories of restaurants (fast-food, sit-down, regional); categories of cost (expensive, medium, practically free). Make notes on each category: kinds within the category, common traits, and so forth. Then write a short essay.

Misused Words: a/an

Use *a* before *consonant sounds* (not just consonants), and use *an* before *vowel sounds* (not just vowels).

> Would you like *a* pear?
>
> Will you attend *a* university or college? (*University* starts with a *y-* sound, which is a consonant sound.)
>
> Would you like *an* apple?
>
> Will you enroll in *an* honors course? (*Honors* starts with a short *o* sound, which is a vowel sound.)

Remember, base your choice on vowel or consonant *sounds*, not on vowels or consonants themselves. Insert either *a* or *an* in the following sentences.

1. Have you had the pleasure of having _____ honest friend?

2. Big eyes seem to have _____ universal appeal.
3. Above all else, Julius Caesar was _____ honorable man.
4. The professor, against all expectation, had _____ understanding heart.
5. Why does the dentist have such _____ happy smile?

Dictionary Practice

Match the following words with their brief definitions.

_____ 1. doleful (p. 310)   a. mournful; sad

_____ 2. *faux pas* (p. 309)   b. a blunder; a breach of etiquette

_____ 3. incendiary (noun, p. 308) c. cannot be penetrated

_____ 4. impenetrable (p. 309)   d. useless; futile; ineffective

_____ 5. ineffectual (p. 310)   e. a person who quarrels, causing dissension

_____ 6. reminisce (p. 309)   f. to remember

CHAPTER **16**

Parallel Structure

Using parallel structure makes your writing sound smoother and, even more important, makes it easier to understand. How can you check for parallel structure? Look to see if related words, phrases, or clauses have been stated with similar forms. For example, compare these two sentences:

Faulty	**Improved**
To give a sentence parallel structure is balancing it.	To give a sentence parallel structure is to balance it.

The improved sentence uses a parallel structure within the sentence. That is, it uses the same verb form, *to give* and *to balance*, rather than *to give* and *balancing*.

Parallel structure not only balances the sentence but also helps readers to see how the different parts of a sentence relate to each other. In the following example, notice how much clearer the sentence sounds with parallel structure.

Faulty	**Improved**
In our house, you shouldn't correct my father, my mother hates teasing, and you should always say something to my sister.	In our house, don't correct my father, tease my mother, or ignore my sister.

The faulty version, the one without parallel structure, sounds so choppy that potential visitors might not bother sorting through the family rules and could end up making complete fools of themselves.

Copyright © 1992 by Harcourt Brace Jovanovich, Inc. All rights reserved.

Because parallel structure makes sentences easier to understand, this structure is extremely important when you are explaining difficult concepts or instructions. But even in the most everyday writing, such as letters to a friend, parallel structure will make reading easier and more enjoyable.

◻ Deciding What to Make Parallel

When listing anything—whether dirty tricks or saintly actions, lengthy clauses or short phrases—you can repeat different amounts of the sentence and still maintain parallel structure. The following examples illustrate this principle. The first sentence starts each parallel pattern with the subject:

> Cousin Eustace used to steal my matchbox cars,
> *he* used to stomp on my silly putty, and
> *he* used to tangle my slinky.

This sentence starts the pattern with the main verb:

> Cousin Eustace *used* to steal my matchbox cars,
> *used* to stomp on my silly putty, and
> *used* to tangle my slinky.

This sentence starts the pattern with the infinitive form (*to* + verb):

> Cousin Eustace used *to steal* my matchbox cars,
> *to stomp* on my silly putty, and
> *to tangle* my slinky.

This sentence starts the pattern with Eustace's different actions:

> Cousin Eustace used to *steal* my matchbox cars,
> *stomp* on my silly putty, and
> *tangle* my slinky.

Which version is best? Depending on your purpose, the one that repeats the least is usually best. When writing a list, therefore, decide what *must* change in a sentence—as little as possible—and change only those parts, whether the list comes at the beginning or the end.

Occasionally, because of particularly long segments, you may decide to repeat one word or phrase throughout the sentence to alert readers that you are beginning another parallel segment. Look at the following sentence:

> The class included *students who had* lived overseas and traveled extensively,
> *students who had* visited every state in the country, and
> *students who had* never left the county.

In the first clause, "lived overseas" and "traveled extensively" sound like the beginning of a pattern. But if you start your repeated pattern with the verbs, the sentence is confusing. By repeating "students who had" before the next clause, the writer alerted the reader to the real pattern. You can use this device of intentionally repeating certain parts of your parallel pattern to enhance clarity.

In the following sentence, the *by* acts like a semicolon, separating groups.

> The twins celebrated their birthday
> *by* picking up their girlfriends,
> *by* driving to Santa Barbara,
> *by* swimming and surfing, and
> *by* eating on the UCSB campus.

In the next sentence, the *how* acts as a break, marking the end of one description and the beginning of another.

> The movie *A Town Like Alice* shows
> *how hard* life became for the Europeans in Malaysia during World War II, especially for the women and children;
> *how strong* they had to be to endure the enforced marches, minimal food, unsanitary water, and inadequate medicines; and
> *how important* this time would become for the ones who did survive.

As you write sentences, then, strive for as little repetition as possible. Just remember that occasionally, for clarity's sake, you must have that repetitive hook to hang your pattern on.

Copyright © 1992 by Harcourt Brace Jovanovich, Inc. All rights reserved.

▢ Parallel Clauses and Phrases

In the following exercises, you will be working to set up parallel structure based on entire clauses and phrases. For example, the repeated pattern in this sentence includes the entire independent clause each time:

> The toilet leaks, the carpet stinks, the floor creaks, and the lights blink. Are you certain you want to rent this apartment?

Practice 1

Combine the sentences in exercise 1 using independent clauses. (Remember to use a FANBOYS when combining two or more independent clauses.)

1. The volleyball team's best server broke her wrist.
   The star setter sprained her little finger.
   The strongest hitter caught the flu.
   Therefore the team will probably lose the game.

Use dependent clauses as you combine the sentences in exercise 2, as in this example:

> Before you say anything, even though you are curious, if you really love me, you'll let me explain why my hair looks like this.

2. The mail might bring a sweepstakes check. (Unless)
   I haven't entered. (which)
   I'll have to pass up spending spring break in Florida.

Use phrases as you combine the sentences in exercise 3, as in this example:

> The dog jumped over the couch, across the rug, into the doorway, and then begged for approval.

3. The sun did this.
   It climbed over the horizon.
   It climbed between the clouds.
   It climbed above the trees.
   Then it invaded my window.

   _____

   _____

Now try exercises 4 and 5 without any pattern provided. Combine the clauses and phrases in each set into a sentence, being careful to create parallel structure.

4. Because Teresita likes to stay active
   She participates in bicycle races.
   teaches skulling
   skis like an Olympic contestant
   She also designs sportswear.

   _____

   _____

5. I sit down to write.
   I tell myself that writing isn't a chore.
   that the word processor isn't an instrument of torture
   I assure myself that my mind only *seems* blank.
   (Repeat the *that* as a hook to keep your readers with you.)

   _____

   _____

▢ Parallel Verb Forms

Sometimes when you fail to use consistent verb forms, you create sentences with faulty parallelism. To avoid this, whenever you are listing two or more actions, be sure to use verbs, infinitives, or the *-ing* verb form consistently.

sprinkle	to sprinkle	sprinkling
melt	to melt	melting
smother	to smother	smothering

Compare the following three sentences.

> To make my favorite dessert,
> *sprinkle* vanilla wafers with chocolate chips,
> *melt* the chocolate in the microwave, and then
> *smother* the whole delicious mess with whipped cream.

> To make my favorite dessert, you need
> *to sprinkle* vanilla wafers with chocolate chips,
> *to melt* the chocolate in the microwave, and
> *to smother* the whole delicious mess with whipped cream.

> Back-to-basics dessert lovers can make my favorite dessert by
> *sprinkling* vanilla wafers with chocolate chips,
> *melting* the chocolate in the microwave, and
> *smothering* the whole delicious mess with whipped cream.

All three sentences use parallel structure, but with a different verb form. The verb form is often a useful hook to hang a list on.

Practice 2

For exercises 1–3, rewrite the sentences according to the examples.

1. Example: *Jonna not only sings but also plays the piano.*

   My moped not only moves fast.
   My moped also is saving on gas.

   _____

   _____

2. Example: *Rutherford shimmied, dipped, strutted, and spun to the music's beat.*

   Ezra bounced the ball.
   The basket became his aim.
   The ball was thrown into the air.
   He hit a perfect shot.

   _____

   _____

3. Example: *When Jumana reached the mall, she had already chosen each gift, added up the cost, and collected the money.*

   This happened when Erich left the gym after swimming practice.
   He felt exhausted all over.
   He felt tortured through and through.
   Practice always discouraged him right down to his bones.

   _____

   _____

In exercises 4 and 5, working without a pattern, combine each set of phrases, clauses, or sentences into a single parallel sentence.

4. when I cannot be bothered with studying
   hang out at the student commons
   catching up on the latest campus news
   to eat chocolate frozen yogurt with sprinkles

   _____

   _____

5. Mom has been here all day.
   She did the laundry.
   She has been cooking enough meals for a week.
   Mom helps me care for my newborn all day.

   _____

   _____

▣ Parallel Nouns and Describing Words

Sometimes by working on parallel structure, you can improve the way you use individual words in a sentence. The following examples show how using parallel structure with nouns and describing words can make your writing smoother.

Faulty	**Improved**
Someone who studies hard and a mother on her own, Keesha also works part-time at surgical nursing.	A *good student* and a *single mother*, Keesha also works part-time as a *surgical nurse*.

Copyright © 1992 by Harcourt Brace Jovanovich, Inc. All rights reserved.

The sentence on the right is improved because it describes Keesha's three roles with three parallel nouns.

Faulty	Improved
She daydreams about Anders, an anesthesiologist, who is aloof and mystifies her.	She daydreams about Anders, an anesthesiologist, who is *aloof* and *mysterious*.

The sentence on the right is improved because it uses two parallel describing words.

Faulty	Improved
In Keesha's dreams, Anders all of a sudden bows before her and in a dramatic fashion asks her to marry him.	In Keesha's dreams, Anders *suddenly* bows before her and *dramatically* asks her to marry him.

The sentence on the right is improved because it uses parallel *-ly* words to tell how he proposes.

Keesha and her daydreams have illustrated how to smooth out your writing with consistent and parallel use of similar elements—nouns, words that describe nouns, and words that describe verbs.

Practice 3

For exercises 1–3, combine each set of sentences according to the example.

1. Example: *Cassie, Tessie, and Mui-Sheung like to go on triple dates.*
   Three people meet at lunch to swim.
   One is Rodney.
   Another is Ted.
   The third is Ali.

2. Example: *Harriet disagrees, but I think Lord Peter Wimsey is prim, fussy, and peculiar.*

   This will happen eventually.
   The car of my dreams will be big.
   It feels comfortable.
   It will keep me safe.

3. Example: *But whether prim or just polite, fussy or just proper, peculiar or just distinctive, Wimsey was certainly clever enough to solve mysteries.*

   It could be new or used.
   It could have fresh paint or rust all over it.
   Pinstripes or polka-dots could be on it.
   For now, the car just has to run.

Now, without a pattern, use your imagination to combine this set of phrases and clauses into a single sentence.

4. The perfect student
   completes assignments accurately
   gets assignments done quickly
   all assignments are handed in on time
   never puts anything off
   probably doesn't exist

Sentence Practice

Set 1

Edit the following sentences to give each one parallel structure.

1. Why is it that the best teachers require the longest papers, allow the fewest excuses, and their tests are so hard?

322 Chapter 16 Parallel Structure

2. I like the teachers who cancel class before most long weekends, let students drop their two lowest grades, and they always tell great stories.
3. My father has planned an exciting spring break for me. While my friends lounge on a beach in Florida, I shall be painting the family room, organizing the basement, and I have to revarnish our hardwood floors.
4. My husband, Randall, is a true-green Boston Celtics fan. He has a subscription to *Celtics Pride*, he throws his wastepaper against a Celtics backboard that sits over his wastebasket, he wears a Celtics jacket, and our green station wagon sports a Celtics bumper sticker.
5. Our cat, Arwen, is fat, grumpy, and never does anything.
6. On a cold night, give me a fire in the hearth, I like my plump cat sitting on my lap, a murder in my book, and I'll be content.
7. Summer afternoons should always be spent at the beach where the waves crashing against the shore, the sun on my back, and the icy lemonade slipping down my throat drive away all consciousness of time or needing to be responsible.
8. Rise above your limitations, or they will be engulfing you in mediocrity.
9. Akiyo had a paper due in anthropology, a test in French, a problem set in physics, and needed to finish an overdue explication for humanities; no wonder she spent Saturday in the library.
10. To make a great salad, mix some black olives, mushrooms, artichoke hearts, and Italian dressing, you need to rub garlic on a big salad bowl, break up some Romaine lettuce, sprinkle lots of Parmesan cheese on it, add a little more cheese, and then toss everything together.

Set 2

Edit the following sentences to give each one parallel structure.

1. Many football teams take their names from animals, such as the Broncos from Denver, the Detroit Lions, the Rams of Los Angeles, and the Seattle Seahawks.
2. When scheduling classes for next semester, try to space out your classes over the week, balance heavy reading classes with lab classes, and you should fit in one easier course.
3. When you first try to ice-skate, resign yourself to falling, to get up, and falling again.
4. Few people realize that during the seventeenth century, the Puritans in England outlawed Christmas. They said it was pagan, of the world, and superstitious.
5. My father told me that the best way to make friends is to find people with similar interests, treat them the way you would like to be treated, and you should also know the number for take-out pizza.
6. If ever you go swimming and meet a shark by accident, be friendly, firm, and swim fleetly.
7. I thought my roommate and I would become great friends, but all she seemed to want was to study her philosophy, listen to her Wagner tapes, and most of all she wanted me to leave her alone.
8. The movie's appeal was its blood, gore, and the wickedly humorous villain.
9. In a crowd, Armelia seemed quiet and unexciting, but one-on-one she could make a child a heroine-worshipper, a woman a friend, a man a lover, and an old man youthful again.
10. The day had all the charms of early summer: lazy, expansive, no responsibility, and free.

Copyright © 1992 by Harcourt Brace Jovanovich, Inc. All rights reserved.

Paragraph Editing Practice

Read through the following paragraphs, and then go back through them, making improvements in parallel structure.

A. For a long time, Christmas morning at our house seemed like a free-grabbing whirl of greed, consumption, and eventually being disappointed. We always received lots of presents: books, toys, things we could wear, and food, but no matter how much we got, we always came up from under our pile of torn wrapping paper, ribbons, and the presents with the same question: "Is that all I get?" Finally, totally disgusted with the process, my parents decided they must either change the method or be giving up gift-giving entirely. They tried collecting all of a person's presents and had us open one present at a time, but inevitably the piles ended up uneven and again there were tears, making sour looks, and the same question: "Is that all I get?" A Christmas without gifts loomed darkly on the horizon. Then my mother read about a different system in a magazine article. Now, each Christmas, we collect the gifts we are giving, rather than getting. In turn, we each hand out our presents, one at a time, so that we can have the pleasure of watching as others receive our gifts. We have so much more fun now in choosing our presents, so much more fun in watching them be received, that none of us doubts any longer that the old words are true: It *is* more pleasant to give than to receive.

B. In 1981, recreational pilot Priscilla Blum and Jay Weinberg, both American Cancer Society volunteers, organized the Corporate Angel Network. This service makes empty seats on corporate planes available to cancer patients who must travel long distances to receive medical care, to see specialists, or who just want to go home for special occasions. Since then, more than 2,500 cancer patients have been given rides, traveling with dignity and they are comfortable, and best of all, at no cost. Blum knows how much this can mean to cancer patients as they work through the pain, how depressing cancer can be, and the trauma that cancer causes. She has recovered from cancer herself.

Essay Editing Practice

Read through the following essay and then go back through it, editing any errors you find. Look especially for faulty parallelism, and watch for misused words.

The Joys of Gardening

When a **novice** gardener first puts her spade in the ground, she probably has visions of lovely flowers, roses bathed in dewy fragrance, tall stalks of brilliantly hued delphinium, and massive bunches of chrysanthemums. More practically, she may see freshly picked tomatoes, corn, green beans, or broccoli, and rows and rows of home-canned produce. The spade goes in one spring morning, the first clump of sod comes up and the gardener never realizes that whatever else she manages to produce in her garden, she will almost certainly develop her own character.

First, gardening will **defer** her satisfaction. In her neighbors' yards, she sees tulips, crocuses, and other bulbs, daffodils, popping there vibrant blooms through ground that was recently covered with snow. She wants the same drama in her own backyard, but she will find no easy gratification in gardening. These neighbors planted their bulbs in November. Now in spring, she can't instantly produce the same display. Once she gets through spading the soil, eliminating the weeds, adding the lime and fertilizer and peat moss and whatever else the dirt needs. She must plant her seeds or seedlings and wait. The dreams of April must **sustain** her through May and sometimes even into June. Ironically, through most of spring, the time she would most like to work on her garden, the only outlet for her energy is some **sporadic** weeding.

Later, when early passions have burned themselves out, she will have more to do than she could ever have imagined. If gardening first teaches a person to defer her satisfaction, gardening next develops perseverance, for every gardener must live with the results when that satisfaction comes to pass. By midsummer, the vegetables need picking, the tomato plants need pruning, the green beans need stringing, the strawberries have gotten thick, and the list goes on and on and on. Even more to the gardeners **dismay**, with the vegetables, the muggy weather appears and the flies and the weeds. Lured by the **enticement** of an afternoon swimming, the excitement of a baseball game, or the attraction of a lazy afternoon sipping lemonade, she must fight harder and harder with herself to tend the garden. For most beginning gardeners, by early fall, fresh tomatoes join rotting ones on the kitchen sideboard, and weeds have taken over the flower garden.

So inevitably gardening teaches a person to set reasonable expectations. If the Canterbury bells bloom at all, they will do so only briefly, and then, just as Robert Frost warned, leaf will subside to leaf. The zucchini plants, set out with such fond dreams of summer abundance, will offer up 2.3 vegetables each, and then wither away. The rose will climb no higher than the first rung on the lattice, and the sweet pea will die in the dust. Only the weeds will flourish. As if an exercise in prepositions, they will thrive in the flower beds, among the vegetables, under the hedges, above the trellis, along the sidewalks, beside the fences, around the swing-set, over the compost heap, and even onto the driveway.

The next spring, the gardener goes to stand in the backyard and surveys her domain. The cold weather of late fall finally subdued the weeds, the snows of winter have scared good manners and breeding

Copyright © 1992 by Harcourt Brace Jovanovich, Inc. All rights reserved.

into her backyard. Even with the snows now melted, a blanket of last year's leaves still cover her failures. Will she attempt the grand schemes again of course she will. Gardening may teach a person to defer satisfaction, may develop perseverance, may purify expectations, but it can do so only with the necessary prerequisite character trait, which is optimism. No matter how grimly her previous efforts have failed, when spring comes it will be no less beautiful, refreshing, or full of hope. Perhaps in some distant year hence, as her experience grows and her perseverance stretches, her results will finally match her expectations.

Writing Practice

Choose one of the following topics to write about.

A. Think of some endeavor you have undertaken that delivers only long-term gains, such as developing a certain skill, saving for a new home, taking up a new sport. Now consider some advantages that only long-term pursuits can give a person. List three, with some examples for each, and write a short essay using your list.

B. If you or your family grows its own vegetables, describe the advantages of this effort. List three particular advantages, with illustrations for each, and then write a short essay using your list.

C. Think of some other hobby, activity, business, or sideline that you or your family pursues. Write a short essay, describing this pursuit in one internal paragraph, and explaining its advantages in two more paragraphs.

Misused Words: than/then

Use *than* with comparisons.

> The orange kitten is more determined *than* the black one.

Use *then* with progression, whether through time, steps in a process, or arguments in logic (if/then).

> If it's 2:30, *then* why is it dark outside?
>
> If it were 5:30, *then* I would understand why it's so dark.
>
> The dog ate lunch. *Then,* because it was so dark outside, he went to sleep.

Write either *than* or *then* in the following sentences.

1. Trust me; Raven is more determined _____ Tom is. She'll find Jeff first and ask him.
2. If she's so determined, _____ why hasn't she managed to find him?
3. He's got a busier schedule _____ anyone I know.
4. _____ Raven will just look harder for him.
5. Rather him _____ me—that's all I can say.
6. Why? Who would you want in your group rather _____ Raven?
7. She works hard, shows up for group meetings, and _____ helps with the finishing touches.
8. But just think of the disappointment when you hear that Raven's looking for you and _____ discover it's only for a group project.

Review Exercises

Provide apostrophes for sentences 1–5.

1. Where is Rozinas entry in the dress-designing contest?
2. Its over there, next to the entry covered with gaudy ribbons and clashing sequins.
3. That one looks like an old, very used painters dropcloth.
4. Rozinas looks dignified next to it—simple, sultry, and shocking all at the same time.

5. Hey, it looks successful as well: The judges ribbon is hanging on it.

In sentences 6–11, circle the verb that agrees with the subject.

6. Whoever bought this sculpture, he or she (needs, need) an enormous living room to display it.
7. An epic, which (is, are) a long narrative poem, often glorifies a race or nation.
8. Where (is, are) the books I brought home from the library or the magazine that came in yesterday's mail?
9. None of the books by my bed (looks, look) boring enough to put me to sleep.
10. Charles Dickens, who (describes, describe) so poignantly the plight of children in the Victorian age, would have been appalled at how many homeless children roam our country today.
11. Dustin's family (needs, need) a car that can carry nine or more passengers.

Dictionary Practice

Match the following words with their brief definitions.

_____	1. defer (p. 325)	a. beginner
_____	2. dismay (p. 326)	b. disappointment
_____	3. entice (p. 326)	c. to tempt
_____	4. novice (p. 325)	d. infrequent
_____	5. sporadic (p. 326)	e. to delay
_____	6. sustain (p. 325)	f. to support; to nourish

Copyright © 1992 by Harcourt Brace Jovanovich, Inc. All rights reserved.

CHAPTER 17

Misplaced Words, Phrases, and Clauses

Can you tell what is wrong with this paragraph?

> While in a dead sleep late one afternoon, the phone woke Kendra. Her boyfriend wanted to bring his family over, whom Kendra had recently agreed to marry. Jimmy only wanted her to fix her delectable lasagna. They would, he told her, arrive at 5. Smashing mozzarella cheese through the food processor, slopping bottled sauce over half-cooked pasta, and crumbling left-over hamburger patties over the lot, the lasagna went into the oven moments before they arrived. When Jimmy decided to ungraciously complain, Kendra wondered why she hadn't just said no.

Writers, who usually know what they want to say, sometimes misplace words—a mistake that can cause either confusion or amusement for the reader. For example, the phone was not in a dead sleep. Also, even if in coming years, Kendra may very well *feel* as if she has married her in-laws, she would never *agree* to do so.

This chapter describes how to avoid misplacing words, phrases, or clauses. It shows what happens when you "dangle" phrases or words that describe, making it hard for the reader to decide exactly what is being described.

■ Misplaced Words

Some words that describe cause little confusion, no matter where they are placed in the sentence, because they clearly can describe only one word.

Copyright © 1992 by Harcourt Brace Jovanovich, Inc. All rights reserved.   331

Chapter 17 Misplaced Words, Phrases, and Clauses

Sleepily, Luis assembled his midnight snack.
Luis *sleepily* assembled his midnight snack.
Luis assembled his midnight snack *sleepily*.

In all these sentences, *sleepily* clearly describes how Luis assembled his snack. In other cases, however, a word could be describing any of several words in a sentence. Therefore, *where* these words appear in the sentence can make a big difference to its meaning.

Words that might describe any of several words in a sentence should be put next to the word they are in fact describing.

Watch out for words that can describe either an action or another describing word, as in the following examples:

Barb gazed hopelessly at the romantic poet.

Barb gazed at the hopelessly romantic poet.

In the first sentence, *hopelessly* describes how Barb gazed at the poet, and in the second, it describes how romantic the poet was. Words of this type that often cause confusion include *only, almost, never, even*, and *nearly*. Of all the words frequently misplaced, *only* is the most common.

The stray dog jumped on the boy.

Only the stray dog jumped on the boy. (Nothing else jumped on him.)

The stray dog *only* jumped on the boy. (It didn't bite the boy.)

The stray dog jumped *only* on the boy. (It didn't jump beside the boy.)

The stray dog jumped on *only* the boy. (It didn't jump on the flowers.)

Be especially careful to place words like *only* with the words they describe.

Practice 1

Rewrite sentences 1 and 2 twice each, inserting the describing words as indicated.

1. Rodney drove over his son's new bike.
   a. Insert *almost* in such a way that Rodney ruined his son's bike.

Copyright © 1992 by Harcourt Brace Jovanovich, Inc. All rights reserved.

b. Insert *almost* in such a way that Rodney was able to get out and move the bike before driving on.

_____

2. Her sister was given a priceless antique.
   a. Insert *nearly* so that this sister now has an expensive antique.

   _____

   b. Insert *nearly* in such a way that this sister was disappointed.

   _____

Misplaced Phrases

Loosely defined, a phrase is a group of words that functions together as a unit.

> **When a phrase describes a noun or an action, that phrase must be placed with the word it describes.**

In this section, you will see several different types of phrases that are often used to describe the word or words before them. In the examples, notice how misplacing one of these phrases confuses the meaning of the sentence.

Prepositional Phrases

Prepositions are little words used with a noun to form a phrase, such as *of laughter, behind the television,* or *except the pickles.* Such phrases are often used to describe other words in the sentence. To place these phrases correctly, put them right next to the word or words they describe.

Incorrect	Correct
The golfer hit her ball into the pine trees *with the lowest score*.	The golfer *with the lowest score* hit her ball into the pine trees.
The elephant pointed its trunk at the peanut vendor *in the* circus ring.	The elephant *in the circus ring* pointed its trunk at the peanut vendor.

Copyright © 1992 by Harcourt Brace Jovanovich, Inc. All rights reserved.

Phrases with Participles

Participles are -*ing* or past-tense verb forms, such as *carrying, giving, adding,* or *carried, given, added*. They can work alone to describe a noun, as in "an *added* advantage," or they can work as part of an entire phrase, as in "the ingredients *added to the recipe*." Used alone as describing words, participles rarely cause confusion, for everyone seems to instinctively put them directly beside the noun they describe. Used as part of a phrase, however, they often cause trouble. Usually, this phrase belongs directly *after* the noun it describes, especially when the phrase is very short.

Incorrect	Correct
The pickup truck almost ran over the squealing pig *driven by the clown*.	The pickup truck *driven by the clown* almost ran over the squealing pig.
The bull didn't notice the crowd *pawing menacingly at the cowboy*.	The bull *pawing menacingly at the cowboy* didn't notice the crowd.

When the entire phrase is longer, it can go *before* the main independent clause. Then you must be extremely careful that the participle describes what the subject of the independent clause is doing. Otherwise you will produce some remarkable and sometimes amusing statements.

Incorrect	Correct
Captivated by a display of swimsuits, *the poodle* escaped from Tassie's leash.	Captivated by a display of swimsuits, *Tassie* let the poodle escape from its leash.
Stretching out beside the pool, *the sun* slowly baked Holt's pale skin.	Stretching out beside the pool, *Holt* let the sun slowly bake his pale skin.

Infinitive Phrases

An infinitive phrase always begins with *to* + verb, for example, *to hear the band*. When your sentence starts with such a phrase, be sure that the *subject* of the following independent clause is what performs the action of the infinitive phrase.

Incorrect	Correct
To simplify using the computer, *a mouse* helps operators move the cursor.	To simplify using the computer, *operators* can use a mouse to move the cursor.
To perform well in the concert, *the audience* was ignored by the pianist.	To perform well in the concert, *the pianist* ignored the audience.

Practice 2

Combine the sentences in each set as instructed.

1. A pumpkin pie was made by Stan.
   He did this to celebrate Thanksgiving.
   (Begin this sentence with *To celebrate*.)

   ____

   ____

2. The horse went around the mud.
   The horse was carrying my roommate.
   (Use *carrying* to attach the second sentence.)

   ____

   ____

3. Her sandwich looks a little like our history professor.
   The sandwich is almost eaten.
   (Use *almost eaten* to attach the second sentence.)

   ____

   ____

4. I had been hoping to catch a new episode of *Murder, She Wrote*.
   A press conference was on instead.
   (Begin this sentence with *Hoping to catch*.)

   ____

   ____

Misplaced Clauses

Because a dependent clause has its own subject and verb, usually it can appear without confusion either at the beginning or the end of a sentence. For sentences with dependent clauses, you just need to guard against pronoun confusion. That is, be sure the reader will know for certain which noun any pronoun stands for.

> Because he was a rival for my affections, Eli refused to acknowledge John.

In this sentence, the reader can't know whether Eli or John is the detested rival. Make very certain that readers know who or what you mean with your pronouns.

> Because John was a rival for my affections, Eli refused to acknowledge him.

Dependent clauses formed with the double-duty signal words *who, which, that,* and *whoever* need to be placed carefully in a sentence. In most cases, such a dependent clause must directly follow the noun or nouns that it describes so that readers can know exactly what the *who* or *which* or *that* refers to. Notice in the following examples how confusing a misplacement can be.

Incorrect	**Correct**
Kimberley picked out a dog at the local Humane Society, *which has floppy ears and a winning personality.*	Kimberley picked out a dog, *which has floppy ears and a winning personality,* at the local Humane Society.
Our furniture would never appear in *House Beautiful, which offers economy rather than elegance*	Our furniture, *which offers economy rather than elegance,* would never appear in *House Beautiful.*
The snow piled up in soft blankets through the night *that buried the pumpkin patch.*	The snow *that buried the pumpkin patch* piled up in soft blankets through the night.

If most of these sentences sound obviously incorrect to you, that's hardly surprising—but it's not always so easy when you are the writer. Because you *know* what you want to say, your sentences may seem completely logical and clear to you, but still sound strange to someone else. Always go back over what you have written and try to see your sentences, paragraphs, and entire essays from the perspective of the reader. If you can do that with your own writing, you will be able to catch these misplaced words, phrases, or clauses, and eliminate possible confusion (as well as a few laughs at your expense).

Practice 3

Combine the sentences in each set, using a dependent clause with *which* or *who* to add the information from the second sentence. (Review the use of commas with such clauses in Chapters 7, 8, and 9.)

1. The chemistry book cost $15 dollars.
   The book cost $43 new last year.

   _____

   _____

2. My '55 pickup behaves perfectly for me.
   The pickup gives my husband fits.

   _____

   _____

3. My neighbor will probably live to be a hundred.
   He goes for a two-mile walk every day, rain or shine.

   _____

   _____

4. The customer left her driver's license on the counter.
   She was just here.

   _____

   _____

Sentence Practice

These sentences contain misplaced words. Rearrange the word order, or rewrite the sentence to eliminate any confusion.

1. Upon arriving at the scene of the attempted burglary, the klutzy burglar was arrested by the police.
2. Did you see the sunburned man standing beside the rusty old pickup wearing cowboy boots?
3. Instead of plastic, little girls used to find dolls under the Christmas tree made of wax.

4. Yolanda returned her new snakeskin boots to the discount shoe store because she nearly paid ten dollars more than they would have cost at a department store.
5. The cockapoo lapped mineral water from the woman's fingers with the silly pink bow around its neck.
6. I cannot give you a higher grade on this final exam to answer your question.
7. Jorge saved his long hair at the barber's from a close shave.
8. In Celtic lore, Tristan and Isolde defy King Mark and his knights whose adulterous love ends in great tragedy.
9. Watering the petunias, the neighbor's cat brushed against my trousers.
10. The audience seemingly suffered through the endless play.
11. Three little batmen came to my house only on Halloween this year.
12. While sticky, quickly put the stamp on the page, being careful to place it within the lines.
13. The woman paid far too much for that old weather-beaten child's rocker.
14. Every Wednesday, Sir Charles places a rose on Lady Angelica's grave, which is the day she died.
15. The chocolate-covered child finally found refuge at the neighborhood Dairy Queen, who had run away from home after she accidentally ruined the carpet with fudge sauce.

Sentence Combining

Combine each set of sentences, being careful to place related words or phrases together.

1. Try to relax before an exam.
   Books should be put down two hours before the exam.

Jogging around the track will also help.
(Begin this sentence with *To relax*.)

_____

_____

2. Captain McNeill catches catfish.
   He catches the biggest catfish I have ever seen.
   He lives three houses down the street.
   (Use a *who* phrase.)

_____

_____

3. Captain McNeill caught a catfish almost as long as his arm.
   After he caught the catfish, he brought it over to my house.
   He brought all the neighborhood cats along with him.
   (Use *bringing* in this sentence.)

_____

_____

4. Doctor bills come on time.
   This always happens.
   Insurance payments do not come on time.
   They never do.
   Why is this?
   (Make this a question.)

_____

_____

5. My psychology professor has just had an article published.
   The article is in *American Psychologist*.
   She is a clinical psychologist.
   She is probably the best in Indianapolis.

_____

_____

6. Ammon writes English composition papers.
   He can write them while he listens to Pat Metheny.
   Ammon writes this way often.
   Pat Metheny plays jazz guitar.

_____

_____

Copyright © 1992 by Harcourt Brace Jovanovich, Inc. All rights reserved.

7. I notice how other people drive.
   They drive carelessly.
   I am doubly afraid to get my driver's license.

8. I live on Hawthorne Street in Portland, Oregon.
   Living there I can do things.
   Hawthorne Street has great restaurants for eating out.
   Hawthorne Street has vintage clothing stores for visiting.
   I can do these things any time I want.
   (Start this sentence with *Living*.)

Essay Editing Practice

As you edit this essay, look for any errors you have studied so far, including misused words.

Community Crossroads

To an opera house come highbrow people. To the stadium come sports fans. To a grocery store, though, come all kinds, for all accept the most prosperous line up behind a grocery cart each week. And who knows maybe even Johnny Carson has made a **clandestine** run for some Dijon mustard. If almost all Americans walk the grocery aisles, however, they do not all do so at the same time of day.

In the mornings, people with young children fill the shopping aisles their babies propped up in the cart between a roll of toilet paper and a two-pound coffee can. Preschoolers hang from the cart, hopping off to help Mom or Dad load milk or to hold a bag open for their sitter to put fruit in. Stores probably hire extra workers in the morning to clean up broken jars of spaghetti sauce and restacking the fruit after little fingers have toppled apple pyramids. With five parts familiarity and one part disregard, the adults ignore the children's water-torture words: "When will we buy animal crackers again?" "Why can't I have some

Misplaced Clauses   **341**

gum?" "I'm thirsty, I want some soda." For these morning trips, adults dress casually in jeans, old sweatshirts, or whatever comfortable and familiar object emerged from the clothes closet. They rarely wear makeup and occasionally sprout curlers. The children come wildly dressed, wearing orange shirts and purple jams, striped socks and untied shoes—the result of little hands in the clothes drawer. With their own line of makeup, they wear oatmeal foundation and fruit-punch lipsticks, but in keeping with the relative **nonchalance** of the morning crowd, neither they nor the adults with them seems to care.

Far from feeling free shoppers in the dread hour before supper are all business. Their clothes, though different, still have in common a feel for work: three-piece suits, jeans and work boots, nurses' uniforms and mechanics' overalls, all chosen carefully for the shoppers profession. These shoppers choose their groceries carefully as well, but almost always ahead of time, arriving with a list, whether written or habitual. They know what brand of orange juice they want, what kind of cheese, what size of detergent, and they move through the store like efficiency experts on parade. They have a focused look, as if wearing blinders. They rarely check prices. Searching out sale items would cost more in time than the dollars they would save. Whether plumbers or teachers, accountants or astronauts, construction workers or librarians, shoppers at this time all have one driving force, they want to get home.

Only late at night does the grocery store show it's true potential to draw Americans together. In the midnight aisles, opera fans meet basketball fans. Owners of seven figure condos encounter owners of cardboard shacks. Shoppers whose sequins dance under the stores glaring lights bump carts with shoppers whose pajamas peek out from under raincoats. Over the last-minute milk gallon and the forgotten bread, the cookies tardily purchased for some child's school party and the pickles purchased for a suddenly ravenous mother-to-be. All social distinctions dissolve into America's melting pot.

Copyright © 1992 by Harcourt Brace Jovanovich, Inc. All rights reserved.

To see the real America, with all its unashamed diversity, delightful **idiosyncrasy**, and easy-going familiarity, tourists can skip the travel book attractions, and visit the grocery store late at night. They will find themselves at a crossroads of American society.

Writing Practice

Write an essay on one of the following topics.

A. What does our country gain by having so many different kinds of people? What are some ways that other cultures, for example, have affected your life (for example, foods, clothes, music, books, entertainment)? Choose three ways you benefit from living in a country that has so much variety, make notes on how you benefit, and then use these notes to write a short essay.

B. Make a list of phrases that would describe American grocery stores for a brand new immigrant. You might address store layout, how stores promote certain products, things to avoid, etiquette, and so forth. From this list, write an essay with three internal paragraphs.

C. Make a list of ideas on how people can cut costs in the grocery store. Then decide how to organize some of your ideas into three paragraphs. You could address one area of the grocery store in each paragraph (produce, frozen foods, canned goods, deli, and so forth), or one kind of food. Choose any organization principle that works for you, and then write an essay with three internal paragraphs.

Misused Words: principle/principal

Use *principle* (always a noun) to mean a conviction, a code of law, or the origin of an idea.

> What has happened to your *principles*?
>
> If our country ever loses its *principle* of equality, it will probably lose its identity at the same time.
>
> The *principle* behind grammar is orderly communication.

Use *principal* as a noun to mean the head of a school or the original money in an investment. Use it as a describing word to describe a person, place, or thing as the foremost or main one in its class.

> Uh-oh—here comes the *principal*.
>
> He won't discuss the loan until we come up with the *principal*.
>
> What is your *principal* reason for wanting more exercise?

Write either *principle* or *principal* in the following sentences.

1. The _____ from my high school called my parents last week.
2. Her _____ reason for calling was to find out how much aid I am getting from my college.
3. My parents refused, on _____, to answer.
4. They have always held to the _____ that financial matters should remain in the family.
5. My parents even have a hard time revealing how much _____ they will be able to provide when discussing a loan with the bank.

Review Exercises

Circle the correct pronouns in these sentences.

1. Andy and (his, him) friend Luke have forgotten (his, their) promise to get each other's approval before getting engaged.
2. The computer can check spelling a lot faster than (me, I).
3. Jason or Lila will have to come back and get (his, her, their) book.
4. Everyone finished (his or her, their) bowl of chili.
5. The salami and sausages have had (its, their) usual bad effect on my stomach.
6. Neither Jeff nor Percy was laid off from (their, his) job last year.
7. The team lost (their, its) first game of the play-offs.
8. Procter and Gamble left (their, its) mark on American culture when it began sponsoring soap operas.

Copyright © 1992 by Harcourt Brace Jovanovich, Inc. All rights reserved.

344   Chapter 17   Misplaced Words, Phrases, and Clauses

9. Most of the treasure found (their, its) way out of the country.
10. At the family reunion, each of my grandmother's priceless gems will be displayed tomorrow in (their, its) new setting.

Dictionary Practice

Look up the words in bold print and provide a brief definition for the word as it appears in the sentence.

1. And who knows, maybe even Johnny Carson has made a **clandestine** run for some Dijon mustard.

    clandestine: _____

    _____

2. To see the real America, with all its unashamed diversity, delightful **idiosyncrasy**, and easy-going familiarity, tourists can skip the travel book attractions and visit the grocery store late at night.

    idiosyncrasy: _____

    _____

3. With their own line of makeup, they wear oatmeal foundation and fruit-punch lipsticks, but in keeping with the relative **nonchalance** of the morning crowd, neither they nor the adults with them seem to care.

    nonchalance: _____

    _____

CHAPTER 18

More on the Mechanics of Writing

Earlier chapters discuss the use of commas and some of the other punctuation marks we use to join or separate parts of a sentence. This chapter explains the use of a few more punctuation marks—quotation marks, question marks, and periods. It also discusses the use of underlining (or italics) and capital letters.

☐ Underlining or Italics

Italic type on the printed page is used to emphasize certain words or set them apart from the rest of the sentence. When you are writing by hand or with a typewriter, or when you are using a printer that does not have italics, then use underlining instead. Following are six common uses for underlining or italics.

1. *Titles of major works.*

   Books: *The Sound and the Fury,* by William Faulkner; *Dare to Discipline,* by James Dobson
   Newspapers: *New York Times; Chicago Tribune*
   Magazines and journals: *TV Guide; Redbook; Organic Chemistry*
   Plays: *Hamlet; Duchess of Malfi; Steel Magnolias*
   Operas: *Marriage of Figaro; Porgy and Bess*
   Other major musical works: *The Messiah; Unfinished Symphony*
   Art works (paintings, photographs, sculptures, and so forth): Picasso's *Paulo as Harlequin;* Rivera's *Delfina Flores;* Nevelson's *Total Obscurity;* Calder's *The Spiral*
   Movies and TV series: *Dick Tracy; Princess Bride; Citizen Kane; All My Children; 60 Minutes*

2. *Names of ships, aircraft and spacecraft.*

   The sinking of the *Titanic* and the *Challenger* disaster have both left their tragic imprint on history.

3. Foreign words.

   Although in Chinese *xie xie* sounds like a sneeze, when the speaker smiles you'll probably discern the true meaning—thank you.

4. *Letters as individual letters, and numbers as individual numbers.*

   Please spell my name with a *k*, not a *c*.
   Robert Indiana's painting has *5*'s painted all over it.

5. *Words referred to as words.*

   I would be more flattered that my daughter's first word was *Mama* if her second and third words hadn't been *want that*!

6. *Anything you want to emphasize.*

   After looking over his sixteenth birthday present, my soon-to-be-disinherited son said, "I wanted a *new* car!"

Practice 1

Provide the underlining in these sentences.

1. Fritz said, "I have six assignments I must read this weekend: an article in the journal Gifted Children Quarterly, the 500 pages of Herman Melville's Moby Dick, T.S. Eliot's major poem The Waste Land, three chapters in Sarah Orne Jewett's book The Country of the Pointed Firs, Thornton Wilder's play The Skin of Our Teeth, and a critique of Rembrandt's painting The Nightwatch. Remind me again, please, why I didn't do all this when it was first assigned?"

2. "Why is he my ex-boyfriend?" Holly said. "Well, just as an example, when Thirtysomething first came on TV he was excited to watch it, but then became oddly disappointed as the title first appeared on the screen. 'Rats,' he said. 'I thought the title was Dirtysomething.' "

3. Unlike Bethany who has only single marks on her papers, usually A's, her sister Brigitta has many marks on her papers, usually comments like Illogical, Awkward, Punc., and grades we will choose to ignore. It

seems strange, but Brigitta's the one who has sold four poems to the regional literary journal Northwest Reader.

◼ Question Marks

Use a question mark to punctuate the end of a question, whether it is at the end of a sentence or has been inserted within either parentheses or dashes.

> We were supposed to have a test *today*?
>
> What was supposed to be on it?
>
> Well, before the test actually begins, Herr Professor—quick, may I cram off your vocabulary list?—could you tell us one more time about your tour of Wittenburg?

Sometimes at the end of a sentence, you have to decide whether to put the question mark inside or outside of quotation marks. Whenever the entire question is a quote, put the question mark inside the quotation marks.

> He didn't have to, but my roommate asked anyway, "Did you eat that entire five-pound can of cheese popcorn tonight?"

Practice 2

Provide punctuation for the following sentences.

1. On their third date Angel said to his date   Now that I know you better may I ask a personal question
2. His date reluctantly nodded   What would you like to know
3. How did your parents choose the name Poinsettia
4. She laughed   You tell me first about Angel
5. He called me audacious   what does that mean anyway   and I didn't know whether to thank him or leave

Copyright © 1992 by Harcourt Brace Jovanovich, Inc. All rights reserved.

▢ Periods

Use periods to end statements or intentional fragments, to end statements phrased as questions (which makes them polite commands), or to tone down exclamations.

> Most Americans throw all their trash conveniently into one container.
>
> A luxury, to be sure.
>
> Would you please get the mail.
>
> What a delicious feeling to be finished.

Use periods to mark abbreviations, dollars and cents, decimals, and numbered lists.

> Ms., Mr., Mrs., Dr., Ph.D., Jr., Ave., Mt. (but not certain abbreviations that are sounded out as letters or pronounced as words, such as VIP, USSR, USA, NFL, SALT talks, NASA).
>
> $10.99, $.59
>
> The atomic mass of carbon is 12.011. One inch is equal to 2.54 centimeters.
>
> Rules of the house:
>   1. Say please and thank you.
>   2. Never *watch* someone work if you can help.
>   3. Kiss the cook.

Periods *always* go inside quotation marks. A comma can follow a period ("James, Jr., had no sons."), but a period never follows a question mark, exclamation, or another period.

▢ Quotation Marks

You probably know the main use of quotation marks, which is to show that the words inside the marks are a direct quote from someone—either written or spoken words.

> James Thurber said, "Humor is emotional chaos remembered in tranquility."

Like italics or underlining, quotation marks are also used to set off some titles—usually titles of shorter works.

> Poems: "The Hired Hand," by Robert Frost
> Essays: "Dialogues Concerning Natural Religion," an essay by David Hume, included in the book *God and Evil*, edited by Nelson Pike
> Short stories: "The Pit and the Pendulum," by Edgar Allan Poe
> Chapters or articles that are part of a bigger work: "The Lost Individual," a chapter from *Individualism Old and New*, by John Dewey; "The Meaning of Dreams," an article by Jonathan Winson in *Scientific American*
> Songs, short musical compositions, and segments of radio programs or individual shows from TV series:
> "You Got It," by Roy Orbison; "The Tollefson Boy Goes to College," a radio episode of *Prairie Home Companion*; "Genesis of the Daleks," a television episode of *Dr. Who*.

You may also use quotation marks to call attention to words with new meanings, words used with obvious irony, or words used in a special sense.

> As though choosing a steak for her dinner, she seemed to stamp me with a blue "USDA Approved" mark.
>
> The professor had some "welcome" news: We have a take-home test due tomorrow.

There are a few rules you should know about using other marks of punctuation with quotation marks.

1. *Periods and commas always go within the quotation marks.*
   "I would like to go," he told me. "I'll go get ready."

2. *Semicolons and colons always go outside the quotation marks.*
   Let me tell you what I mean by "exciting": free choice at a sports car lot; a late-night reading of Poe's "The Fall of the House of Usher"; and a date with Camilla, who lives down the hall.

3. *Question marks and exclamation points go within the quotation marks only when they apply directly to the quoted words. If they apply to a larger sentence and not just the quoted words, these marks go outside the quotation marks.*

Copyright © 1992 by Harcourt Brace Jovanovich, Inc. All rights reserved.

Would anybody want to eat "Puppy Chow?" If it's the new snack made of rice cereal dipped in melted milk-chocolate bars and peanut butter, and then rolled in powdered sugar, I'll have some "Puppy Chow"!

4. *Use single quotation marks when you need to quote something within double quotation marks.*

"I'm going to read my English homework, a short story named 'The Bride Comes to Yellow Sky,' by Stephen Crane," I told my roommate.

Practice 3

Provide the correct punctuation for these sentences. Exercises 2 and 3 each contain a dialogue with two speakers.

1. I have written a short story about a visit to my uncle's house that I think I'll call No Joy in Mudville.

2. Can you come to the party? my sister asked.

    No, but I will send my replacement, a cassette of Rudolph the Red-Nosed Reindeer.

    Why are you sending that?

    I sniffed. If you could see my nose—Neon Nose, I call it—you would understand why!

3. I just finished reading a short story by Flannery O'Connor, Tally told her study partner. O'Connor is a twentieth-century writer who lived in Georgia. She wrote stories about the Deep South.

    Tally listed the unsympathetic characters in A Good Man Is Hard to Find: the son, Bailey; the escaped convict, called The Misfit; and, of course, the awful grandmother.

    Oh, no, another story about weird people! her partner exclaimed. What's the story like?

    An escaped convict takes a family hostage and kills everyone, Tally answered. How is that for a charming plot?

    It sounds gruesome!

    Maybe, but just at the end, just before The Misfit kills the grandmother, she looks up at him and says, Why you're one of my babies. You're one of my own children! Tally shook her head. As awful as that grandmother was, bad-tempered and complaining all the time, in the end she forgot herself. Faced with almost certain death, I guess she started thinking about eternity and saw the eternal value in The Misfit. The story's really about hope, not just about how awful people can be.

■ Capitalization

Use a capital letter to begin the first word of a sentence or an intentional sentence fragment.

> I made a New Year's resolution to exercise twenty minutes every day. What a joke!

Use a capital letter to begin every new line of traditional poetry or verse.

> EPITAPH ON CHARLES II
> Here lies our Sovereign Lord the King
> Whose word no man relies on,
> Who never said a foolish thing,
> Nor ever did a wise one.

(As you may know, some poets use no capital letters or follow their own rules of capitalization and punctuation for artistic effect. This is called "poetic license.")

Always capitalize proper nouns. There are many categories of proper noun; they include the following:

> Names or any word used as a name: Mary, Junior, Bubba
> Cities, countries: China, Calcutta, Sri Lanka
> Historical periods: Renaissance, Middle Ages, Roaring Twenties
> Languages: French, English, Hindi

Capitalize certain words in titles—always the first and the last words, and every other word except *a, an, the,* conjunctions, and short prepositions.

> *Idylls of the King, A Portrait of the Artist as a Young Man*

Capitalize nouns used as labels, titles, or names that identify a certain entity.

> Titles or positions used as names or with names: Captain, Governor Diego, Aunt Elsa)
> Specific classes: Biology 121, Political Science 201, Introduction to Art History
> Specific regions: the West, Underworld, Lunar Fields

Avoid using capitals with words that *describe* rather than *label* a noun.

No capitals	Capitals
She's our president.	Did you see President Webster walk into our class?
The library is too hot in summer.	Let's study in Fisher Library.
Our biology textbook cost over $50.	The book for Biology 201 will cost less.
The eastern section of our ranch has water.	She's moving to the East.

Practice 4

Edit these sentences, adding punctuation, underlining, and capital letters where needed.

1. jerry went to the library yesterday to find some books for his spanish professor. dr ortega wanted some interesting novels about the west. jerry thought books by zane grey and louis l'amour would be just right for dr ortega's trip through wyoming, nevada, and california. unfortunately his professor was hoping for some easy reading about

the spanish occupation of southern california, which means a book about zorro would have been a better choice.
2. when the trustees of the university dropped by chemistry 121, it was the first time that they had stepped into the science building. slophill hall desperately needed renovations, and everyone from the president to the janitor knew it. the labs could have been used unchanged as the fifties setting in back to the future or as a textbook example in a recruitment film entitled science facilities you want to avoid.

Sentence Practice

Edit these sentences, paying attention to the mechanics of writing.
1. In his essay Goodbye, Proud Barns, Dan Guillory recalls glorious visits with his grandfather, a cotton farmer in the deep south who had a barn packed full of "the wonderful whiteness."
2. If president lincoln were alive today, would he rather watch masterpiece theatre or monday night football.
3. mr. lincoln liked to attend the theater himself, so he would certainly like masterpiece theatre, but then he also wrote about four score and seven, so he would probably like football, too.
4. colleen, hurry up and rsvp to that ms. so-and-so—what was her name, anyway—because we don't want to miss her fascinating workshop on mla and apa documentation or do we
5. Please get me a tube of colgate, a bottle of tabu cologne, and some bausch & lomb saline contact cleaner.

Paragraph Editing Practice

Read the following paragraph first for content. Then read back through it, editing as you read.

A. The egyptian pharaoh Psammetichus (664–610 bc) was perhaps the first in a long line of linguistic theorists to experiment on the possibility of an original language from which all other languages had descended. Like most people, he believed that in the dawn of time, early humans spoke a primitive, "natural" tongue and that this tongue was still being spoken. Certain that this mother tongue was his own, he decided to conduct an experiment. Putting humanity and kindness aside for this scientific cause, he placed two infants in the care of a slave and **banished** all three to an isolated retreat. If the slave uttered one word to them, she would be killed. As the story goes, the children's first **intelligible utterance** was the word bekos. From the scholars that he had retained for just such an occasion, Psammetichus learned that the word meant bread in phrygian, a language spoken in what is now the northwest corner of turkey. For many years after that, because of the pharaoh's experiment, people believed that this ancient language was the first ever to be spoken on earth.

Essay Editing Practice 1

As you edit this essay, concentrate on errors in writing mechanics as described in this chapter.

A celebration of the past

The chinese New year, figured according to the lunar calendar, occurs somewhere between January 21 and February 19. During its two weeks, chinese people around the world celebrate with feasting, parades, dragon dances, and fireworks. Many of these celebrations have their roots in Chinese mythology.

One example is the custom of pasting inscriptions on doorways. Before the old year finishes, traditional chinese either purchase or write for themselves two inscriptions on long strips of red paper (the color of happiness). They then paste these inscriptions on either side of their doors. Written in two parts, the sayings reflect the chinese people's customary love of nature and concern for humanity. For example, the two sentences might say:

Eternal sky and earth exclaim, be renewed again.

Each mountain and river declares, let us meet in peace.

If the family has recently suffered a death, the inscriptions go onto green or yellow paper (the colors of mourning) and reflect the customary **veneration** of ancestors:

Of all words, let reverence and honor be your watchwords.

Then heaven will say, see how they remember things past.

Where did this custom of pasting up inscriptions come from. According to a chinese myth, on a peach tree standing at the top of tu-shuo mountain a spirit door stands waiting for good spirits to enter and find their home. Two spirits, Shen Tu and Yu Lu, stand beside this door, driving away evil spirits. Some people believe that originally the new year's custom began with pasting pictures of these two spirits beside doorways of homes so that they could prevent evil spirits from entering. The chinese, fond of putting words on their walls (for the chinese characters themselves make beautiful pictures), eventually replaced the pictures of the spirits with inscriptions. Naturally, at new year's, these sayings were words of good fortune.

In another, more exciting new year's custom that also grew out of superstition, chinese people set off firecrackers of many different sizes and varieties. When heated, the gunpowder inside these firecrackers explodes, causing a loud bang. Traditional chinese people find out from a fortune teller the exact moment when the new year will begin and, at that moment, set off firecrackers. Although most people set off firecrackers for fun now, originally they did so to ward off evil spirits.

Many people believe that this custom pre-dates gunpowder, for the word for firecracker, pao zhu, means to burn bamboo. When heated, the joints in the bamboo explode with a loud bang. According to one story, this practice of burning bamboo started with another spirit of the mountain, this one evil. Shan-sao was only about a foot and a half tall, wore no clothes, and had absolutely no fear of people. It would come down from the mountain, find some people, and watch them. The only way the people could get rid of this evil spirit was to burn bamboo, for while the spirit did not fear people, it did fear the sound of exploding bamboo. As time passed, firecrackers took the place of bamboo, but the custom of making loud noises at new year's to ward off the influence of evil spirits continued.

Besides these two customs, chinese people practice many other new year's customs that have their roots in the stories of the past. Of course, many modern chinese no longer believe in the spirits and stories that gave birth to these traditions. Nevertheless, they do retain an abiding respect for their ancestors, and a deep commitment to living a life that brings honor to their family. That is one aspect of Chinese mythology that will never change.

Writing Practice 1

Choose one of the following topics to write about.

A. Is there an ethnic or religious holiday that your family celebrates in a way unfamiliar to many other people? Jot down the main steps in this celebration, and for each step write down descriptions, stories, illustrations, or details that will help explain this celebration to your readers. Then write a short essay with three internal paragraphs.

Copyright © 1992 by Harcourt Brace Jovanovich, Inc. All rights reserved.

B. Are you familiar with an ethnic cuisine? Jot down some distinguishing features of this cuisine, and add examples, explanations, or details that will help your reader understand or appreciate this cuisine. Then write a short essay with three internal paragraphs.

C. What is your favorite holiday? Jot down as many reasons as you can for your choice, and choose three of these reasons. For these, write down descriptions, stories, illustrations, or examples that will help your reader understand why this holiday is your favorite. Then write a short essay with three internal paragraphs.

Dictionary Practice 1

Look up the words in bold print and provide a brief definition for each word as it appears in the sentence.

1. Putting humanity and kindness aside for this scientific cause, he placed two infants in the care of a slave and **banished** all three to an isolated retreat.

   banish: _____

2. As the story goes, the children's first **intelligible utterance** was the word *bekos*.

   intelligible: _____

   utterance: _____

3. If the family has recently suffered a death, the inscriptions go onto green or yellow paper (the colors of mourning) and reflect the customary **veneration** of ancestors.

   veneration: _____

Essay Editing Practice 2

This essay includes errors that have been discussed in Chapters 1–18. Designed as a comprehensive review, this slightly longer essay has over twenty-five errors. First read straight through it to make whatever sense of it you can. Then go back through the essay, sentence by sentence, looking for fragments, comma splices, and run-ons; comma errors; subject-verb agreement and pronoun-antecedent errors; faulty shifts in perspective (first-, second-, or third-person) and in verb tense; faulty parallelism; misplaced words; and punctuation errors. Watch for misused words as well.

Code words

Registration time has arrived. All across campus, you and other students pour over schedules, meet with advisors, and chat with friends, hoping to establish the perfect schedule that allows them to both learn all the necessary content and skills for their eventual career and taking full advantage of the college years opportunities for fun and friendship. Faced with a roster of professors, these advisors and friends frequently fall back onto certain code words. These code words will often reveal the practices of a certain teacher, knowledge that can be useful as you choose your classes.

Inevitably, on almost every campus, a few professors earn the description of "blowoff". These men and women require little or no thinking for any of they're assignments. To complete a business analysis paper for one such professor, for example, you might have to transfer a description of the company a list of directors charts of performance and financial forecasts and so forth onto your computer, print it, and then turn it in. As long as you have everything she asks for and in the right order, you will get an a. These assignments are so straightforward her assistants grade them. When someone—usually from among the other professors in their division—complain, this professor might require that we find additional information, or turn in more papers during the semester. Even so, busywork remains busywork bad teaching remains bad teaching.

If these professors give tests at all, and many don't, you rarely have to understand anything. A **cursory** reading of the textbook and your lecture notes prepared you. And since these professors, raised on the philosophy of behavior that keep asking, "How would you feel if this happened to you?" rarely give grades below a B. You can end up with a wonderful grade point average. Before jumping into these professors' boats, however, take a moment to check their classes for seaworthiness. Almost inevitably, students whom sail with her **founder** in the waters of their eventual endeavors. They make the grade in college but not in their careers. Unless you enjoyed wasting your time and tuition. You would be wise to avoid these professors.

When students start **bestowing** upon professors' praise that only a **deity** deserves, be equally cautious. Code words like "she's fantastic or he's the best" will start dropping from devotees' lips when you ask about these professors. Bring up tests, papers, or projects and these worshippers will appear blissfully ignorant, and in fact, they neither noticed nor cared what their **paragons** required. To set at their heroes' feet, to hear their pronouncements, and to bask in their glory was all these idolizers needed.

Be cautious about these professors. Some do deserve praise, but a few **mavericks** have long since lost perspective on both their purpose in teaching and their ability to teach, being in their class could disillusion **Pollyanna**. They often teach their own pet theories exclusively, refusing to recognize even a shred of value in any opposing thought. If a professor's speciality is Camus, for example, he will devote four or five weeks of the semester to this one author even in a survey course. As for your future in the class, if you dont make it into his little circle of followers, nothing you write on Camus will ever please this man. Even the deserving ones pose problems, for many will have little time for you, and those that do may have personalities that don't appeal to you. Investigate them if you choose, but maintain your objectivity as you do so.

Unfortunately, the best teachers on campus have earned the repu-

Copyright © 1992 by Harcourt Brace Jovanovich, Inc. All rights reserved.

tation of being "tough, but good." These men and women will almost certainly demand true learning's pound of sweat, study, and sacrifice. They rarely wink at a student's failure and even more rarely take upon themselves responsibility for a students failure. To complete these professor's assignments, students must journey through entire worlds of thought, return to make their report, and then contend with the evaluation of a more seasoned traveler. The **antithesis** of armchair tourists, like travel stickers these professors display the evidence of their continued learning on their bulging bookshelves, in their perceptive lectures and many scholarly publications, or even their idle conversation shows how much they know. These "tough, but good" ones know their stuff and therefore offer students the best value. From these professors' classes, students will emerge exhausted, but also enlightened and invigorated and ready to tackle the most difficult challenges in life.

With an understanding of these "three catch phrases," than, students can discover the true ability and value of prospective professors—at least students can if they know the professors' identities. As for the classes taught by the **ubiquitous** "staff," students can only pick up the dice and roll.

Writing Practice 2

Choose one of the following topics to write about.

A. Many colleges and universities ask students to evaluate their professors. Write a paper in which you define a "good" or a "bad" teacher. Introduce your paper with a little story about a good or bad teacher you have had, and use as your insight this sentence: "In at least three ways,———exemplified a [good/bad] teacher." Then take three paragraphs to explain and illustrate the qualities of a "good" or "bad" teacher. Conclude with a short description of the effect the teacher in your introductory paragraph had upon you.

Copyright © 1992 by Harcourt Brace Jovanovich, Inc. All rights reserved.

B. In a balanced essay—one that explains both sides and refuses to take sides—explain the advantages and disadvantages of asking students to write evaluations of their professors. Introduce the essay with a short explanation of the practice and a description of the kinds of questions that students must respond to in these evaluations. Then take one long or two short paragraphs to explain why asking students to write evaluations is a good idea and another one or two paragraphs to explain the opposite. You may have to do a little informal research on this, perhaps finding out the effect that these evaluations have on professors' careers, whether anyone pays any attention at all to them, and so forth. (On most campuses, professors are ready to give anyone and everyone an earful on this topic.) Conclude with some implications for students: Required to complete these evaluations and given the advantages and disadvantages to the practice, how should students respond?

C. Write a descriptive essay about three teachers you have known who were interesting, bizarre, excellent, horrible, or whatever. Introduce your essay with a brief explanation of how important teachers can be in shaping a person's life, and then use this for your insight: "In my past, three teachers in particular stand out as having had an effect on my life." Use a paragraph to describe each teacher, ending each paragraph with a sentence or two on why this teacher had an effect. Then conclude briefly with a response to this discussion—perhaps an acknowledgment and brief description of how students affect their teachers' lives.

Dictionary Practice 2

Look up the words in bold print and provide a brief definition for each word as it appears in the sentence.

1. Some do deserve praise, but a few **mavericks** have long since lost perspective on both their purpose in teaching and their ability to teach.

   maverick: _____

   _____

2. As for the classes taught by the **ubiquitous** "staff," students can only pick up the dice and roll.

   ubiquitous: _____

   _____

Copyright © 1992 by Harcourt Brace Jovanovich, Inc. All rights reserved.

Match the following words with their brief definitions.

_____ 3. antithesis (p. 360)   a. hasty

_____ 4. bestow (p. 359)   b. to sink; to fail

_____ 5. cursory (p. 358)   c. to give; to convey

_____ 6. deity (p. 359)   d. a god

_____ 7. founder (verb, p. 359)   e. opposite

_____ 8. paragon (noun, p. 359)   f. a cheerful, loving, optimistic person

_____ 9. Pollyanna (p. 359)   g. a model of virtue or excellence; commendable person

PART 2

The Writing Process

CHAPTER **19**

Preparing to Write

Whether you're writing a paragraph, essay, or full-length book, trying to go directly from an assignment to a first draft is like jumping off a diving board without first checking that you have enough water to keep yourself intact. Small wonder that if you jump straight into the draft, you can end up temporarily paralyzed and unable to finish. Even less wonder that you might never want to climb up on the diving board again. You will find the entire task of writing much less daunting if you follow a process in your writing. We recommend three steps.

1. *Preparing to write:* Choosing a topic, audience, and stance; choosing a purpose and a form; generating ideas; deciding on an insight; and choosing the actual content for your paper.
2. *Drafting your paper:* Drafting your internal paragraphs, introduction, and conclusion.
3. *Revising your paper:* Checking for organization; making sure you have kept your audience and your relationship to this audience in mind; making certain you have strong words and sentences; checking for errors in punctuation, grammar, and spelling.

This chapter describes most of the work you'll be doing in the first step, preparing to write.

☐ Preliminary Choices

As you begin a writing project, you need to define certain aspects of the project: your topic, audience, stance, purpose, and form. Some of these you will be able to choose for yourself; others your professor will choose for you.

Topic

If the teacher does not assign a topic, write down two or three possible subjects—things that you are interested in, know about, or have spent a lot of time doing. From this short list of subjects, you can choose one subject and proceed through the writing process, coming back to the list if you discover you don't want to use your first choice.

Audience

Your teacher may also assign a specific audience. If not, then your second step is to decide who your reader will be. Why is this so important? Think about it this way: Have you ever had the phone ring and picked it up, only to find that you couldn't hear the person on the other end? It could have been your sister, an obnoxious salesperson, a wrong number, or your boss. Without hearing anything from the other person, you couldn't respond at all and probably just hung up.

And yet you sometimes write an entire essay without having any idea of the person who will be reading your work. No wonder you have trouble deciding what to include. If writing for grade school children, you might develop a paper on the offensiveness of Smurfs one way, but write a quite different paper on the same subject for a presidential commission on children's television programming. This may seem like an extreme example, but the advantages of developing your paper to suit your audience apply to anyone and any subject.

Of course, you probably always have at least a vague notion of the kind of person you are writing to. Ideally, however, when you write a paper, you will have in mind a real person who can *represent* your audience, someone with skin on his or her face: not "someone in high school" but your little brother; not "a colleague at work" but Mona, who drinks coffee with you every day; not "someone who thinks watching professional sports is dumb" but your girlfriend's stepmother, the one who's always complaining about Super Bowl mania.

Only when you know your audience on this very real level can you decide if you have developed your points to their best advantage. Through your writing, you are trying to help your readers gain an insight that you have into a subject. To do this you need to make contact with your readers, to touch whatever will make them pay attention and respond to your insight. As you write, you may be trying to entertain your readers, enrich them, advise them, or provoke anger, frustration, or disgust. Depending on your audience, you may need to explain at greater length, be funnier or more subdued, use the latest slang, or write so formally that you could be quoting from the King James Version of the Bible. But unless you know what your readers will be like, you won't be able to judge their response and know what specific examples or illustrations they need to be able to understand. So try to narrow your audience down to one person who represents your audience, someone whose reactions you can judge.

Stance

Before proceeding on your paper, you also need to decide *who you will be* as you write. This is called your *stance*. "Who *I* am?" you say. "Well, I know who *I* am!" In fact, you are many people: a sibling, a friend, perhaps a spouse, maybe an enemy, a supporter, a doubter, a dissatisfied customer, an expert, an employer, and many other people. As an employer, you can tell your employees how they should improve their work; as a colleague, you can discuss ways that your co-workers could improve their work; and as an employee, you will probably keep your mouth shut unless specifically asked for suggestions. In each case, your tone will change based on your relationship with the listener.

But let's get practical. What should your stance be for your college papers? In general, when your audience is your professor, write respectfully but with confidence. Too many students slip into the stance of humble, ignorant student, and their papers consequently scream the repeated message, "Is this right? Have I said the right thing? Am I doing okay?" If you must write as student to professor, first *separate your opinions from your facts*. Then don't apologize for your opinions, and be certain enough of your facts to state them confidently.

Sometimes your professor will give you a choice of audience so that you can write your paper more casually, as though to a friend, your grandmother, your little sister, or your roommate. Then you can choose your stance freely, your attitude toward your chosen audience determining who you will be. (Even so, you might want to save the story about rubbing Ben-Gay on the quarterback's jock strap for a real letter to your high school buddy. When you write an assigned paper, after all, whomever you choose to write to, your professor always hovers between you and your intended audience.)

Purpose

At different times, we write for different reasons—sometimes to give information, sometimes to tell a story or create a picture in words, sometimes to argue a controversial issue.

If your teacher leaves the assignment open, then you may want to postpone deciding on your purpose until after you have generated ideas on your subject and know what your particular insight is. Some insights lend themselves to persuasion, others to description, instruction, or narration (a story).

If your teacher gives a detailed assignment, however, this is the time to choose how best to complete that assignment. What you want to accomplish (your purpose) will help determine the way you write your paper (your strategies). If you want to write a story, you will proceed along a completely different course than if you want to write a persuasive essay, explain how to do something, or describe something.

Form

Writing projects take many forms, most commonly stories, reports, and poems, but also letters of complaint, autobiographies, scripts, brochures, advertisements, and many more. Again, if you have the choice of format, this is the time to narrow your options, including the length of your project. A short essay, such as those assigned in this book, calls for a narrow topic, with perhaps an introduction, three or four main paragraphs, and a conclusion. A twelve-page paper would require a much broader topic, and a book even broader.

Practice 1

Class discussion topic: A student has been assigned a paper on college majors, sports, or movies. He decides to write on basketball. He will wait to decide the purpose of his paper, but as his audience, he chooses his professor, a woman in her thirties who, he knows, has little interest in or knowledge about any sport except tennis. He therefore writes as a comparative expert, but writing to his teacher, he will use a respectful tone.

Copyright © 1992 by Harcourt Brace Jovanovich, Inc. All rights reserved.

Given this audience, try to classify the following basketball terms according to these categories:

    C   Too casual for use within a college paper.
    D   Formal enough, but needs a definition or identification.
    OK   Acceptable as is.

Answers will vary, but in your discussion try to come to a consensus on the best category for each word.

_____	zone	_____	breakaway foul
_____	three-point shot	_____	juke
_____	jump shot	_____	sky hook
_____	professional teams	_____	jump ball
_____	NCAA	_____	the basket
_____	bounce pass	_____	zebras
_____	offense	_____	dribble
_____	Wilt Chamberlain	_____	Earl the Pearl
_____	charging	_____	key
_____	the Palace	_____	skying
_____	technical foul	_____	referee
_____	shot-clock	_____	Magic
_____	slam-dunk	_____	guard
_____	charity stripe	_____	hang-time
_____	hoops	_____	free throw

Practice 2

Class discussion topic: A student decides to write a persuasive paper on why music shouldn't be censored. The professor knows little about rock music, so the student must consider the following terms. Classify each as one of the following:

    C   Too casual for use within a college paper.
    D   Formal enough, but needs a definition or identification.
    OK   Acceptable as is.

Copyright © 1992 by Harcourt Brace Jovanovich, Inc. All rights reserved.

370 Chapter 19 Preparing to Write

Answers will vary, but try to come to a class consensus on the best category for each word.

_____	CD	_____	Talking Heads
_____	guitar licks	_____	MC Hammer
_____	lyrics	_____	mix
_____	rhythm section	_____	Dead Head
_____	British Invasion	_____	cut
_____	powerhouse jam	_____	MTV
_____	independent label	_____	audiophile
_____	censorship	_____	soundstage
_____	sound quality	_____	rocker
_____	*Rolling Stone*	_____	punk
_____	committed fan	_____	"Material Girl"
_____	rap	_____	acoustic
_____	R&B	_____	ballad
_____	synthesizer	_____	Grammy
_____	electronic drums	_____	*Abbey Road*
_____	lead guitar	_____	boogie
_____	music video		

Practice 3

The following terms would be appropriate if you were writing a note to a close friend. For each term, provide an equivalent word or phrase that would be appropriate for a formal paper.

1. kids _____
2. clobbered _____
3. wiped out _____
4. pucker up _____
5. blown away _____
6. brown nose _____
7. kinda gross _____
8. get it? _____

Copyright © 1992 by Harcourt Brace Jovanovich, Inc. All rights reserved.

9. like, wow! _____

10. bugged me _____

11. spilled my guts _____

12. pig out _____

13. blow it off _____

14. chill out _____

▣ Generating Ideas

Having decided on your topic, audience, stance, purpose, and form, you can move on to generating ideas for your paper. How you proceed with deciding on your content will depend on your assignment. This section suggests some different strategies for generating ideas, varying with the kind of assignment the professor gives.

Expository Essay

An expository essay explains or clarifies something and therefore imparts information to readers. Sometimes, when teachers assign this kind of paper, you will have a hard time deciding how to begin. Some writers find that it helps to begin with random visual images. Ask yourself what picture comes to mind when you say your chosen topic, and write down whatever stands out most strongly from this picture. Then play out this idea, first with general observations, and finally with questions. Once you have questions, you have the possibility for answers, which is the information you will clarify or explain.

For example, if you are writing on "Fast-food restaurants," you might begin with a list like this:

What Comes to Mind	**What You Write Down**
A vision of a certain employee at the neighborhood taco place	Uniforms: Don't fit well, usually boring Not much variety Why do they need to wear them? Identify workers Team spirit Help with cleanliness?

Copyright © 1992 by Harcourt Brace Jovanovich, Inc. All rights reserved.

Getting a cup with a movie tie-in at a hamburger place	Promotional items: Glasses, plastic figures, sweepstakes, contests What do chains have to pay for the right to use tie-ins? Is it competitive? How do they choose what to do? Do sales go up during contests?
Nearby restaurant being remodeled	Remodeling: Is there a common decorating style? Lots of plants, pastel colors Nostalgia—pictures of old things Flowers, light Why do they use a certain style? Are there decorating no-no's?

As you can see, pictures or ideas that come to mind as you are mulling over a topic can easily lead to questions. Those questions are valuable: If *you* are wondering about something, chances are your eventual readers will share your curiosity. Answering the questions that come to your own mind will help you write interesting content.

Descriptive Essay

For a paper in which you will be describing something, you could begin with each of the five senses and branch out from there. For example, here's a list of ideas you might come up with for a paper on a symphony concert.

Look	audience all looking forward, nice clothes in expensive section, more casual in the balcony, bright lights on stage, active conductor, movement of violins, percussion instruments at back of stage, black skirts on women, white blouses and shirts, black tuxedos, isolated movements in audience
Sound	smooth notes of violin, loud and sudden percussion, mellow cello, rustle every now and then in audience, conductor turning pages, person nearby popping gum (yuck)
Smell	stale cigarettes, wood, body odor, dust, polish, wool, occasional whiff of perfume or aftershave

Feel	slight roughness of seat, elbow of person in next seat (sharing arm of seat), seat bottom comes up whenever anyone moves, slight slope of floor toward stage
Taste	lingering taste of punch, after-dinner coffee, lipstick, breath-mint

For a descriptive paper, you can use many schemes to gather your ideas. Try going visually from right to left, or from prominent to background features. You might start with dominant sensual features and go to more subtle features. Just remember that the strongest description involves *all* the senses.

Narrative

For a story, you might list the events in the story, grouping them according to beginning (where you explain the circumstance that is the reason for the story), the middle (where you try different ways to resolve the circumstance), and the end (where you finally resolve everything).

Beginning	Deciding where to go to college
	Dad said, go where he graduated from or no money.
	I wanted to stay home, go to a local college—girlfriend here, have a decent part-time job—up for a supervisor job
Middle	Tried to put off decision; tried to change his mind—explained about job (left out Julie); had a big argument—Dad stayed determined—not even mad, or defensive, just "Go there or pay your own way."
	Tried to tell him his school had changed since he went there—he didn't seem to care (still read alumni magazines from cover to cover and contributed money).
	I looked into costs. Got a commitment from Dad on what he'd pay. He reminded me to check out education, but both colleges were pretty good.
End	Finally decided, if he was that determined, better just go. Got him to agree to one semester and then a transfer if I hated it. In the end, broke up with Julie anyway, and like this school a lot. Dad's being nice—hasn't rubbed my face in it.

How detailed you become in your story will depend on how long you want your story to be. If you want a fairly long story, you would probably add much more detail to your list. If you want to write a short narrative essay, you might break the events down into four or five paragraphs.

Persuasive Essay

For a persuasive essay you can start by listing reasons to support your claim, expanding each reason with examples. For example, here's an idea list for an essay on why homes should not have televisions.

Reason	Examples, Expansions
Build personal relationships	Talking, esp. at meals Playing card or board games together Pursuing hobbies together Have time to write letters
Build your mind	Read more Take evening classes Join discussion groups Avoid TV media's biases and value judgments, and make choices on more in-depth analyses and real-life events
Build your health	Spend time doing physical activities See fewer food commercials so resist eating Get to sleep earlier Avoid anxiety of seeing too much violence on TV

Again, the length of your paper will help determine how deeply you cover each of these reasons.

These are only four examples of the ways you can collect ideas on a topic. At this stage, don't limit yourself. As you gather your ideas for a paper, let your thoughts roam freely. You want as long a list as possible so that you can select the most intriguing and productive ideas for your essay. Always try to fill up a page or two of these random ideas if you possibly can.

Copyright © 1992 by Harcourt Brace Jovanovich, Inc. All rights reserved.

Sample: Generating Ideas

Earlier in this chapter, we introduced a student who is writing a paper on basketball. See pages 368–369 to review his chosen audience and stance. We will keep coming back to this student in Chapters 19–22, following along as he develops his paper. At this point, he is generating ideas.

As he begins, he finds himself making a list comparing professional basketball and college basketball—something he has been thinking about lately. Please notice how choppy these notes are. The writer has made no attempt to write in complete sentences or to bend his notes into any special organization, other than the two main headings. That's fine at this stage when you want ideas, not coherent writing.

College	**Pro-**
younger players	more seasoned capable players
lower scores	
longer shot-clock (45 sec)	shorter shot-clock (24 sec)
shorter season	longer season—all the way till June
only four years	sometimes up to ten years or more—whole careers
usually four years together—or rather, predictable departures from team, although sometimes players leave early	unexpected trades
school to do at the same time	full-time job

different defenses
    Georgetown-Princeton
    What difference between them?
	only man-to-man defense
	technical fouls/illegal defense

more control	more stars, less teamwork
lots of fun to watch	can be really exciting
younger, some still growing	cold, professional, a job to them sometimes arrive at games tired come in flat
shorter three-point range	longer three-point range

Copyright © 1992 by Harcourt Brace Jovanovich, Inc. All rights reserved.

Practice 4

Choose one of the following general topics, assume that your audience is a professor, and choose a purpose for your paper (to instruct, to describe, to tell a story, or to persuade). Then generate a list of random thoughts (like the earlier examples) for a short essay.

> Talk-show ethics
> Drugs
> Living arrangements in college
> Violence in our society
> Homelessness
> Ethnic foods

☐ Deciding on Your Insight

After making a long list of ideas, you need to go back and choose a central idea to focus your writing on, something you want to describe, explain, or argue. This central idea is your *insight* (also called a *thesis*), the special perspective that you have on a topic, the aspect of the topic that you, as an individual—can best discuss. In some cases, you will choose this insight based on what you already know and have experienced. In other cases, you will choose this insight based on what you are willing to find out: Your curiosity about some aspect of the topic will drive you on until you arrive at an insight. Occasionally, an insight will seem irresistible because it offers a humorous, suspenseful, or emotional approach to a topic.

As you proceed through the writing process, everything in your paper will eventually relate in some way to this insight, whether your paper is a short essay or a full-length book. Whatever your choice, your insight should lend itself to some kind of development. It can't be so obvious or simple that you can't expand it. For an essay, look for an insight that you can expand into a presentation of three or four sub-points. These sub-points will form the body of your paper. For longer papers, your insight might expand into two or more sections, each of which can be broken into sub-points. Books need an even broader beginning point. Chapter 20 explains how to choose these internal sections. For now, as you look at your list of ideas, if sub-points begin to emerge under a heading, you may have found your insight.

How would this work with the expository essay on fast-food restaurants? Perhaps you might come up with some great explanations on why fast-food employees have to wear such ugly clothes. Or you might notice a humorous approach to these restaurants' decor. For the descriptive essay on the symphony concert, you might want to share your insight on which characteristics of the setting help a concert-goer concentrate on the music and which distract. For the story about choosing a college, the insight may be the necessity for compromise when two people disagree or, alternatively, what happens when one person holds the winning cards (in this case, a bank card). And for the persuasive paper on TV, you could make it personal by claiming your own life would have been better without television. Whatever you choose from your list of thoughts, this central idea will be your insight. Everything else in your paper should help your reader to gain this same insight.

Through the entire process of deciding what to say in your writing, you should relax and not worry about how you write your ideas down. Use single words, phrases, sentences, or a series of sentence fragments to collect your ideas. In the preliminary steps of writing, *what* you write—the ideas and information—is far more important than *how* you write it.

You might write even your insight as a short phrase to begin with. Before you begin to draft your paper, however, you should try to state your insight as a single sentence. As you proceed, this sentence may change because writing requires flexibility. You need to be willing to keep what works, change what doesn't, and throw out some ideas entirely. But getting your insight into a sentence at this point will help to keep your paper focused.

What will this sentence look like? If you look back over the essays in this book, you will find many examples of insight sentences. The following examples, grouped according to purpose, have been taken from essays in this book, as noted by page number. Notice the many different ways this central focus is introduced: some in detailed, descriptive sentences, and others in only brief statements. Each serves to let the reader know what the writer's perspective on the topic will be.

Expository Essays

"Tomato Trees and a Cure for AIDS"   (page 114)

Insight: If we have developed the technology to transport millions of gallons of crude oil across our precious oceans, then we had better develop the technology to clean up our inevitable messes.

Copyright © 1992 by Harcourt Brace Jovanovich, Inc. All rights reserved.

"The Real Miracle" (page 135)

Insight: The way television commercials portray family life is especially unrealistic.

"Code Words" (page 358)

Insight: These code words will often reveal the practices of a certain teacher, knowledge that can be useful as you choose your classes.

Descriptive Essays

"Community Crossroads" (page 340)

Insight: To a grocery store, though, come all kinds, for all except the most prosperous line up behind a grocery cart each week.

"My Wife the Scientist" (page 172)

Insight: Still, I wonder if anyone begins to understand how difficult it is to be married to a scientist.

Narrative

"Odysseus and the Cyclops" (page 110)

Insight: With his ship and his boatload of men, he (Odysseus) wandered the Aegean Sea looking for trouble, and when, after a great storm, he finally reached an island and managed to lead his weary crew onto shore, he found it.

"Painted Faces" (page 220)

Insight: These women spend a fortune (no exaggeration) trying to balance their act somewhere between the Gerber Baby and the Joker.

Persuasive

"College Reasons" (page 250)

Insight: In college, students should have better reasons for identifying sources than just to avoid the charge of plagiarism.

"Who Are the Greatest?" (page 252)

Insight: In more ways than one, though, basketball players stand taller than anyone else among the giants of professional sports.

With some topics you will know immediately what your insight will be, probably because the topic is one you have thought about many times. If you are a pro-basketball fan, for example, assigned to do a comparison-contrast paper, you may know immediately that you want to write a paper comparing the Celtics and the Bulls, with the insight that the Celtics show more teamwork. If your topic seems obvious, so that you can skip these first two steps of listing ideas and choosing an insight, that's fine. But letting the insight arise out of your random thoughts liberates you from that original panic of an unfamiliar topic and allows you to choose the best of many ideas.

Sample: Choosing an Insight

The student writing on basketball looks over his list (see page 375) and decides that the most important differences are as follows:

> The man-to-man defense in the professional games versus the variety in college.
> The shorter shot-clock in professional games.
> The greater ability in professional games.

These create definite differences, but the student still thinks that both games provide a lot of excitement. Therefore, as a preliminary insight for his comparison-contrast paper, this student writes:

> *Insight:* College and professional basketball have differences—like defense, the shot-clock times, and pro-teams are a lot better. But still, they're both great.

Remember, however, that this student is not yet ready to begin writing his paper just because he has an idea for his insight. This is a *preliminary* insight designed to direct further preparation for writing. The words *better* and *great*, in particular, are too vague and subjective for a final draft: Could two people agree on what this writer meant with these terms? Even so, the writer is doing well to get his insight down in words—even if these words are not outstanding—because this gives him something to work from.

Practice 5

Given the following set of random thoughts, locate three ideas, comparisons, categories, or reasons, and write a preliminary insight. (Use different TV shows if you prefer.)

Television
Kinds of shows: sitcoms, soap operas, police shows—and detective, cartoons
    drama shows—Star Trek   Murder, She Wrote
   sitcom—Cosby Show   Growing Pains   Designing Women
   soap operas—???
   police-detective shows—too many to list

Copyright © 1992 by Harcourt Brace Jovanovich, Inc. All rights reserved.

380 Chapter 19 Preparing to Write

Why so many detective-cop shows?
    puzzle—people like to figure something out
        Murder, She Wrote   Perry Mason   Matlock
        Some clubs get together to watch Murder, She Wrote and try to figure it out before she does
    great leads—Magnum PI
        tough—Mike Hammer, crazy—Rockford, clever—McGyver
        great disguises—Mission, Impossible
    interest feeds interest—the more they have on TV, the more people like them
    good vs. bad—Hawaii 5-O   Spenser for Hire   Wild, Wild West
    exciting—McGyver
    get to see the seamy side of life—sex, violence, crime, drug world
        Hill Street Blues   Miami Vice
    a mixture of drama and romance—Moonlighting   Scarecrow and Mrs. King

Appeal of sitcoms—laughter, poke fun at our own lives, short, usually painless—sometimes not, All in the Family
    people we can like, things always turn out okay for them—Growing Pains   Cosby Show
    candy-coated lessons—Designing Women   Head of the Class
    just crazy fun—Bob Newhart   Dick Van Dyke   Lucy Show

Appeal of other shows
    soap operas: romance, love, divorce, misunderstanding
    cartoons—keeps the kids quiet
    dramas—who knows? never have liked them much, except maybe L.A. Law and that has quirky characters, rich people, a little suspense
    news shows—gives a person a chance to watch self-righteous, know-it-all newscasters feed their egos—also interesting

Insight: _____

_____

_____

Exercise

Return to the list of ideas you created for Practice 4 on page 376. Look carefully over your list of random thoughts and write a preliminary insight for a short essay. (If you did not do Practice 4, go back and do it now, and then write your insight.)

Copyright © 1992 by Harcourt Brace Jovanovich, Inc. All rights reserved.

CHAPTER **20**

Deciding What to Include

Once you have chosen your topic, audience, stance, purpose, and form, have generated a list of ideas, and have written a preliminary insight, most of your preparation is done. But one task remains before actually beginning to write your paper. Using your insight as a reference point, you need to choose the information that will form the body of your paper. Then, when you know what will be in the internal portion of the paper, you can write an introduction about it. The conclusion will also depend on the body and is best left until the rest of the paper has been written.

◻ Generating Topic Sentences

Your next step is to generate some ideas to use as topic sentences for the internal paragraphs. Chances are good that as you went through the process of generating ideas for your insight, you already listed some possible ideas for internal paragraphs. Use these to begin a new list, adding ideas that will help you clarify, demonstrate, support, or give an account of your insight. List as many ideas as you can, even as many as eight or ten if possible, so that you can look back over the list and choose the three with the best potential for being developed into a paragraph. Later if you can't find anything to say about one of these ideas, you can go back and choose another.

Practice 1
For each of the following insight statements, list three or four specific ideas from which you could develop the topic sentences for your internal paragraphs.

Descriptive Essay

1. Description of People: *Professional athletes can serve as role models for courage in the face of adversity.* List people you can describe that demonstrate this insight.

   _____

   _____

   _____

Expository Essay

2. Comparison-Contrast: *Although television and movies seem similar, they affect viewers differently.* List ways that television and movies differ in their effect on viewers.

   _____

   _____

   _____

3. Definition: *Freedom has many meanings, but to a college student, freedom means the ability to choose.* List aspects of college that will clarify this definition.

   _____

   _____

   _____

4. Classification: *Even given all the different cars that people drive, only three (or four?) kinds exist.* Choose three or four categories for cars.

   _____

   _____

   _____

5. Cause and effect: *In a crisis, Americans from many different economic and social backgrounds cooperate in order to solve a problem.* List crises, nationally publicized or others you know of, that you can use to illustrate cooperation.

   _____

   _____

   _____

Copyright © 1992 by Harcourt Brace Jovanovich, Inc. All rights reserved.

Narrative

6. **Story:** *Every now and then, a father (or mother, sibling, friend) does something that makes everyone who knows him (or her) proud.* List the main events in this story.

_____

_____

_____

7. **Process:** *Although for most classes I study hard, I have a reliable method of cramming for emergencies.* List the steps in the process.

_____

_____

_____

Persuasive Essay

8. **Argument:** *Whatever anyone else says, I like (dislike) working out.* List reasons why this is so, especially reasons that will convince someone you are right.

_____

_____

_____

When you have a list of ideas for your topic sentences, limit your list to what you can cover in the assigned length. Then you can decide in what order you want these ideas. This is a crucial step, for even the best ideas will lose their force if poorly organized. Some topics offer an obvious structure. In a process paper, you can almost always structure your paper according to the sequence of the process. In a narrative, you might follow a time sequence (although, in a story, you might want to vary this structure).

But when you are confronted with three distinct ideas, such as for a persuasion or a classification paper, in what order do you put your internal paragraphs? You might save your best idea for last, whether that is your strongest reason, funniest feature, most interesting category, or most richly detailed characteristic. Then you can select your second-best idea for your first internal paragraph and bury your third idea in the middle. (Once you begin writing, of course, you may want to rearrange the sequence of your ideas.)

Copyright © 1992 by Harcourt Brace Jovanovich, Inc. All rights reserved.

Your next step is to write out some preliminary topic sentences. When you do so, include transition words that will help make your organizational structure obvious to your readers (or even just to yourself as you proceed with writing). For example, if your structure is a sequence, you might use transition words like these:

> First . . . Next . . . Finally . . .

If your structure is a list—of categories, differences, reasons, consequences—you might use transition words like these:

> First . . . Second . . . Last . . .
>
> One [reason] . . . Another . . . A final . . .

Sample: Ideas for Topic Sentences

The following examples show how the student writing on basketball starts to define his internal paragraphs with topic sentences. Because he is still in the preliminary stages of his writing project—in other words, still deciding what he wants to say—he hasn't yet revised his insight to eliminate the weak terms *better* and *great*. This means his thinking on his insight is still a little fuzzy; he still doesn't know himself why pro-teams are better or exactly how both teams are great. Fussing too much now over the exact wording of his insight would mean denying the power of learning that occurs as he organizes and composes his thoughts into a coherent message. Eventually, writing the internal paragraphs will sharpen his insight into his topic. In the same way, his first topic sentences are wordy, choppy, and in some places almost like notes (in the final draft, he will surely eliminate the dashes). *Ideas count at this stage, not form, so don't put too much pressure on yourself to polish your writing.*

> *Insight:* College and professional basketball have differences —like defense, the shot-clock times, and pro-teams are a lot better. But still, they're both great.
>
> *Topic Sentence 1:* First, pro-teams must use man-to-man defense —college teams can use the zone, too, and that means that they can have a lot more different kinds of games.
>
> *Topic Sentence 2:* Pro-teams also play a lot faster because their shot-clock gives about half the time—24 seconds, and college teams play a lot slower because their shot-clock is 45 seconds.

Copyright © 1992 by Harcourt Brace Jovanovich, Inc. All rights reserved.

Topic Sentence 3: Finally, pro players have played a lot longer, so they can play a lot better—score more, defense better.

Practice 2

Use the ideas that you listed under one of the insight statements in Practice 1 (pages 376–379) and write three topic sentences for a short paper.

1. _____

2. _____

3. _____

▪ Choosing the Content

Whatever kind of paper you are writing, your ultimate purpose is to share your insight with your readers. How can you select the ideas that will allow you to do this? You can do this best by using specific, concrete examples and illustrations to communicate your insight.

These specific, concrete details add spice to writing because your reader can picture something. Write down *pizza* rather than *food*, *sweats* rather than *comfortable clothes*, and *Maserati* rather than *expensive car*, and your reader will know *precisely* what you are writing about. Abstract words, such as *food*, *clothes*, or *car*, give your reader too many options to choose from and make it harder for you to communicate an idea.

Let's suppose that you believe comfort counts for more than looks in choosing clothes. If you write *comfortable clothes*, to your reader these words could mean old jeans, baggy shorts, oversized shirts, a gathered skirt and polo shirt, or many other items. If you give your readers that many options, they probably won't bother choosing any one of them to form a picture, and you'll lose the benefit of giving them something they can feel, touch, taste, or smell. Mention *sweats* instead, and they will feel the softness of the fleece on their legs and the baggy fit over their seats, the stretch in the waist and the ease in bending. With these sensations, won't they be more inclined to agree with your argument?

Furthermore, your readers will be more likely to gain your insight if they can follow for themselves the same course that you followed in gaining the insight yourself. This means giving them the reasons why you have an insight. If you tell your reader that your friend Harriet does weird and crazy things (your insight), your reader may or may not be willing to take your word for it. If you follow this statement with a specific incident (one of your reasons for the insight), such as the time Harriet stood at the entrance of Jumping Joe's Burgers and handed out straws to everyone, then your readers can decide for themselves that you are right—your friend does do some strange things. Specific, vivid, concrete details and examples will allow readers to decide for themselves that your insight is valid.

Of course, your readers will also expect some ideas from you that are not specific and concrete. Without at least a framework of abstract ideas, you'll sound like a wordy four-year-old who hasn't yet developed an ability to perceive any design to events, any similarities, patterns, or categories in the world. An ability to create, use, and understand abstract words like *beauty, truth, love,* and *infinity* sets humans apart from other living creatures. Your readers will want these abstract ideas in your papers. In your insight sentence and topic sentences, in particular, you will probably have to depend on abstract words to be able to state your idea.

As you decide how to expand your more abstract topic sentences into full paragraphs, however, choose the most vivid, concrete, and specific examples and details that you can. These will help you communicate your insight most effectively. If it helps, think of your specific details as the pontoons under a raft on which your abstract ideas will have to travel—from you, across a vast expanse of boredom, indifference, and competition, to your reader. Given today's busy world, your ideas will have a rough trip. Load too many abstract ideas into an essay with only a few specific, vivid details to support it, and the essay and your insight will sink. Stick to only a few abstract ideas, float them out on vivid details, and your ideas will have an easy trip.

Copyright © 1992 by Harcourt Brace Jovanovich, Inc. All rights reserved.

How can you generate vivid details? As you take notes for the final content of your paragraphs, use words that evoke a picture in the mind—something your readers can see, smell, feel, hear, or taste.

Your last step in preparing to write, therefore, is to write down your insight and your topic sentences. Then, for each topic sentence, list the most vivid, specific, and concrete examples, illustrations, explanations, or descriptions that will support and expand your topic sentence. You will use these notes to write your paragraphs.

Sample: Listing Specific Examples

The following lists show how the student writing on basketball chose specific examples for his three topic sentences. With such detailed notes, he should have little trouble actually drafting the paragraphs.

Notice that while these notes sometimes look like finished sentences, they are often only isolated words or phrases. Notice as well that while listing examples that he might use, this student decided to alter his original plans, changing his second and third topic sentences. This is the flexibility that writing offers.

> *Topic sentence 1:* First, pro-teams must use man-to-man defense—college teams can use the zone, too, and that means that they can have a lot more different kinds of games.
>
> Princeton-Georgetown game: Princeton, heavily expected to lose, controlled the game by using a zone defense and slowing the game down. They usually took the entire 45-second clock. 1989 NCAA tournament. Georgetown finally won—a few crucial shots going in, maybe the excitement of Princeton, lack of experience—but Princeton almost won.
>
> Pro-teams: less team strategy (or maybe just can set it up more quickly?). Star quality really develops. When a player (Michael Jordan?) starts having a hot streak, the rest of the players can pull away from the key. Draws the defense away. Leaves open lane. Jordan "jukes" his own man, gets past and POW! slam-dunk.
>
> *Topic sentence 2:* Pro-teams also play a lot faster because their shot-clock gives about half the time—24 seconds, and college teams play a lot slower because their shot-clock is 45 seconds.

But maybe pro-teams can just set up their offensive plays more
   quickly.
Also don't always need a second chance—better shooters.
Can adjust more easily.
45-second clock an allowance for college students.
Other allowances: shorter three-point shot.
Shorter game.

Revised topic sentence 2: The rules give college players certain allowances, such as the 45-second clock, the shorter three-point shot, and the shorter game, because of college teams' inexperience.

Topic sentence 3: Finally, pro players have played a lot longer, so they can play a lot better—score more, defense better.

Already covered in paragraph 2?
Example of college inexperience: NCAA final in the 80s. Georgetown player tossed the ball into James Worthy in the last few
   seconds (North Carolina) and lost the championship.
But Isiah Thomas tossed ball into Larry Bird in '86 championship
   game, Boston went on to finals with Lakers . . .
Both exciting, both can get excited about winning (though pros
   usually during play-offs), both make mistakes.
Dennis Rodman down the court with fist in the air.
College players jumping over victory, crushed when they lose.

Revised topic sentence 3: The teams are different, but they're the same, too.

James Worthy example
Excitement
Take a lot of practice, skill, natural ability

Practice 3

For practice in thinking of vivid, concrete details, list four or five specific examples for each of these abstract terms.

1. water sports: _____

2. city life/country life: _____

3. great music: _____

4. flattering statement: _____

5. hairstyle: _____

6. a popular vacation spot: _____

7. hiking gear: _____

8. late-night snacks: _____

9. faddish clothes: _____

10. movie heartthrobs, both male and female: _____

11. high school activities: _____

12. college activities: _____

13. happy home life: _____

14. the trouble with preschoolers: _____

15. political issues: _____

Practice 4

A few years ago Charles Schultz, the creator of "Peanuts," gave our popular culture the saying, "Happiness is a warm puppy." In doing so, he took an abstract concept, happiness, and gave it a specific picture. For the following abstract concepts, provide a specific incident in which the person might experience or demonstrate the concept. The first three have been done as an example.

1. Loneliness

    a. For a college student: <u>opening an empty mailbox</u>

    b. For separated spouses: <u>making only one cup of coffee in the morning</u>

    c. For parents whose last child went off to college: <u>buying only one half-gallon of milk each week—and not finishing even that</u>

2. Tension

    a. For a college student: _____

    b. For a parent: _____

    c. For an employee: _____

3. Relief

    a. For a college student: _____

    b. For an elementary-aged child: _____

    c. For a professional athlete: _____

4. Adventure

    a. For a college student: _____

    b. For a baby: _____

    c. For a movie-goer: _____

Copyright © 1992 by Harcourt Brace Jovanovich, Inc. All rights reserved.

5. Success
   a. For a college student: _____

   _____

   b. For a scientist: _____

   _____

   c. For anyone: _____

   _____

6. Foolishness
   a. For a college student: _____

   _____

   b. For a parent: _____

   _____

   c. For anyone: _____

   _____

7. Decency
   a. For a college student: _____

   _____

   b. For a tourist: _____

   _____

   c. For a sister or brother: _____

   _____

8. Courage
   a. For a college student: _____

   _____

   b. For a high school teacher: _____

   _____

   c. For anyone: _____

   _____

Copyright © 1992 by Harcourt Brace Jovanovich, Inc. All rights reserved.

☐ Preparing to Write: A Summary

Preparing to write usually requires four steps.

1. Make certain you know your topic, audience, stance, purpose, and form, whether these matters are determined by your teacher or decided by you.
2. List random ideas on your topic until you gain an insight that you want to share.
3. Decide what the body of your paper will cover, drafting your ideas as topic sentences for the internal paragraphs. (For the shorter essays assigned in this book, this means listing three or four topic sentences.)
4. Generate the concrete, specific illustrations and examples that will support each topic sentence.

Exercise

Choose one of the following topics and work through the four steps of prewriting.

A. Martin Luther King and Mahatma Gandhi each helped to bring about radical changes in their societies through a policy of nonviolence. Compare the advantages and disadvantages of violent and nonviolent intervention.

B. Convince an adult to learn to read.

C. Describe how you decide when it is acceptable (if ever) to lie.

D. Define the qualities or characteristics that make a person a good friend.

E. Write an account of what it would be like to be homeless, using one day as an example.

F. Defend the decision that a person should (or should not) be willing to create an advertising campaign for a product he or she knows is defective or harmful (such as cigarettes).

Copyright © 1992 by Harcourt Brace Jovanovich, Inc. All rights reserved.

CHAPTER **21**

Writing a Draft

After you have worked through the prewriting tasks discussed in Chapters 19 and 20, you are ready to draft your paper. While the structure of your paper may vary somewhat depending on its particular purpose and form, the essays assigned in this book call for three main sections: an introduction, two or more internal paragraphs, and a conclusion.

The introduction, which sets the context for your insight, will draw your readers into the paper. The content of the internal paragraphs will provide the examples, illustrations, descriptions, and details that allow the readers to decide for themselves that each topic sentence is true, and in that way accept that the insight itself is true (or so you hope). A reader is then ready to hear your conclusion—the statement at the end that answers the question, "So what?"

This may be the sequence within the paper—introduction, internal paragraphs, and conclusion—but you don't have to draft them in that order. That is, you might begin by writing the internal paragraphs. Having already listed (during prewriting) the specific examples, illustrations, or descriptions that you will use in your paragraphs, you should be able to write this part of the paper quite readily—that is the advantage of doing so much work on preparing to write.

As you write your internal paragraphs, you need to keep in mind three important characteristics of a paragraph: unity, coherence, and logical sequence of ideas.

■ Internal Paragraphs

Unity

Each paragraph must focus on one and only one idea. The topic sentence will determine what the paragraph is about. Whatever the topic sentence says, everything in the body of the paragraph must support

Copyright © 1992 by Harcourt Brace Jovanovich, Inc. All rights reserved.

that idea. After drafting a paragraph, read it through and ask yourself: "Does everything in this paragraph relate to the topic sentence?" This will ensure that your paragraph is unified.

What is wrong with the following paragraph?

> Like many holidays, Valentine's Day has had some strange superstitions associated with it. In the 1700s, girls pinned bay leaves to their pillows, hoping they would dream of their sweethearts. If a girl did dream of her lover, she was to marry him before the year was out. An even more devoted sweetheart boiled an egg the night before Valentine's Day, took the yolk out, filled the space with salt, and ate the egg, shell and all. She would then go to sleep without drinking or speaking. Doubtless, after such a repast, she dreamed, though whether pleasantly, one couldn't be sure. For good luck, young people rose early on Valentine's Day and tried to catch an owl and two sparrows, for with their capture, these creatures brought good luck throughout the year.[1] In much the same way, the fresh dew of the early May Day morning is also thought to bring good luck to those who bathe their faces in it.[2]

Up to the last sentence, the paragraph returns again and again to the topic of superstitions on Valentine's Day. Notice how the words *Valentine's Day* keep repeating. This repetition emphasizes the paragraph's focus. Then in the last sentence, the paragraph strays off the main subject, creating a flaw in the paragraph. In your own paragraphs, then, no matter how witty the comment, how interesting the information, or how bright the insight, leave it out unless you can show clearly that it relates to your main topic.

This does not mean that your topic sentence must come at the beginning of the paragraph. If you think it belongs in the middle or at the end, put it there. But wherever you put it, your reader should be able to discern what your topic is.

Coherence

All the parts of a paragraph must relate to each other. You might enjoy bringing seemingly divergent or different ideas to a topic, and that's

---

[1] J. Walker McSpadden, *The Book of Holidays* (New York: Thomas Y. Crowell, 1958), p. 30.
[2] McSpadden, p. 74.

not wrong—in fact it may be a very creative approach. Just be sure that you always show how these divergent ideas relate to the main point of your paragraph. Furthermore, make sure that the sentences flow smoothly from one to the next. Transition words can help you establish this coherent flow. Following are some common transition words and their uses.

> To show contrast: *however, nevertheless, instead*
> To show progression: *first, next, second, after this, then*
> To show similarity: *in the same way, likewise, similarly, also*
> To show example: *for example, this is, one example, for instance*
> To show cause: *for this reason, consequently, and so, thus*
> To show concession and acknowledgment: *even though, of course, although, though*
> To show passage of time: *first, next, then, later, afterwards, until, when, finally*
> To show place: *in the foreground, in the background, at the left, in the middle, at the right*

In this paragraph about stamp collecting, notice how the underlined transition words hold the series of examples together.

> Stamp collecting offers more than just a hobby; it offers a glimpse into the country of origin. Stamps regularly feature major landmarks or buildings. Stamps from India, <u>for example</u>, show the Taj Mahal, and those from Ghana show its main port. Australia, <u>in its turn</u>, has had an entire series on its distinctive animals, and the United States has had a series on the state birds. New Zealand stamps have <u>instead</u> highlighted major exports, and Japanese stamps have shown national treasures. One long stamp from Singapore presents its four main religions through a picture of a Buddhist temple, an Islamic mosque, a Hindu temple, and a Christian church. Of all themes, <u>though</u>, flags take pride of place. Perhaps as they imagine letters and packages from their country traveling throughout the world, stamp designers like to imagine their most durable national symbol traveling with them.

Through the underlined transition words, the writer first shows the fundamental structure to be used (*for example*), then marks the first few progressions onto new examples (*in its turn, instead*), and finally highlights the last one (*though*). In this way, the transition words guide the reader through the paragraph, making the content coherent by showing how each part relates to the whole.

Copyright © 1992 by Harcourt Brace Jovanovich, Inc. All rights reserved.

Please note, however, that too many transition words can make a paragraph sound stilted. Related sentences often flow together without any transition words; not *every* sentence in the stamp-collecting paragraph carried a transition. If you are having to rely heavily on transition devices, ask yourself whether you are trying to fit too many divergent ideas together in one paragraph.

Logical Sequence

Part of writing a unified, coherent paragraph is choosing an effective sequence for your sentences. Often this sequence arises out of the topic.

If your topic calls for . . .	You will probably . . .
Examples	List them, saving the most convincing for last.
Proofs or reasons	List them, saving the most convincing for last.
Details	List them according to space (such as right/left, or moving from one characteristic to another).
Instructions	List them in order of procedure.
Explanation	Give details beginning with what the reader understands and progressing to new understanding.
Illustration	Tell the story from beginning to end, choosing details that relate to the topic sentence.

Whatever sequence you choose, look over your drafted paragraph with a critical eye. Make certain that a reader will understand what you are saying and at least be able to restate your point—if not agree. If so, then you have a well-developed paragraph.

Sample: Drafting a Paragraph

The student writing on basketball uses his notes to develop his first internal paragraph. Notice that at this point, the paragraph still has errors. The writer needs to remember his chosen audience: a teacher who knows little about basketball. Will that reader know the word *key*, much less *juke*? Will she know what the NCAA championship is? Writing as an expert to someone who knows little about a subject, the writer needs to be especially careful to define terms and stay away from slang.

Copyright © 1992 by Harcourt Brace Jovanovich, Inc. All rights reserved.

The paragraph also has weak verbs (*was, is, have*), faulty parallel structure, and punctuation errors—but these are issues of style and mechanics, and need not be a concern in a first draft. As this writer gains skills, he will be able to eliminate these problems earlier and earlier in the writing process. For now, it is enough that the paragraph develops its argument well. The writer will have a chance to revise this first draft before he turns his paper in.

NOTES

Topic sentence 1: First, pro-teams must use man-to-man defense—college teams can use the zone, too, and that means that they can have a lot more different kinds of games.

Princeton-Georgetown game: Princeton, heavily expected to lose, controlled the game by using a zone defense and slowing the game down. They usually took the entire 45-second clock. 1989 NCAA tournament. Georgetown finally won—a few crucial shots going in, maybe the excitement of Princeton, lack of experience—but Princeton almost won.

Pro-teams: less team strategy (or maybe just can set it up more quickly?). Star quality really develops. When a player (Michael Jordan?) starts having a hot streak, the rest of the players can pull away from the key. Draws the defense away. Leaves open lane. Jordan "jukes" his own man, gets past and POW! slam-dunk.

DRAFT PARAGRAPH

Because pro teams have to use man-to-man, and college teams can use the zone as well, college teams have more different plays in their offense. In the 1989 NCAA tournament, Georgetown, who was favored to win, was almost beat by the low-ranked Princeton team. Princeton slowed the game down with a zone. They used the entire 45-second clock each time down the court. Then they sank enough shots so that Georgetown barely pulled the game out. Professional teams on the other hand must use man-to-man, so everyone knows what their games will be like. Rather than team plays, these teams sometimes rely on getting the hot shooter free. So if the Bulls' star player, Michael Jordan, is shooting well (and he usually is), the defense is pulled out from the key to leave a lane open for Jordan. Then he can juke his guard and slam-dunk the ball. So with different rules on defense, college and professional games have different strategies.

Copyright © 1992 by Harcourt Brace Jovanovich, Inc. All rights reserved.

Practice 1

Suppose that you are writing a short essay based on the following information. Choose *one* of the three topic sentences. On a separate sheet of paper, generate some ideas, and then write a unified and coherent paragraph for that sentence.

> *Topic:* Entertainment.
> *Audience:* Interested adult, such as colleague at work.
> *Stance:* You are a fellow colleague or acquaintance, with neither more nor less knowledge than your reader, but with good ideas.
> *Purpose:* Expository (to explain or clarify something).
> *Insight:* Although many people enjoy mysteries, these mysteries appeal for different reasons.
> *Topic sentence 1:* Some mysteries gain their appeal from the threat of violence.
> *Topic sentence 2:* Other mysteries gain their appeal from the question of who did something.
> *Topic sentence 3:* The best mysteries, the ones that can be enjoyed a second time, gain most of their appeal from the characters.

☐ Writing an Introduction

A good introduction pulls your readers into your paper, sparking their interest and getting their attention. Like the bright displays that sit at the entrances of stores at the mall, the introduction should make your readers stop and take notice. Having caught them, you can then entice them to find out what you really want them to gain: your insight, which usually comes at the end of your introduction. In general, you can use three devices to pull your reader into your paper: the funnel, the bait, and the challenge.

The Funnel

With the funnel, you start with your general topic and lead your readers sentence by sentence to your particular insight. Suppose this is your insight: "The way television commercials portray family life is especially unrealistic." You might begin a funnel by talking about television, then pull the reader farther toward your insight by talking about commercials, and finally put everything together in the last sentence, as this paragraph illustrates:

Americans love television. They eat their Crunch-Munchies in front of the morning news programs, pretend to dust during the soaps, and let Johnny make them drowsy enough for sleep. But whatever Americans watch, as long as they are tuned to the networks, they see a lot of commercials. These thirty-second slices become the basis for people's individual dreams and desires, even though the life that the commercials present is so often unattainable. The way television commercials portray family life is especially unrealistic. (From "The Real Miracle," page 135.)

Like a funnel that opens wide and then narrows to a point, the introduction starts with a general observation and pulls the reader closer and closer to the particular insight. Such an introduction might include definitions of necessary but unfamiliar terms, or possibly a brief historical background.

With the funnel approach, be careful that your opening statement isn't completely off the subject. Even the most general observation should relate directly to your central topic. Alternatively, you might start with a comparison, a little story, or a quotation that addresses the topic generally, then gradually shift down to your particular thesis. The essay "Tomato Trees and a Cure for AIDS" (page 114), for example, begins with a reference to a news event in 1989, draws the reader down toward bioengineering, and then settles on the insight that bioengineering still seems too hazardous for most people. The essay then goes on to refute this statement and, in the conclusion, gives the insight that the benefits of bioengineering may be worth the risks. Here is the introduction:

In 1989, the Exxon oil freighter *Valdez* ran aground in Alaska, dumping over ten million gallons of crude oil into the pristine waters of Prince William Sound. Some scientists immediately considered a bioengineered solution. A tiny organism developed in the laboratory could actually eat the long carbon chains that made up the crude oil and during digestion turn these chains into environmentally safe by-products, such as alcohol. No one accepted the scientists' proposal, for even though tipsy otters would have been better than dead ones, bioengineering still seems to pose too many hazards for widespread use.

Copyright © 1992 by Harcourt Brace Jovanovich, Inc. All rights reserved.

The Bait

In starting an essay with the bait, you intentionally use a device that will catch a reluctant reader's interest. Few of us can resist listening in to someone else's conversation. At the grocery store, the movie theater, or the library, we instinctively perk up and listen when we hear someone talking. You can use your readers' curiosity and begin an introduction with a quotation, especially when that quotation is part of a short anecdote or story. The following introduction to the essay on summer internships (page 155) shows how this technique works.

> "What are you doing this summer?"
> One by one the four college friends sharing their last meal before the summer described their summer jobs, one in a fast-food restaurant, one in a family business, and one at a nearby amusement park.
> "What about you?" All eyes turned toward the fourth friend at the table.
> "Don't you remember? I'm going out to Redmond, Washington. I've got an internship with Microsoft."

In this introduction, the conversation pulls readers toward the topic (internships) and eventually to the insight sentence: "An internship, usually set up through the career development center at colleges or universities, offers more than just a nice salary."

The essay entitled "Who Are the Greatest?" (page 252) uses the bait when it starts with the obscure statement, "They are all great." This causes the reader to wonder, "Who is great and in what way?" These questions pull the reader into the essay.

> They are all great. That needs to be said first. The issue here is relative greatness, not absolute greatness. Who could fail to recognize that Larry Bird, Marcus Allen, or Nolan Ryan excel? All sports, however, do not require the same level of athleticism. They are all great athletes, just not equally great.

In this essay, the writer saves her insight for the last paragraph: "In more ways than one, though, basketball players stand taller than anyone else among the giants of professional sports."

The essay "No Lunch Boxes for Jason" (page 192) also baits the reader, using the odd circumstance that Jason never goes to school.

Copyright © 1992 by Harcourt Brace Jovanovich, Inc. All rights reserved.

> On any school day that he chooses, ten-year-old Jason can go to his front picture window and watch the neighborhood children going to school, knapsacks slung over their shoulders, lunch boxes at their sides. Jason will never go with them. With two sisters and a preschool brother to keep him company, Jason figures his fractions, scrawls out his compositions, and masters his science at home, all under the watchful eye of his mother. Jason is a homeschooler. Even though parents who teach their children at home will readily acknowledge that they have taken on a challenge, they believe they have good reasons for doing so.

These techniques, all examples of the bait, make readers curious and so pull them into the essay.

The Challenge

As a variation on the bait, you might want to start with a debatable observation. This works on the readers' instinctive desire to prove themselves right. The essay "Wasted on the Young" (page 177) begins with the debatable observation that young people don't make use of their education.

> My mother tells me that education is wasted on the young. I often have to agree. Given all the pressures, questions, adjustments, and fears that I am dealing with as an eighteen-year-old college student, I wonder sometimes if I should have waited a year or two after high school before beginning college. My classwork often gets slighted. In fact, twenty seems like a better age than eighteen to begin college.

Another kind of challenge is to begin with a question, which works on the readers' instinctive desire to know the answer or to give their own opinions. The essay "Painted Faces" (page 220) begins with questions that pull the reader into the essay.

> How much makeup is enough? How much is too much? Many women concern themselves with these questions on a daily basis. Of course, where one woman might prefer to leave her face *au naturel*, another has mastered the art and never needs to check whether her foundation and eye shadow show in streaks or her lipstick has bled halfway down her

chin. Each of these women looks perfect for any occasion. But many women are not blessed with cosmetic confidence. These women spend a fortune (no exaggeration) trying to balance their act somewhere between the Gerber Baby and the Joker.

A debatable statement or a question sometimes works well, but it has its dangers. A debatable observation can easily put you at a disadvantage. Readers might decide you aren't serious about the observation and will then feel manipulated, or readers will disagree so strongly with the statement that they will be unwilling to accept anything else you say. A blunt question at the beginning of an essay is a device that can be overused and thus become trite and predictable. In this book, note that only one essay ("Painted Faces") begins that way, and rightly so. Either the funnel or the other kinds of bait will usually seem more subtle and therefore more effective. Each technique offers its own dangers, so use them sparingly and carefully.

Whichever method you use—the funnel, the bait, or the challenge—the purpose of the introduction is the same: to pull your reader down to your insight, which usually concludes the introduction, and on into the internal paragraphs of your paper.

Sample: Drafting an Introduction

Our student writing on basketball, after considering his audience, decided to use the bait for his introduction. First he tried to think of a situation in which an uninterested reader would be likely to encounter basketball. Then he constructed the following anecdote to bring this reader into his essay.

> "So what if it's a college or professional basketball game? What's the difference?"
> Someone who rarely watches basketball might ask these questions as he or she walks through the TV lounge and sees a game on television. A true fan, however, sees many differences between college and professional games, especially in the different rules that college and professional teams play under. Even with these different rules, however, both games share the element of excitement.

If you have been following the evolution of this paper, please notice that here, finally, the insight sentence is carefully written. The writer has shifted the direction of the paper toward a comparison of rules, rather than a comparison of the subjective notion of which kind of basketball is "better." Also, instead of "great," the writer has made his praise more specific by mentioning the games' "excitement."

Original	Revision
College and professional basketball have differences—like defense, the shot-clock times, and pro-teams are a lot better. But still, they're both great.	A true fan, however, sees many differences between college and professional basketball games, especially in the different rules that college and professional teams play under. Even with these different rules, however, both games share the element of excitement.

Please notice as well that the writer has eliminated the dashes and the poor construction of his original sentence, which he wrote casually, almost as notes. But even now, the writer can still improve his writing: Does he realize that he repeats *college and professional teams* and *however*? Little flaws like this can detract from his insight. However, they can be fixed during the last step in the writing process: revising and polishing the first draft.

Because the writer's change in his insight alters the direction of the paper, his three topic sentences must change as well. After drafting this introduction, the writer revised his topic sentences once more, both to reflect his new slant and to sharpen the sentences' style as well.

Topic sentence 1: First, because rules require pro-teams to use man-to-man and allow college teams to use the zone as well, college teams have more variety in their offense.

Revised topic sentence 2: The rules give college players certain allowances, such as the 45-second clock, the shorter three-point shot, and the shorter game, because of college teams' inexperience.

Revised topic sentence 3: In spite of these differences in the rules, both games offer the fan plenty of excitement.

As is so often the case, writing the introduction helped this student to focus his paper even more specifically on one aspect of his topic.

Copyright © 1992 by Harcourt Brace Jovanovich, Inc. All rights reserved.

404 Chapter 21 Writing a Draft

Practice 2

Look at the introduction of each of the following essays (appearing earlier in this book). Identify the format as F for funnel or B for bait.

_____ 1. The Hardest Lesson (page 112)

_____ 2. "But I Studied!" (page 195)

_____ 3. How I Spend My Summer Vacations (page 55)

_____ 4. My Life as a Forty-Year-Old Student (page 96)

_____ 5. Genius by Design (page 255)

_____ 6. Clothes for College: Don't Sweat It (page 99)

_____ 7. Odysseus and the Cyclops (page 110)

_____ 8. Steel-Toed Boots and a Seat at the Game (page 137)

Practice 3

A student, Julie Mayberry, wrote the following essay for her English class, but after this draft decided that the introduction did not effectively draw the reader down to her insight: the way Washington Irving uses sayings in his short story "The Devil and Tom Walker." In this, her first draft, the insight arrives too abruptly at the end of the first paragraph. Eventually these paragraphs (without the insight) became the three internal paragraphs.

Take a sheet of paper and, based on these body paragraphs, write two different introductions for Julie's essay, one using a bait and one using a challenge. For bait, use something to catch the reader's interest. You might quote an old saying, perhaps, or start with an obscure statement, such as, "He didn't know what he was saying." Or you might begin with a question or with a debatable statement, such as, "Sometimes short-story writers don't mean what they say." Whatever you choose, remember that the introduction should draw the reader toward the insight, which in this case relates to the sayings.

   In the story "The Devil and Tom Walker," Tom and his wife hoard money. They always seem to try to outwit each other so they can take the best for themselves. Tom meets the devil in the woods and makes a deal with him. When Tom's wife learns of the deal, the devil kills her. Tom tries to put up a very "Christian" front to fend off the devil, but in the end the devil takes Tom away. Throughout the story, Irving uses familiar sayings to create certain effects.

   Washington Irving illustrates the saying, "The devil take me . . ." by describing the following scene. After Tom secretly charges more than is needed, he claims that the devil will take him if he has made any money off of the customer. The next

Copyright © 1992 by Harcourt Brace Jovanovich, Inc. All rights reserved.

moment there is a knock on the door and the devil comes in to take Tom away. Likewise, Irving uses the saying, "The devil would have his due." In most cases, this saying is only an expression, but in this case it is very real. The devil gets Tom's wife and even Tom. In the end, the devil gets everything.

In contrast, Irving gives an ironic twist to some of the sayings he uses. One of these sayings, "I'll drive them to the devil," is ironic because while Tom was going to church and acting like a Christian, he drove himself to the devil. Another saying, "Charity begins at home," is ironic because what Tom was doing could hardly be considered charity. He acted as a friend to a certain client while waiting to foreclose a mortgage that would ruin the man. The last saying Irving uses, "a friend in need," is ironic because Tom was hardly a friend at all. He appeared friendly to the people, but when they became his clients, he took advantage of them.

For her own paper, Julie decided to use the funnel technique for her revised introduction. The insight and the topic sentences have been italicized. As you read her final draft, notice how she *concludes* the essay—the subject of the next section of this chapter.

For years people have used sayings to reinforce a thought. Sometimes, though, a saying will become overused and lose its punch. When this happens, a saying needs to be used differently to regain its impact. *In "The Devil and Tom Walker," Washington Irving gives familiar sayings a new strength by using them first to emphasize the lesson in a situation and second to emphasize the irony in a situation.*

In the story, Tom and his wife hoard money. They always seem to try to outwit each other so they can take the best for themselves. Tom meets the devil in the woods and makes a deal with him. When Tom's wife learns of the deal, the devil kills her. Tom tries to put up a very "Christian" front to fend off the devil, but in the end the devil takes Tom away. *Earlier in the story, Washington Irving lets the reader know this end result through his use of sayings.* After Tom secretly charges more than is needed, he says, "The devil take me . . ." if he has made any money off of the customer. The next moment there is a knock on the door and the devil comes in to take Tom away. Likewise, Irving uses the saying, "The devil would have his due." In most cases, this saying is only an expression, but in this case it is very real. The devil gets Tom's wife and even Tom. In the end, the devil gets everything.

In contrast, Irving gives an ironic twist to some of the sayings he uses. One of these sayings, "I'll drive them to the devil," is ironic because while Tom was going to church and acting like a Christian, he drove himself to the devil. Another saying, "Charity begins at home," is ironic because what Tom was doing could hardly be considered charity. He acted as a friend to a certain client while waiting to foreclose a mortgage that would ruin the man. The last saying Irving uses, "a friend in need," is ironic because Tom was hardly a friend at all. He appeared friendly to the people, but when they became his clients, he took advantage of them.

The sayings that Irving uses give the reader a sense of how serious the situation really was. Though it appeared humorous, it was serious in every case because the devil dominated everything. He made lying and cheating appear good to Tom so the devil could profit from it. For the most part the sayings that Irving uses, both ironic and serious, reinforce the idea that the devil can control people and sometimes succeeds.

☐ Writing a Conclusion

While reading an essay, readers give their attention to the writer's arguments, analyses, descriptions, or story, letting the writer take them by the hand and lead them down the forest path. When they reach the conclusion, readers want to see where they have been heading and, more importantly, why they have come. Usually they do not want just a review of the path itself. It's true: No matter what you have heard, readers usually want more from a conclusion than just a summary. A conclusion might *include* a summary, but good conclusions offer something more, too. At their best, along with a summary (if necessary), conclusions also answer the question "So what?" by emphasizing some aspect of the essay or by suggesting some implications of the thesis.

A Simple End for a Story

Occasionally, of course, the walk through the forest is itself the destination, and especially so with narrative essays. In narratives, which tell a story, the essay often needs no other conclusion than the end of the story. The story entitled "Twice-Told Tails" (page 292) concludes this way:

> "Ajax," Palm-Olive squeaked from the kitchen, "Dad scavenged some especially moist cake and some nice green grapes for tonight's supper."

The walk is important as well to essays whose main purpose is to entertain. Notice how brief the conclusion to "The Hardest Lesson" (page 112) is.

> Even then, however, students who really hate to get up in the morning will probably still forget to set the alarm in the first place.

This ironic exposé of getting up in the morning deserves little more.

A Review

When your purpose is to teach readers, the content again counts more than the conclusion. For these essays, a summary alone may be an appropriate way to end. Looking back over the essays in this book, you will find that several include summaries. For emphasis and review, the essay entitled "College Reasons" (page 250) ends with a summary of reasons why a student should not plagiarize.

> Nevertheless, if students gain this or any other information from a book, article, interview, video, or any reference material other than their own common knowledge, they must always proceed with caution. By not citing a source, they not only risk the charge of plagiarism, but they also lose credibility and block from readers an avenue for further research.

A Parting Shot

In some essays, you can use the concluding paragraph to advantage by emphasizing some aspect of your essay, sending a parting shot at your reader. This parting shot might be to contradict something you have already discussed. In the essay "Clothes for College: Don't Sweat It" (page 99), the writer has presented sweats as a good option throughout the essay, but in the last sentence, she raises the possibility that they are *too* trendy.

> You can let sweats show the world your style, your spirit, your very essence. Even better, because all but a few die-hard punks will be wearing sweats, you will certainly fit in with the college crowd. Of course, if you would rather not join the crowd, shop anywhere but the athletic department.

The parting shot might also be a new and especially good argument. In the essay "Summer Jobs" (page 155), the writer saves her best reason for last: In internships, students will be treated as adults.

> For students who have been there, however, one advantage towers over all the rest. Many students feel that in college they are in a holding pattern between adolescence and adulthood. An internship puts students over the top, for professionals on the job usually treat students as contributing colleagues who must be mature if they are to fulfill job requirements. Perhaps, more than the internship itself, this new vision of themselves as adults becomes the lasting benefit of internships for students.

In the essay comparing the bowl system for college football play-offs and the NCAA basketball tournament (page 158), the writer again reserves her best reason for keeping bowl games: A tournament would disrupt professional football.

> So the bowl system, for all its obvious flaws, clearly satisfies in three ways. It multiplies the post-season winners, it takes little time in an already overloaded season, and it causes fewer injuries to the players. The clincher for football fans, however, is the effect of a tournament on the vastly lucrative and enormously satisfying pro-football play-offs and Super Bowl. As soon as fans remember that a college tournament would encroach on their beloved professional football, even the most avid tournament supporters will settle in happily for the New Year's Day extravaganza of bowl games.

Coming at the end, your conclusion is your last chance to convince your readers. You might well win them over by emphasizing your best points or by springing one last shot.

The Implications

You can also use concluding paragraphs to your advantage by spelling out the implications of your topic for your readers. In the essay on nontraditional students ("My Life as a Forty-Year-Old Student," page 96), the writer uses his last paragraph to spell out what his essay means for readers: not that they should be offended, but that they should recognize what he is going through.

> Calm down, reader. If you are one of the eighteen-year-old students I am writing about, please know that I do understand that you also face problems. I haven't completely forgotten my own younger years. Can you believe now, however, that when I show up for class with my assignments finished and my papers neatly typed, I have had to pay as exacting a price as you must pay for your own completed work?

The conclusion of the essay on bioengineering (page 114) also explains the implications for readers: Even if bioengineering involves hazards, because of our great needs, we must deal with these hazards.

> True, we take a risk with bioengineering. However, we risk food poisoning when we eat in a restaurant. We risk terrorists when we fly across the Mediterranean. For these hazards, we set up health standards and security measures, and then we live with the risks. We can do the same with bioengineering. If we have developed the technology to transport millions of gallons of crude oil across our precious oceans, then we had better develop the technology to clean up our inevitable messes.

In a more roundabout way, the writer who describes women's gains in "Steel-Toed Boots and a Seat at the Game" (page 137) concludes by describing the implications for readers and for himself: After years of discrimination, any gains women have made have come justly.

> After so many centuries of limited choices, of corsets and high heels, of bound dreams and fettered intellects, women's multiplicity of choices probably comes fairly and behind time. Even so, will they eventually share their gains? I grant them their dresses freely, of course, and have no desire to take up their barbaric habit of leg-shaving, but what about a Wednesday afternoon poker game? Now *that* I could handle.

In your conclusions, then, make it clear to readers why they have read the paper. A simple end to a story, a review of a lesson, a parting shot, or a statement of implications can do this. Whatever the approach, by the end of a good conclusion, readers have a definite sense of completion.

Copyright © 1992 by Harcourt Brace Jovanovich, Inc. All rights reserved.

410 Chapter 21 Writing a Draft

Sample: Drafting a Conclusion

For his conclusion on basketball, our writer finished describing how the rules allow both college and professional games to be exciting for fans. Looking back over his introduction and three internal paragraphs, he noticed how both the introduction and his third paragraph talk about fans. He decided to highlight this thread in his conclusion.

> So even though the different rules under which college and professional teams must play cause some definite differences in the games themselves, both games still offer much to basketball fans. What about the casual observer who walked through the TV lounge and asked about the difference between college and professional games? Even after a long explanation, this observer may not care to watch the rest of the game, but the fans around the TV won't notice: The second half has started.

Practice 4

Look at the conclusion of each of the following essays (appearing earlier in this book). Identify the technique the writer uses (some writers might use more than one technique), writing E for *ending* (for a story), P for *parting shot*, S for *summary*, or I for *implications*.

_____ 1. My Home, the Space Colony (page 70)

_____ 2. Odysseus and the Cyclops (page 110)

_____ 3. A Castle in the Clouds (page 174)

_____ 4. Wasted on the Young? (page 177)

_____ 5. No Lunch Boxes for Jason (page 192)

_____ 6. Painted Faces (page 220)

_____ 7. Supper's Ready! (page 223)

_____ 8. Who Are the Greatest? (page 252)

_____ 9. Genius by Design (page 255)

_____ 10. Money in the Bank (page 272)

_____ 11. Different Characters (page 274)

Copyright © 1992 by Harcourt Brace Jovanovich, Inc. All rights reserved.

CHAPTER 22

Revising Your Paper

Once you have completed an essay's internal paragraphs, its introduction, and its conclusion, you may think your work is done. But you have one more step in the writing process: revising your paper. For this step, you need to read through the essay, evaluating it, editing it, and then reading it again, continuing this loop until either the essay satisfies you or your time runs out. You should reserve enough time to go through your papers at least twice, and preferably three times. It's a good idea to concentrate on a different aspect of your paper with each rereading.

■ First Reading: Organization

In your first reading, check for organization. You can have wit so entertaining that you could be a stand-up comedian, descriptions so specific that two people working independently could draw the house you describe, sentences so well constructed and complex that your teacher puts them on the board for everyone to admire, but if you do not have a well-organized essay, your readers may never gain your insight. Okay, the sermon's over. How should you check for organization?

First, take a separate sheet of paper and write out your insight and the topic sentences from your internal paragraphs. You will end up with a list of four or five sentences, like the list in the practice exercise on pages 384–385. These sentences should present the basic structure of your essay and, with appropriate transition words in the topic sentences, should fit together as one piece. All essays that you read will not show such simple organization, especially narrative and descriptive essays. Even so, isolating the insight sentence and your paragraphs' topic sentences provides a quick review of your organization. Your insight sentence, in particular, is important. It should provide a focus for your paper and must be written in such a way that all the topic sentences relate directly to that insight.

Next, read through each internal paragraph, making certain that everything in each paragraph relates to the topic sentence—and relates so clearly that your reader will have no doubts about the relationship. If necessary, include extra sentences, phrases, or transition words to clarify this unity and to improve the flow from sentence to sentence.

Finally, when checking organization, read the introduction to evaluate how well it draws your reader into the essay and leads them to the insight. Then read the conclusion to evaluate how well it brings that feeling of finality.

☐ Second Reading: Audience and Stance

In this next read-through, check that you have covered everything that your chosen reader needs to know. In the basketball essay that compares college and professional games, the author sometimes used words his reader probably would not understand, such as *juke* and *key*. The writer would likely need to define *NCAA tournament* as well. If his reader had been a fan, of course, defining all these terms would have been demeaning, so including definitions will always depend on the chosen reader. Make certain that your words neither confuse nor demean your reader.

Make equally certain that your reader will feel comfortable with your choice of words, tone, perspective, grammar, and punctuation. If you write a newsy, informal essay, full of slang words and grammatical and punctuation errors, for a professor, it will almost always produce trouble for you. Write a formal letter, full of technical words and overly polite language, to your little sister back home, and she'll think you're crazy. So make certain that your reader will feel comfortable with your presentation.

Copyright © 1992 by Harcourt Brace Jovanovich, Inc. All rights reserved.

Third Reading: Strong Words and Sentences

Use Concrete Nouns

If you collected your ideas in lists during prewriting, you should already have the first requisite: strong nouns. By strong, we mean *specific* and *concrete*, words that evoke a picture in your reader's mind. As you read your paper a second time, look for ways to make your nouns more specific and concrete, for this will help ensure that your readers gain your insight.

Use Active Verbs

At this time, also check to be sure that you have chosen the strongest verbs. Strong verbs *do* something. They describe an action and in that way elicit a picture of movement, provide variety, and help keep the reader from becoming bored. How, specifically, can you strengthen verbs?

Get rid of the passive voice wherever you can. What does this mean? Look for sentences where the subject is acted upon rather than does the action. In the following passive sentence, the subject (*ball*) is acted upon by Chris:

> The ball was hit by Chris.

In this circumstance, who does the action? Chris does, of course. We can rewrite the sentence in the active voice so that *Chris* rightfully becomes the subject of the sentence.

> Chris hit the ball.

Using *Chris* as the subject does three things. First, *Chris* makes the sentence more interesting because by nature we gravitate toward movers and shakers, and especially more toward people than objects.

Second, using *Chris* as subject shortens the sentence. Every essay writer struggles with this challenge: to keep readers' attention. If you put a lot of empty, needless words into your sentences, you will wear out your readers' patience and lose them. Using *Chris* as subject eliminates needless words and therefore improves the sentence.

Third, using *Chris* as subject simplifies the sentence by presenting the information chronologically. The reader first meets Chris, who began the action, then proceeds through the hit, and ends with the ball. With the passive voice, the reader has to work backwards from the ball to Chris, putting the ball before the girl, to paraphrase an old saying.

Practice 1

Rewrite the following passive sentences so that they are in the active voice, beginning with the person or object that *did* something and then telling what that subject did. You may need to provide information, specifically the new subject.

1. The beaker was placed upon the burner.

2. A car was purchased last week.

3. The fruit was distributed among the children.

4. A lot of issues were discussed.

5. These notes were then reprinted.

Eliminate "to be" Verbs

Verbs like *is, are, was,* and *were* will almost certainly come easily to you, yet these verbs describe a state of being rather than an action and are therefore less vivid and interesting. Why do these weak verbs get used so much? If I ask you to close your eyes and think of your bedroom, car, family, or favorite holiday, you will probably imagine a picture, not a movie. In other words, you will see a condition, not an action, so this condition is what you describe. But just as we would all rather see a movie than a filmstrip, so also our readers would prefer to see action rather than condition. To reach our readers, to entertain them and keep them, we must purposely switch from condition verbs (describing a still picture) to action verbs (describing a movie in which someone *does* something).

Weak	Stronger
Last Christmas was exciting. The tree was on the floor when we came down for breakfast. My mother's Christmas platter was broken, the crèche was scattered, and the holly was under the table. There were holes in one of the presents, which we later found out was filled with a cheese ball. There must have been a chase the night before, with our cat after some mice.	Last Christmas Eve, burglars broke into our house and almost got one of our presents. Fortunately, our watch-cat chased them off, but in the process, she scattered the crèche, buried the holly under the table, knocked the tree on the floor, and broke my mother's Christmas platter. She probably loved the chase, but she should have just let the mice have the cheese ball.

Using action verbs takes practice and discipline, but it will certainly improve your writing.

We have already explained one way to eliminate *to be* verbs: by eliminating the passive voice wherever possible. (That is, change "The ball *was* hit by Chris" to "Chris hit the ball.") Frequently, you can also eliminate *to be* verbs by replacing them with another verb that is buried somewhere in the sentence—often hidden in a word that is not itself a verb. In the following examples, the "buried verb" has been underlined. Notice how eliminating the *to be* verb often helps to eliminate other unnecessary words as well.

Weak	Stronger
We are <u>hopeful</u> that we can finish on time.	We hope to finish on time.
Stamp collecting is <u>entertaining</u> for young and old alike.	Stamp collecting entertains young and old alike.

Copyright © 1992 by Harcourt Brace Jovanovich, Inc. All rights reserved.

416 Chapter 22 Revising Your Paper

> The report on rate adjustments is <u>satisfactory</u> for our needs.
>
> The report on rate adjustments satisfies our needs.
>
> That movie is the <u>scariest</u> I have seen.
>
> That movie scared me more than any I have seen.

In all these sentences, the underlined words describe a condition. These words can just as easily and more effectively describe an action. As you read through your paper, look for such constructions.

Practice 2

Sentences 1–6 follow a pattern of *subject + was + word that describes the subject*. Revise each sentence, turning the describing word into an active verb. Again, you may have to provide extra information. The first sentence has been done as an example.

1. The speech was inspirational.

   The speech inspired everyone who heard it.

2. The noise was both shocking and amusing.

3. The woman was knowledgeable about bird songs.

4. The earthquake was destructive.

5. The storekeeper was suspicious of the departing customer.

6. The accountant was dependent upon his computer.

Sentences 7–12 follow a pattern of *subject + was + word that describes the subject + action*. When you rewrite a clause in this pattern, use the action as the verb and change the describing word to describe this action rather than the subject. Sentence 7 has been done as an example.

7. The student was successful at writing her paper.
   <u>The student wrote her paper successfully.</u>

8. The child was scared about jumping off the wall.

9. The cat was graceful when stretching.

10. A state trooper is diligent about chasing speeders.

11. A psychologist is reluctant to give advice.

12. The teenager was always willing to borrow money.

You can also eliminate *to be* verbs by simply replacing them with more active verbs. When describing a chair, a writer might say, "The chair is over there." It's a straightforward description, yet one that uses a weak verb. A chair, of course, not being alive, cannot really *do* something, but in the search for strong verbs, you can often ignore this. The following examples show how this and similar sentences can be rewritten with stronger verbs.

Weak	**Stronger**
The chair is over there.	The chair awaits/[lures/beckons/invites] me.
The dew is on the ground.	The dew shimmers on [glistens on/moistens/covers] the ground.

Copyright © 1992 by Harcourt Brace Jovanovich, Inc. All rights reserved.

    The Grand Canyon is wonderful.   The Grand Canyon amazes [inspires/delights/intrigues/surprises/astounds] visitors.

    The baby is cute.   The baby enchants [charms/disarms/captivates/attracts] everyone. (You could even say "looks cute," though this barely improves the original.)

Practice 3

Rewrite the following sentences with active verbs, so that the subject *does* something rather than simply *is* something. For example:

    The tree by the house was big.

    Replace *was big* with the active verb *to tower*.

    The tree towered over the house.

1. The problem is difficult. _____

2. The class is dull. _____

3. The car is fast. _____

4. The girl was happy. _____

5. My class was hard. _____

6. Her keys are lost. _____

7. The sky is pretty. _____

8. The shadows were mysterious. _____

Copyright © 1992 by Harcourt Brace Jovanovich, Inc. All rights reserved.

Eliminate "There is" and "It is"

Here is another way to strengthen your sentences: Try to eliminate every sentence or independent clause that begins with *There is/are* or *It is/They are*. The following examples show how you can do this.

Weak	**Stronger**
There are three books I should read.	I should read three books.
It is such a surprise to see you.	I'm surprised to see you. Seeing you surprises me. You surprised me.
There is an easy answer to that.	I can answer that easily. That answer comes easily.
They are the best books on the subject.	These books will answer your questions. These books will cover that subject.
These are the friends who went with me.	These friends went with me.
It is Joe who followed you last night.	Joe followed you last night.

Occasionally, sentences beginning with *There is* or *It is* come naturally and work well, but you can quickly overuse this construction. By eliminating as many as possible, you will probably end up with an effective number.

Practice 4

Rewrite the following sentences to eliminate the *There is/was* or *It is/They are*. In each case, find or create a subject that can *do* something. The first sentence has been done as an example.

1. There was only one apple in the dish. <u>The dish held only one apple.</u>

2. There is a movie that I want to watch. _____

3. There were too many reasons not to audition. _____

4. It is a wonderful idea. _____

Copyright © 1992 by Harcourt Brace Jovanovich, Inc. All rights reserved.

5. It had been a slow morning. _____

_____

6. There were toothbrushes stuck in the glove compartment. (Don't resort to a passive construction!) _____

_____

7. It would have been the first day I could have slept in. _____

_____

Try to Combine Sentences

As you read your paper with an eye to strong words and sentences, look also for places you can combine your sentences. This step will help eliminate extra words and will make your presentation more complex and interesting for your readers. Throughout this book, we suggest different ways to combine sentences. Here is a brief review.

Create a dependent clause:

> Anabelle might forget this test.
>
> She will probably still pass it.
>
> If Anabelle forgets this test, she will probably still pass it.

Attach phrases with infinitives (*to* + verb):

> Ross called his mother last night.
>
> He needed some money.
>
> Ross called his mother last night to ask for some money.

Attach phrases with participles:

> Shirelle searched through the card catalog.
>
> She needed a book about large families.
>
> Shirelle searched through the card catalog, looking for a book about large families.

Attach descriptive phrases:

> Gavin has no trouble getting along with his roommate.
>
> Gavin is the last of six children.

Gavin, the last of six children, has no trouble getting along with his roommate.

Attach dependent clauses:

Brittany will play Portly Otter in *The Wind in the Willows*.

She is short and bouncy.

Brittany, who is short and bouncy, will play Portly Otter in *The Wind in the Willows*.

Eliminate repetitive verb phrases by combining subjects:

Joella wrote a computer program for her math class.

Bonnie wrote a computer program for her math class.

Joella and Bonnie wrote computer programs for their math class.

Eliminate repetitive subjects by combining verb phrases:

Nell trained as an accountant.

She taught a high school bookkeeping class.

Nell trained as an accountant and then taught a high school bookkeeping class.

▣ Every Reading: Punctuation and Grammar

As you work through your essay, remember that organization, audience and stance, and strong words are more important to your writing than grammar and punctuation are, so address those improvements first. Later, however, you do still need to look for mechanical errors. If you leave too many mistakes, they might confuse your reader. Misplaced commas, run-on sentences, shifts in verb tense or from third person to first person, and especially the careless use of pronouns—all of these can make your writing difficult to understand. Additionally, lots of errors might make your reader think that you don't care enough about your message to polish it.

For these reasons, to make certain that you have eliminated as many errors as possible, read through your essay one last time after you have

Copyright © 1992 by Harcourt Brace Jovanovich, Inc. All rights reserved.

typed it. This will give you a chance to check everything presented in the first section of this book, including the following questions:

1. Do you have any inadvertent fragments, comma splices, or run-on sentences? (See Chapters 1–6.)
2. Do you have commas only where you need them? (See Chapters 7–9.)
3. Have you left out any necessary apostrophes? (See Chapter 10.)
4. Do your subjects and verbs agree? (See Chapter 11.)
5. Can your reader tell easily what nouns the pronouns refer to? (See Chapter 12.)
6. Do your pronouns and antecedents agree? (See Chapter 12.)
7. Have you maintained a consistent first-, second-, or third-person perspective? (See Chapter 13.)
8. Have you maintained a consistent verb tense? (See Chapter 14.)
9. Have you written balanced sentences with a parallel structure? (See Chapter 16.)
10. Have you misplaced any words? (See Chapter 17.)
11. Have you used periods, underlining, colons, quotation marks, and other punctuation marks correctly? (See Chapter 15 and Chapter 18.)
12. And, finally, have you spelled your words correctly? Use a dictionary and spell-checker (either the computer or roommate/friend variety) to go over your spelling if you usually have trouble with this.

▪ Revising Your Paper: A Summary

In review, then, remember four steps for editing your paper.

1. Check for organization.
2. Make sure you have kept your audience and your relationship to this audience in mind.
3. Make certain you have strong words and sentences.
4. Check for errors in punctuation, grammar, and spelling.

Exercise

In Chapters 19–22, you saw how a writer developed, step by step, an essay comparing college and professional basketball. Now here is the entire essay for you to edit. Work through the essay several times, editing for organization, stance, strong words and sentences, and punctuation and grammar.

Copyright © 1992 by Harcourt Brace Jovanovich, Inc. All rights reserved.

Different Rules, Same Game

"So what if it's a college game? What's the difference?"

Walking through the living room, seeing basketball on television, someone who doesn't know much about basketball might easily ask this question. A true fan, however, is aware of many differences between college and professional games, especially in the different rules that college and professional teams play under. Even with these different rules, however, both games share the element of excitement.

Because pro teams have to use man-to-man, and college teams can use the zone as well, college teams have more different plays in their offense. In the 1989 NCAA tournament, Georgetown, who was favored to win, was almost defeated by the low-ranked Princeton team. Princeton slowed the game down with a zone. They used the entire 45-second clock each time down the court. Then they sank enough shots so that Georgetown barely pulled the game out. Professional teams on the other hand must use man-to-man, so everyone knows what their games will be like. Rather than team plays, these teams sometimes rely on getting the hot shooter free. If the Bulls' star player, Michael Jordan, is shooting well (and he usually is), the defense is pulled out from the key to leave a lane open for Jordan. Then he can fake out his guard and slam-dunk the ball. So with different rules on defense, college and professional games have different strategies.

The rules also give college players certain allowances, such as the longer shot-clock, the closer three-point shot, and a game that's shorter, because of college teams' inexperience. A longer shot clock is good because college players take longer to set up, and when they miss a first shot and manage to get the rebound, the longer shot-clock lets them set up again. The shorter shot-clock works well for professional players because they are quicker in reacting to the defense and shoot more accurately. In his recent autobiography, Larry Bird says he can remember where certain players like to shoot from and how certain combinations of players will set up. Most college players just haven't developed that kind of game sense yet, and so the rules for college games make allowances for their inexperience.

In spite of these differences in the rules, however, plenty of excitement is offered by both games. The youthful, infectious spirits of college players can generate emotion during even the most unimportant games. In contrast, the workmanlike spirits of professional players, who come into a game flat from overnight travel, can sometimes leave their fans disappointed, but in the bigger games even the most tired pros reveal their love for the game: Dennis Rodman running down the court with his fist in the air or the entire bench rising as one to applaud a good play. Part of the excitement comes, too, from the predictable unpredictability of both kinds of basketball. Mistakes are made by both kinds. Who can forget the young Georgetown player tossing the ball into North Carolina's James Worthy and losing the game in the last seconds, or Detroit's Isiah Thomas tossing the ball into Larry Bird's hands and also losing the game in the last seconds? Last-minute losses, last-minute wins, a three-point shot from a forward, a guard driving to the basket, and coaches having fits—these belong to both games, and fans of both prove their pleasure by screaming themselves hoarse.

So even though the different rules under which college and professional teams must play cause some definite differences in the games themselves, both games still offer much to basketball fans. What about the casual observer who walked through the TV lounge and asked about the difference between college and professional games? Even after a long explanation, this observer may not care to watch the rest of the game, but the fans around the TV won't notice: The second half has started.

Copyright © 1992 by Harcourt Brace Jovanovich, Inc. All rights reserved.

Appendix
Commonly Misused Words

a/an

Use *a* before *consonant sounds* (not just consonants), and use *an* before *vowel sounds* (not just vowels).

> Would you like *a* pear?
>
> Will you attend *a* university or college? (*University* starts with a *y-* sound, which is a consonant sound.)
>
> Would you like *an* apple?
>
> Will you enroll in *an* honors course? (*Honors* starts with a short *o* sound, which is a vowel sound.)

Remember, base your choice on vowel or consonant *sounds,* not on vowels or consonants themselves.

a lot

Please remember that *a lot,* meaning more than a little, always requires two words. *Alot* should look as incorrect to you as *alittle.*

accept/except

Accept means to take something willingly.

> Will you *accept* this offer?
>
> Nicole walked up to stage to *accept* the award.

Except excludes something. *Except* carries the meaning of putting a big X on something to eliminate it, and this gives an easy way to remember the meaning: Think "X-cept."

> I will have everything *except* the pasta.
>
> Simon dated every girl in the class *except* one—who happened to be his sister.

affect/effect

Almost always, *affect* is a verb and *effect* is a noun.

Affect as a verb means to influence.

> How could a diet of pizza and coke *not affect* you?

Effect as a noun means a consequence or result.

> The *effect* of too much pizza is too much middle and behind.

Very rarely, *effect* becomes a verb and means to bring about.

> We can *effect* a compromise.

fewer/less

Use *fewer* to describe items—things you can count one by one, such as seashells, serpents, surprises, and salamanders.

> Otis has *fewer* trophies on his shelf, but he has more prestigious ones.

Use *less* to describe amounts—things that come in a lump or all together, like pie filling, fear, fan support, or laughter.

> Otis may have fewer trophies, but he doesn't have any *less* pride.

it's/its

It's is a short form of "it is." Use this contraction only when you can insert *it is* in its place.

> *It's* a gray day when the home team loses.
>
> How could you forget that *it's* our one-month anniversary?

Its signifies possession. As a possessive pronoun, *its* serves the same function in a sentence as *his* does.

> The family piano lost *its* rhythm when my brother left home.
>
> My roommate hopes to pass *his* test.
>
> My pet dog hopes to find *its* bone.

Copyright © 1992 by Harcourt Brace Jovanovich, Inc. All rights reserved.

lay/lie

Lay requires an object, something that gets set down.

> *Lay* your head on my shoulder.
>
> The trainer *laid* the injured player's helmet on the bench.

Lie describes what a subject does, whether that subject is a person, place or thing.

> (You) *Lie* down beside me.
>
> The book *lies* under the pillow.

Additional confusion comes from *lay* being the past tense of *to lie*.

> After the accident last week, the injured player *lay* down on the bench.
>
> When an accident happens, the injured players *lie* down on the bench.

If you just remember that *to lay* requires an object and *to lie* requires only a subject, you'll be all right.

passed/past

Passed is what the quarterback did in the game, what your angry roommate did without even saying "Hi," what even the worst day did. *Passed* is something a person, place, or thing does.

> Our room *passed* inspection—barely.
>
> The elevator *passed* our floor again.

Past relates to a period of time and is part of the phrase *past, present, and future*.

> The *past* looks quite attractive until I remember polio and smallpox.

Past also describes where something went and, for this use, can be replaced with the word *by*.

> The balloon sailed serenely *past* the airplane window.

Copyright © 1992 by Harcourt Brace Jovanovich, Inc. All rights reserved.

principle/principal

Use *principle* (always a noun) to mean a conviction, a code of law, or the origin of an idea.

> What has happened to your *principles*?
>
> If our country ever loses its *principle* of equality, it will probably lose its identity at the same time.
>
> The *principle* behind grammar is orderly communication.

Use *principal* as a noun to mean the head of a school or the original money in an investment. Use it as a describing word to describe a person, place, or thing as the foremost or main one in its class.

> Uh-oh—here comes the *principal*.
>
> He won't discuss the loan until we come up with the *principal*.
>
> What is your *principal* reason for wanting more exercise?

set/sit

Set is something a person does to something else. When you use the word *set*, you need an object to go with it—the thing that gets set down, whether that is a plate of food or pillow.

> Please *set* the plate of rumaki beside me.
>
> *Set* your pillow down beside me, you gorgeous creature.

Sit is something a person, place, or thing does itself; *sit* requires no object because the subject of the sentence is doing the sitting.

> (You) *Sit* down beside me.
>
> The rest of my family *sits* across the field from me.

suppose/supposed

When using the words *supposed to,* remember to include the *d* at the end of *suppose*.

> You were *supposed to* drive the car, not push it.

than/then

Use *than* with comparisons.

> The orange kitten is more determined *than* the black one.

Use *then* with progression, whether through time, steps in a process, or arguments in logic (if/then).

> If it's 2:30, *then* why is it dark outside?
>
> If it were 5:30, *then* I would understand why it's so dark.
>
> The dog ate lunch. *Then,* because it was so dark outside, he went to sleep.

their/there/they're

Use the word *their* to show that something belongs to *them*. *Their* shows possession.

> Which is *their* scuba equipment?

Use *there* to show direction or to point out something.

> The oxygen tanks are over *there.*
>
> *There* are flippers and face masks, too.

Use the contraction *they're* to take the place of *they are.*

> Better hide—*they're* coming now.

to/too/two

To comes from the word *toward*. If you can substitute *toward,* you need the word *to*. You also use *to* with infinitives and with certain common phrases, such as *in addition to*.

> He carried the suitcases *to* the car.

Too has an extra *o*, so use it when you are discussing something extra, such as *too much energy* or *too little luck*.

> The trunks were *too* heavy for him.

Two rarely causes problems; use it for the number.

Copyright © 1992 by Harcourt Brace Jovanovich, Inc. All rights reserved.

use/used

In the expression "I *used to* do something," meaning a habit or practice that you have had in the past, be careful to use the past participle *used*. After hearing so many people slur *used to* together, some writers forget to add the *d*.

who/whom

Use *who* as the subject of a clause, the thing in a sentence that does something.

>*Who* wants to come with me?

>The little girl, *who* looks like Shirley Temple, probably has a perm.

Use *whom* as the object; it receives the action of a sentence and is also used with prepositions.

>You buried *whom* in the chocolate pudding?

>I saw the dancers, each one of *whom* had a sleek shape.

In brief, *who* does the action, and *whom* receives the action.

Index

a/an, 311–312, 425
a lot, 179, 425
accept/except, 81, 425
active voice, 413–417
address, comma in, 150
adverbial conjunctions (transition words), 88–91, 147–149, 394–396
affect/effect, 38–39, 426
agreement
   of person, 261–274
   of pronoun, 233–257
   of subjects and verbs, 201–223, 252–254
apostrophes
   essay practice, "No Lunch Boxes for Jason," 192–194
   paragraph practice, 191–192
   to form plurals, 189–190
   to make contractions, 189
   to show possession, 184–188
appositives, 144–145
audience, 366–367, 412
   choosing an audience, 412

be verbs, 413–421
brackets, 305–306

capitalization, 351–352
choosing
   audience, 366–367
   form, 368
   insight (thesis), 376–379
   purpose, 368
   stance, 367–368
   topic, 366
choosing the content for an essay, 385–387
clauses
   dependent clauses, 26–35, 48–51, 86–87, 123–124
   described, 25–34
   identifying clauses, 30–34, 36–37
   independent clauses, 25, 30–32, 84–87, 121–123
   making clauses parallel, 316–317
   misplaced, 335–337
   non-restrictive, 145–146
   relative, 29, 49
   restrictive, 146–147

   that describe something without limiting it, 145–146
   that limit something, 146–147
coherence in paragraphs, 394–396
colons, 301–303
combining sentences, 420–421
comma errors, 163–180
   before dependent clauses at the end of a sentence, 165–166
   between subject and verb, 164
   between verb and object, 165
   essay practice, "A Castle in the Clouds," 174–176; "My Wife, the Scientist," 172–173; "The Real Miracle," 135–136; "Summer Jobs," 155–157
   paragraph practice, 133–134, 154–155, 171
   separating only two items, 166–167
commas
   addresses, 150
   after introductory dependent clauses, 123–124
   after other introductory elements, 124–125
   between equal describers, 126–127
   between independent clauses, 121–123
   clarity, 125–126
   dates, 149
   description following the noun, 143–147
   items in a series, 129
   places, 150
   quotations, 127–128
   transition words, 147–149
comma splices, 83, 87–98
   essay practice, "My Life as a Forty-Year-Old Student," 96–98
   paragraph practice, 95–96
conclusions, 406–410
   implications, 408–409
   parting shot, 407–408
   review, 407
   simple end, 406–407
conjunctions
   adverbial (transition words), 88–91, 147–149, 394–396
   coordinating (FANBOYS), 43–45, 84–86, 88, 121–123

subordinating (dependent signals), 26–27, 48–51
consistency
  of person, 261–274
  of verb tense, 281–291
coordinating conjunctions (FANBOYS), 43–45, 84–86, 88, 121–123
cumulative essay practices (in order)
  "Steel-Toed Boots and a Seat at the Game," 137–139
  "Why Is the College Bowl System Better?" 158–159
  "Wasted on the Young," 177–179
  "But I Studied!" 195–197
  "Supper's Ready," 223–224
  "Genius by Design," 255–256
  "Different Characters," 274–276
  "Twice-Told Tails," 292–294
  "Of Pizza Smears and Salad Spices," 308–310
  "The Joys of Gardening," 325–327
  "Community Crossroads," 340–342
  "A Celebration of the Past," 354–356
  "Code Words," 358–360

dangling modifiers, 334–335
dashes, 304
dates, commas in, 149
dependent clauses
  commas, 123–124, 165–166
  described, 26–29
  fragments, 48–51, 64–65
  identifying, 30–32
  introductory with commas, 123–124
  signals, 26–30, 49–50
  using to combine clauses, 48–49, 86–87
dependent signals, 26–27
  double-duty signals (*who, which, that, whoever*), 28–29, 49–50
  telling the difference between transition words and dependent signals, 26–30
describing words, commas in, 126–127
descriptive essays
  generating ideas, 372–373
double-duty signals, 28–29, 49–50

emphasizing words, 346
end marks
  period, 248
  question mark, 347
essays
  conclusions, 406–410
  descriptive, 372–373
  expository, 371–372
  introductions, 398–406
  narrative, 373–374
  persuasive, 374
expository essays
  generating ideas, 371–372

FANBOYS (coordinating conjunctions), 43–45, 84–86, 88, 121–123
fewer/less, 102, 426
first-person perspective, 261–263
  essay practice, "Money in the Bank," 272–273
  paragraph practice, 269–272
foreign words, 346
form, choosing, 368
fragments
  dependent clause fragments, 48–51, 64–65
  described, 41–81
  essay practice, "How I Spend My Summer Vacation," 55–56; "My Home, the Space Colony," 70–71; "Test Anxiety," 78–80
  extra information, 62–65
  incomplete thought fragments, 48–51
  infinitive fragments, 63–64
  paragraph practice, 54–55, 69–70
  participles, 62–63
  without subjects, 42–45
  without verbs, 45–48

generating ideas for essays
  descriptive, 372–373
  expository, 371–372
  narrative, 373–374
  persuasive, 374
gerund, 7, 8

helping verbs, 8–9, 12–13
hyphens, 304–305

identifying
  clauses, 30–34, 36–37
  dependent clauses, 30–34
  independent clauses, 30–34
indefinite pronouns, 211–213, 240–243
independent clauses
  described, 25
  identifying, 30–34
  joining, 84–87
  punctuating with commas, 121–123
infinitives
  described, 6, 61
  fragments, 63–64
  misplaced infinitive phrases, 334–35
-ing words, 7, 8, 61
insight (thesis), 376–379

introductions, 398–406
  bait, 400–401
  challenge, 401–402
  funnel, 398–399
italics, 345–47
it is, 419–420
it's/its, 57–58, 426

lay/lie, 294–295, 427
logical sequence in paragraphs, 396

mechanics of writing
  paragraph practice, 354
misplaced clauses, 335–337
misplaced phrases, 333–335
  infinitive, 334–35
  participial, 334
  prepositional, 333
misplaced words, 331–333
misused words (list), 425–430

narrative essays
  generating ideas, 373–374
non-restrictive clauses, 145–146
noun
  described, 5
  making parallel, 319–320

object pronouns, 230–231
organization, 381–385; 411–412

paragraphs
  coherence, 394–396
  concluding, 406–410
  internal, 393–398
  introductory, 398–406
  logical sequence, 396
  unity, 393–394
parallel structure, 313–325
  clauses, 316–317
  deciding what to make parallel, 314–315
  describing words, 319–320
  nouns, 319–320
  paragraph practice, 324–325
  phrases, 316–317
  verb forms, 317–319
parentheses, 303
participles
  described, 8, 9, 61
  fragments, 62–63
  misplaced participial phrases, 334
passed/past, 197–198, 427
passive voice, 413–418
periods, 348
persuasive essays
  generating ideas, 374

phrases
  described, 35–36
  making parallel, 316–317
  misplaced, 333–335
possessive pronouns, 231
prepositions
  described, 16–18
  misplaced prepositional phrases, 333
principle/principal, 342–343, 428
pronouns
  object, 230–231
  possessive, 231
  refer to subject, 232
  reflexive pronoun, 232
  subject, 229–230
  usage chart, 229
pronoun agreement
  antecedent confusion, 233–234
  collective nouns, 245–246
  compound antecedents, 236–237
  either/or, neither/nor, 237–238
  essay practice, "College Reasons," 250–251, "Who Are the Greatest?" 252–254
  indefinite pronouns, 240–243
  paragraph practice, 248–249
  pronoun preceding antecedent, 239
  quantities, 246
  relative pronoun, 243
  singular nouns with plural forms, 246–247
  titles, 246
punctuation
  brackets, 305–306
  colons, 301–303
  dashes, 304
  hyphens, 304–305
  paragraph practice, 307–308
  parentheses, 303
  periods, 348
  question marks, 347
  quotation marks, 348–350
  semicolons, 86–87, 299–301
purpose, choosing, 368

question marks, 347
quotations
  commas in, 127–128
  marks, 348–350

reflexive pronoun, 232
relative clauses, 29, 49
restrictive clauses, 146–147
revising your paper, 411–424
run-on sentences, 87–92

Index

run-on sentences (*continued*)
　essay practice, "My Life as a Forty-Year-Old Student," 96–98
　paragraph practice, 95–96

second-person perspective, 261, 264–265
　essay practice, "Money in the Bank," 272–273
　paragraph practice, 269–272
semicolons, 86–87, 299–301
sentence errors
　essay practice, "Clothes for College," 99–100; "The Hardest Lesson," 112–113; "Odysseus and the Cyclops," 110–111; "Tomato Trees and a Cure for AIDS," 114–116
　paragraph practice, 109–110
sentence patterns, 11–24
sentence structure
　analyzing structure, 103–104
　combining, 420–421
　comma splices, 87–92
　fragments, 41–49, 61–65
　run-on sentences, 87–92
series, commas in, 129
set/sit, 225–226, 428
sexist language, 234–235
stance, 367–368, 412
style, 413–421
　active verbs, 413–414
　combining sentences, 420–421
　concrete nouns, 413
　eliminating "there is" and "it is," 419–420
　eliminating "to be" verbs, 414–418
subject
　described, 5
　identifying the subject, 5
　in sentence patterns, 11–18
subject pronoun, 229–230
subject-verb agreement
　collective nouns, 216
　compound subjects, 203–204
　either/or, neither/nor, 204
　essay practice, "Painted Faces," 220–222; "Who Are the Greatest?" 252–254
　indefinite pronouns, 211–213
　inverted sentences, 205–206
　paragraph practice, 219–220
　participial phrases, 207–208
　phrases that add information, 208

　prepositional phrases, 206–207
　quantities, 216–217
　relative pronouns, 213–214
　singular nouns with plural forms, 217
　titles, 217
subordinating conjunctions (dependent signals), 26–27, 48–51
suppose/supposed, 160, 428

than/then, 327–328, 429
their/there/they're, 277–278, 429
there is, 419–420
thesis (insight), 376–379
third-person perspective, 261, 266–269
　essay practice, "Money in the Bank," 272–273
　paragraph practice, 269–272
titles, 345
to/too/two, 139–140, 429
topic, choosing, 366
topic sentences, 381–385, 402–403
transition words, 88–91, 147–149, 394–396
　commas in, 147–149

underlining, 345–347
unity in paragraphs, 393–394
use/used, 430

verb
　described, 3
　making parallel, 317–318
　recognizing, 3–4
verb tense
　essay practice, "Each Sport In Its Time," 290–291
　future, 285–287
　paragraph practice, 288–289
　past, 283–285
　present, 281–283
　printed matter, 287
　quotations, 287
verbals
　gerunds, 7–8
　infinitives, 6, 61, 63–64, 334–335
　participles, 8, 9, 61, 62–63, 334

who/whom, 257–258, 430
writing, beginning steps
　audience, 366
　choosing a topic, 366
　form, 368
　purpose, 368
　stance, 367